THE PARADOX OF AMERICAN POWER

THE PARADOX

OF AMERICAN

POWER

*WHY THE WORLD'S
ONLY SUPERPOWER
CAN'T GO IT ALONE*

Joseph S. Nye Jr.

OXFORD
UNIVERSITY PRESS

OXFORD
UNIVERSITY PRESS

Oxford New York
Auckland Bangkok Buenos Aires Cape Town
Chennai Dar es Salaam Delhi Hong Kong Istanbul
Karachi Kolkata Kuala Lumpur Madrid Melbourne
Mexico City Mumbai Nairobi São Paulo
Shanghai Taipei Tokyo Toronto

Copyright © 2002 by Joseph S. Nye Jr.

First published by Oxford University Press, Inc., 2002
First issued as an Oxford University Press paperback, 2003
198 Madison Avenue, New York, New York 10016

www.oup.com

Library of Congress Cataloging-in-Publication Data
Nye, Joseph S.
The paradox of American power:
why the world's only superpower can't go it alone / Joseph S. Nye, Jr.
p. cm. Includes index.
ISBN 0-19-515088-0 (cloth) ISBN 0-19-516110-6 (pbk)
1. United States—Foreign relations—Philosophy.
2. United States—Relations—Philosophy.
3. United States—Foreign relations—2001–.
4. Power (Social sciences)—United States.
5. International cooperation.
6. Globalization.
7. Information technology—Political Aspects—United States.
I. Title.

E183.7 .N94 2001   327.73—dc21   2001052369

5 7 9 8 6

Printed in the United States of America

For Molly

CONTENTS

PREFACE

The tragedy on September 11, 2001, was a wake-up call for Americans. We became complacent during the 1990s. After the collapse of the Soviet Union, no country could match or balance us. We had unsurpassed global military, economic, and cultural power. The Gulf War at the beginning of the decade was an easy victory; and at the end of the decade, we bombed Serbia without suffering a single casualty. The economy grew and the stock market boomed. We resembled Britain in its mid-Victorian glory, but with even greater global reach.

But Americans were largely indifferent and uncertain about how to shape a foreign policy to guide this power. Polls showed the American public focused on domestic affairs and paying little attention to the rest of the world. Between 1989 and 2000, the television networks closed foreign bureaus and cut their foreign news content by two-thirds. TV executives found that "young adults cared more about the Zone diet than the subtleties of Middle East diplomacy." The president of MSNBC blamed "a national fog of materialism and disinterest and avoidance."[1] And many of those Americans who did pay attention to foreign policy became arrogant about our power, arguing that we did not need to heed other nations. We seemed both invincible and invulnerable.

All that changed on September 11. The direction of the change, if not the timing, could have been foreseen. Earlier in the year, the final report of a commission on national security chaired by former senators Gary Hart and Warren Rudman warned that America's military superiority would not protect us from hostile attacks on our homeland: "Americans will likely die on American soil, possibly in large numbers."[2] The report was largely ignored. In 1997, James Woolsey and I had written that the highest priority in U.S. national security policy should be given to catastrophic terrorism, but we feared that "the very nature of U.S. society makes it difficult to prepare for this problem. Because of our 'Pearl Harbor mentality,' we are unlikely to mount an adequate defense until we suffer an attack."[3]

The terrorist attack was a terrible symptom of deeper changes that are occurring in the world. As I will show in chapter 2, a technological revolution in information and communications has been diffusing power away from governments and empowering individuals and groups to play roles in world politics — including wreaking massive destruction — that were once reserved for the governments of states. Privatization has been increasing, and terrorism is the privatization of war. Moreover, the processes of globalization have been shrinking distances, and events in faraway places — such as Afghanistan — are having a greater impact on American lives. The world has been changing from the Cold War era to the global information age, but until very recently, American attitudes and policies were not keeping pace.

Where do we go from here? Americans are still wrestling with how best to combine our power and our values while reducing our vulnerabilities. As the largest power in the world, we excite both longing and hatred among some, particularly in the Muslim world. As one Pakistani physician and religious leader put it, "You are blind to anyone beyond your borders. . . . America is the world's biggest bully. Is it any wonder that so many cheer when the bully finally gets a bloodied nose?"[4] At the same time, the tragedy also produced an enormous upwelling of sympathy for the United States in most parts of the world.

Some Americans are tempted to believe that we could reduce these hatreds and our vulnerability if we would withdraw our troops, curtail our alliances, and follow a more isolationist foreign policy. But isolationism would not remove our vulnerability. Not only are the terrorists who struck on September 11 dedicated to reducing American power, but in the words of Jordan's King Abdallah, "they want to break down the fabric of the U.S. They want to break down what America stands for."[5] Even if we had a weaker foreign policy, such groups would resent the power of the American economy, which would still reach well beyond our shores. American corporations and citizens represent global capitalism, which is anathema to some.

Moreover, American popular culture has a global reach regardless of what we do. There is no escaping the influence of Hollywood, CNN, and the Internet. American films and television express freedom, individualism, and change (as well as sex and violence). Generally, the global reach of American culture helps to enhance our soft power—our cultural and ideological appeal. But not for everyone. Individualism and liberties are attractive to many people but repulsive to some, particularly fundamentalists. American feminism, open sexuality, and individual choices are profoundly subversive of patriarchal societies. One of the terrorist pilots is reported to have said that he did not like the United States because it is "too lax. I can go anywhere I want and they can't stop me."[6] Some tyrants and fundamentalists will always hate us because of our values of openness and opportunity, and we will have no choice but to deal with them through more effective counterterrorism policies. But those hard nuggets of hate are unlikely to catalyze broader hatred unless we abandon our values and pursue arrogant and overbearing policies that let the extremists appeal to the majority in the middle.

What policies should guide our power, and can we preserve it? The United States has been compared to the Roman Empire, but even Rome eventually collapsed. A decade ago, the conventional wisdom lamented an America in decline. Best-seller lists featured books that described our fall. The cover of a popular magazine depicted the Statue of Liberty with a tear running down her cheek. Japan was eating our lunch and would soon replace us as number one. That view was wrong at the time, and I said so. When I wrote *Bound to Lead* in 1989, I predicted the continuing rise of American power. But power has its perils.

In his election campaign, President George W. Bush said, "If we are an arrogant nation, they'll view us that way, but if we're a humble nation, they'll respect us." He was right, but unfortunately, many foreigners saw the United States in 2001 as arrogantly concerned with narrow American interests at the expense of the rest of the world. They saw us focusing on the hard power of our military might rather than our soft power as we turned our backs on many international treaties, norms, and negotiating forums. In their eyes, the United States used consultations for talking, not listening. Yet effective leadership requires dialogue with followers. American leadership will be more enduring if we can convince our partners that we are sensitive to their concerns. September 2001 was a start toward such sensitivity, but only a start.

The problem is more than a partisan one. President Bush has declared that he is not a unilateralist, and President Clinton originally touted "assertive multilateralism" but subsequently backed away from United Nations peacekeeping efforts. Nor was he able to follow through on many of his multilateral initiatives. One reason was that Americans were internally preoccupied and relatively indifferent to our extraordinary role in the world. Both Republicans and Democrats in Congress responded largely to domestic special interests and often treated foreign policy as a mere extension of domestic politics. Congress tried to legislate for the rest of the world and imposed sanctions when others did not follow American law—for example, on trade with Iran or Cuba. Not only did Congress refuse to ratify more than a dozen treaties and conventions over the last decade, but it reduced foreign aid, withheld our dues to the United Nations and other international agencies, slashed spending at the State Department, and abolished the U.S. Information Agency. We must do better than that.

I am not alone in warning against the dangers of a foreign policy that combines unilateralism, arrogance, and parochialism . A number of American adherents of realist international relations theory have also expressed concern about America's staying power. Throughout history, coalitions of countries have arisen to balance dominant powers, and the search for new state challengers is well under way. Some see China as the new enemy; others envisage a Russia-

China-India coalition as the threat. Still others see a uniting Europe becoming a nation-state that will challenge us for primacy. But as I will show, while the realists have a point, they are largely barking up the wrong tree.

In fact, the real challenges to our power are coming on cat's feet in the night, and ironically, our desire to go it alone may ultimately weaken us. The contemporary information revolution and its attendant brand of globalization are transforming and shrinking our world. At the beginning of this new century, these two forces have increased American power, including our ability to influence others through our attractive or "soft" power. But with time, technology spreads to other countries and peoples, and our relative preeminence will diminish. For example, today our twentieth of the global population represents more than half of the Internet. Many believe that in a decade or two, Chinese will be the dominant language of the Internet. It will not dethrone English as a lingua franca, but at some point the Asian market will loom larger than the American market. Or to take other examples, in international trade and antitrust matters the European Union already balances American economic power, and Europe's economic and soft power is likely to increase in years to come.

Even more important, the information revolution is creating virtual communities and networks that cut across national borders. Transnational corporations and nongovernmental actors (terrorists included) will play larger roles. Many of these organizations will have soft power of their own as they attract our citizens into coalitions that ignore national boundaries. As one of America's top diplomats observed, NGOs are "a huge and important force . . . In many issues of American policy, from human rights to the environment, NGOs are in fact the driving force."[7] By traditional measures of hard power, compared to other nations, the United States will remain number one, but being number one ain't gonna be what it used to.

Globalization—the growth of networks of worldwide interdependence—is putting new items on our national and international agenda whether we like it or not. Many of these issues we cannot resolve by ourselves. International financial stability is vital to the prosperity of Americans, but we need the cooperation of others to ensure it.

Global climate change, too, will affect Americans' quality of life, but we cannot manage the problem alone. And in a world where borders are becoming more porous than ever to everything from drugs to infectious diseases to terrorism, we are forced to work with other countries behind their borders and inside ours. To rephrase the title of my earlier book, we are not only bound to lead, but bound to cooperate.

How should we guide our foreign policy in a global information age? Some in the current foreign policy debates look at our preponderance in power and see a modern empire. For example, self-styled neo-Reaganites advocate a foreign policy of "benign American hegemony." Since American values are good and we have the military power, we should not feel restrained by others. In their eyes, "Americans should understand that their support for American pre-eminence is as much a boost for international justice as any people is capable of giving. It is also a boon for American interests and for what might be called the American spirit."[8]

But many conservative realists as well as liberals believe that such views smack of hubris and arrogance that alienate our friends. Americans have always viewed our nation as exceptional, but even our Declaration of Independence expressed "a decent respect for the opinions of mankind." If we are truly acting in the interests of others as well as our own, we would presumably accord to others a substantial voice and, by doing so, end up embracing some form of multilateralism.[9] As our allies point out, even well-intentioned Americans are not immune to Lord Acton's famous warning that power can corrupt. As we shall see in chapter 5, learning to define our national interest to include global interests will be crucial to the longevity of our power and whether others see the hegemony as benign or not.

Americans are divided over how to be involved with the rest of the world. At the end of the Cold War, many observers were haunted by the specter of the return of American isolationism. The debate today, however, is not only between isolationists and internationalists but also within the internationalist camp, which is split between unilateralists and multilateralists. Some urge a new unilateralism in which we refuse to play the role of docile international citizen, instead unashamedly pursuing our own ends. They speak of a unipolar world because of our unequaled military power. But as we will see in the pages that follow, military power alone cannot produce the outcomes we want on many of the issues that matter to Americans.

As a former assistant secretary of defense, I would be the last to deny the continuing importance of military power. Our military role is essential to global stability. And the military is part of our response to terrorism. But we must not let the metaphor of war blind us to the fact that suppressing terrorism will take years of patient, unspectacular work, including close civilian cooperation with other countries. On many of the key issues today, such as international financial stability, drug smuggling, or global climate change, military power simply cannot produce success, and its use can sometimes be counterproductive. As President Bush's father said after the September tragedy, "Just as Pearl Harbor awakened this country from the notion that we could somehow avoid the call of duty and defend freedom in Europe and Asia in World War II, so, too, should this most recent surprise attack erase the concept in some quarters that America can somehow go it alone in the fight against terrorism or in anything else for that matter."[10]

The initial American response followed this advice. Congress suddenly approved a big dues payment and confirmed our ambassador to the United Nations. The president sought UN support and stressed coalition building. The Treasury and White House, which earlier had undercut international cooperation on money-laundering tax havens, rapidly became proponents of cooperation. But unilateralism is far from banished. "At first, the Pentagon was even unwilling to have NATO invoke the alliance's mutual-defense clause. The allies were desperately trying to give us political cover and the Pentagon was resisting it. Eventually Secretary of Defense Donald Rumsfeld understood it was a plus, not a minus, and was able to accept it."[11] Other officials, however, worried that coalitions would shackle the United States and that invoking the international authority of the UN or NATO would set a bad precedent. Internal debates about how to implement the Bush doctrine of eliminating the scourge of terrorism raised concerns in other countries that the United States would be the unilateral judge of whether a country is supporting terrorism and the appropriate methods of response.[12] In the Congress, at the same time that our ally Britain was ratifying the treaty creating an international criminal court, Senator Jesse Helms was pressing legislation that would authorize "any necessary action to free U.S. soldiers improperly handed over to the court, a provision dubbed by some delegates as 'the Hague invasion clause.'"[13] How long the new multilateralism will last and how deep it goes remains an open question.

Any retreat to a traditional policy focus on unipolarity, hegemony, sovereignty, and unilateralism will fail to produce the right outcomes, and its accompanying arrogance will erode the soft power that is often part of the solution. We must not let the illusion of empire blind us to the increasing importance of our soft power.

How should we act in this time of unparalleled power and peril? Can we learn how to use our hard and soft power in productive combination to not only defeat terrorism but deal with the other issues of a global information age? Can we wisely use our lead during these years early in the century to build a framework for the long term? Can we promote and ensure our basic values of freedom and democracy? Are our domestic attitudes and institutions up to the challenge, or will we fritter away our advantage through inattention or arrogance? Why we are having such a hard time defining our national interest in this global information age?

This book was originally planned as a wake-up call to Americans as well as a suggestion of how to use our unprecedented power. Now the alarm has been sounded far more effectively than any pen could accomplish, but we still need to determine how to use the current decades of our preeminence to advance long-term national and global interests. Our historical test will be to develop a consensus on principles and norms that will allow us to work with others to create political stability, economic growth, and democratic values. American power is not eternal. If we squander our soft power through a combination of arrogance and indifference, we will increase our vulnerability, sell our values short, and hasten the erosion of our preeminence.

I want to emphasize in closing that this book should not be read primarily as a response to the terrorist attacks on our country, though it indeed has much to say on the subject. My concern is deeper than the terrorists attacks, horrible though they were. It is really about America's future—about how we can increase and take advantage of the power that emanates from our deepest values and how we should face the principal challenges that confront us in a global information age.

ACKNOWLEDGMENTS

No book is an island, and my debts are great. This work is an out-
growth of the Visions of Governance for the Twenty-first Century
Project at Harvard's John F. Kennedy School of Government. I am
grateful to the Carnegie Corporation, the Xerox Foundation, Roy
Ash, Daniel Rose, and others for their support of the project, as well
as to the numerous faculty and student participants in its various
study groups and publications. Some of the early work in these pages
was supported by the Century Foundation, and I am grateful to the
foundation and its president, Richard Leone. I wrote the first draft of
this book while I was on leave as a visiting fellow of All Souls College,
Oxford, and I am grateful to the college for its support as well as the
quality of conversation and cuisine at its high table.

Numerous colleagues read and commented on earlier drafts. Above
all, I am indebted to Robert O. Keohane. Not only was he a patient
reader and critic, but I am sure he is the origin of many of the ideas in
chapters 2 and 3 that draw on some of the earlier work we have done
together. After so many years of fruitful collaboration, I no longer
know how to disentangle the origins of some of our joint thoughts.
Thus I grant him a simultaneous blanket credit and exoneration, with
deep gratitude for his friendship over the years. Neal M. Rosendorf
served not only as a tireless research assistant but as resident cultural

historian and critic who also provided a number of ideas. Alexandra Scacco filled in ably after he left. Neal and Kurt Campbell helped suggest that I write this book.

It would be impossible to mention all those whose intellectual inspiration gave rise to my thoughts, though I have tried, as best I can remember, in some of the notes. I can, however, identify and thank those who read and commented on early drafts: Kurt Campbell, Robert Darnton, John Donahue, Jeff Frankel, Stanley Hoffmann, Anne Hollick, Karl Kaiser, Robert Lawrence, Dan Nye, Molly Harding Nye, Robert O'Neill, Iqbal Qadir, Dani Rodrik, John Ruggie, and Stephen Walt.

I want to thank Tim Bartlett and his assistant, Farahnaz Maroof, at Oxford University Press, for some of the most thoughtful and helpful editing I have encountered in a long career. I'm lucky to have had Helen Mules as production editor and Sue Warga as my copyeditor— both contributed greatly to the final product. Rafe Sagalyn provided general good counsel in placing the book. Jeanne Marasca was infinitely patient in seeing me through many drafts.

Ever since we first went to Africa together four decades ago, Molly Harding Nye has lived and shared all my books. No debt is greater than the one I owe to her, and that explains the dedication of this book.

1

THE AMERICAN COLOSSUS

Not since Rome has one nation loomed so large above the others. In the words of *The Economist,* "the United States bestrides the globe like a colossus. It dominates business, commerce and communications; its economy is the world's most successful, its military might second to none."[1] French foreign minister Hubert Védrine argued in 1999 that the United States had gone beyond its superpower status of the twentieth century. "U.S. supremacy today extends to the economy, currency, military areas, lifestyle, language and the products of mass culture that inundate the world, forming thought and fascinating even the enemies of the United States."[2] Or as two American triumphalists put it, "Today's international system is built not around a balance of power but around American hegemony."[3] As global interdependence has increased, many have argued that globalization is simply a disguise for American imperialism. The German newsmagazine *Der Spiegel* reported that "American idols and icons are shaping the world from Katmandu to Kinshasa, from Cairo to Caracas. Globalization wears a 'Made in USA' label."[4]

The United States is undoubtedly the world's number one power, but how long can this situation last, and what should we do with it?

Some pundits and scholars argue that our preeminence is simply the result of the collapse of the Soviet Union and that this "unipolar moment" will be brief.[5] Our strategy should be to husband our strength and engage the world only selectively. Others argue that America's power is so great that it will last for decades, and the unipolar moment can become a unipolar era.[6] Charles Krauthammer argued in early 2001 that "after a decade of Prometheus playing pygmy, the first task of the new administration is to reassert American freedom of action." We should refuse to play "the docile international citizen. . . . The new unilateralism recognizes the uniqueness of the unipolar world we now inhabit and thus marks the real beginning of American post–Cold War foreign policy."[7]

Even before September 2001, this prescription was challenged by many, both liberals and conservatives, who consider themselves realists and consider it almost a law of nature in international politics that if one nation becomes too strong, others will team up to balance its power. In their eyes, America's current predominance is ephemeral.[8] As evidence, they might cite an Indian journalist who urges a strategic triangle linking Russia, India, and China "to provide a counterweight in what now looks like a dangerously unipolar world,"[9] or the president of Venezuela telling a conference of oil producers that "the 21st century should be multipolar, and we all ought to push for the development of such a world."[10] Even friendly sources such as *The Economist* agree that "the one-superpower world will not last. Within the next couple of decades a China with up to 1 ½ billion people, a strongly growing economy and probably a still authoritarian government will almost certainly be trying to push its interests. . . . Sooner or later some strong and honest man will pull post-Yeltsin Russia together, and another contender for global influence will have reappeared."[11] In my view, terrorism notwithstanding, American preponderance will last well into this century—but only if we learn to use our power wisely.

Predicting the rise and fall of nations is notoriously difficult. In February 1941, publishing magnate Henry Luce boldly proclaimed the "American century." Yet by the 1980s, many analysts thought Luce's vision had run its course, the victim of such culprits as Vietnam, a slowing economy, and imperial overstretch. In 1985, economist Lester Thurow asked why, when Rome had lasted a thousand years as a republic and an empire, we were slipping after only fifty.[12] Polls showed that half the public agreed that the nation was contracting in power and prestige.[13]

The declinists who filled American bestseller lists a decade ago were not the first to go wrong. After Britain lost its American colonies in the eighteenth century, Horace Walpole lamented Britain's reduction to "a miserable little island" as insignificant as Denmark or Sardinia.[14] His prediction was colored by the then current view of colonial commerce and failed to foresee the coming industrial revolution that would give Britain a second century with even greater preeminence. Similarly, the American declinists failed to understand that a "third industrial revolution" was about to give the United States a "second century."[15] The United States has certainly been the leader in the global information revolution.

On the other hand, nothing lasts forever in world politics. A century ago, economic globalization was as high by some measures as it is today. World finance rested on a gold standard, immigration was at unparalleled levels, trade was increasing, and Britain had an empire on which the sun never set. As author William Pfaff put it, "Responsible political and economic scholars in 1900 would undoubtedly have described the twentieth-century prospect as continuing imperial rivalries within a Europe-dominated world, lasting paternalistic tutelage by Europeans of their Asian and African colonies, solid constitutional government in Western Europe, steadily growing prosperity, increasing scientific knowledge turned to human benefit, etc. All would have been wrong."[16] What followed, of course, was two world wars, the great social diseases of totalitarian fascism and communism, the end of European empires, and the end of Europe as the arbiter of world power. Economic globalization was reversed and did not again reach its 1914 levels until the 1970s. Conceivably, it could happen again.

Can we do better as we enter the twenty-first century? The apocrypha of Yogi Berra warns us not to make predictions, particularly about the future. Yet we have no choice. We walk around with pictures of the future in our heads as a necessary condition of planning our actions. At the national level, we need such pictures to guide policy and tell us how to use our unprecedented power. There is, of course, no single future; there are multiple possible futures, and the quality of our foreign policy can make some more likely than others. When systems involve complex interactions and feedbacks, small causes can have large effects. And when people are involved, human reaction to the prediction itself may make it fail to come true.

We cannot hope to predict the future, but we can draw our pictures carefully so as to avoid some common mistakes.[17] A decade ago, a more careful analysis of American power could have saved us from the mistaken portrait of American decline. More recently, accurate predictions of catastrophic terrorism failed to avert a tragedy that leads some again to foresee decline. It is important to prevent the errors of both declinism and triumphalism. Declinism tends to produce overly cautious behavior that could undercut our influence; triumphalism could beget a potentially dangerous absence of restraint, as well as an arrogance that would also squander our influence. With careful analysis, we can make better decisions about how to protect our people, promote our values, and lead toward a better world over the next few decades. We can begin this analysis with an examination of the sources of our power.

THE SOURCES OF AMERICAN POWER

We hear a lot about how powerful America has become in recent years, but what do we mean by power? Simply put, power is the ability to effect the outcomes you want, and if necessary, to change the behavior of others to make this happen. For example, NATO's military power reversed Slobodan Milosevic's ethnic cleansing of Kosovo, and the promise of economic aid to Serbia's devastated economy reversed the Serbian government's initial disinclination to hand Milosevic over to the Hague tribunal.

The ability to obtain the outcomes one wants is often associated with the possession of certain resources, and so we commonly use shorthand and define power as possession of relatively large amounts of such elements as population, territory, natural resources, economic strength, military force, and political stability. Power in this sense means holding the high cards in the international poker game. If you show high cards, others are likely to fold their hands. Of course, if you play your hand poorly or fall victim to bluff and deception, you can still lose, or at least fail to get the outcome you want. For example, the United States was the largest power after World War I, but it failed to prevent the rise of Hitler or Pearl Harbor. Converting America's potential power resources into realized power requires well-designed policy and skillful leadership. But it helps to start by holding the high cards.

Traditionally, the test of a great power was "strength for war."[18] War was the ultimate game in which the cards of international politics were played and estimates of relative power were proven. Over the centuries, as technologies evolved, the sources of power have changed. In the agrarian economies of seventeenth- and eighteenth-century Europe, population was a critical power resource because it provided a base for taxes and the recruitment of infantry (who were mostly mercenaries), and this combination of men and money gave the edge to France. But in the nineteenth century, the growing importance of industry benefited first Britain, which ruled the waves with a navy that had no peer, and later Germany, which used efficient administration and railways to transport armies for quick victories on the Continent (though Russia had a larger population and army). By the middle of the twentieth century, with the advent of the nuclear age, the United States and the Soviet Union possessed not only industrial might but nuclear arsenals and intercontinental missiles.

Today the foundations of power have been moving away from the emphasis on military force and conquest. Paradoxically, nuclear weapons were one of the causes. As we know from the history of the Cold War, nuclear weapons proved so awesome and destructive that they became muscle bound—too costly to use except, theoretically, in the most extreme circumstances.[19] A second important change was the rise of nationalism, which has made it more difficult for empires to rule over awakened populations. In the nineteenth century, a few adventurers conquered most of Africa with a handful of soldiers, and Britain ruled India with a colonial force that was a tiny fraction of the indigenous population. Today, colonial rule is not only widely condemned but far too costly, as both Cold War superpowers discovered in Vietnam and Afghanistan. The collapse of the Soviet empire followed the end of European empires by a matter of decades.

A third important cause is societal change inside great powers. Postindustrial societies are focused on welfare rather than glory, and they loathe high casualties except when survival is at stake. This does not mean that they will not use force, even when casualties are expected—witness the 1991 Gulf War or Afghanistan today. But the absence of a warrior ethic in modern democracies means that the use of force requires an elaborate moral justification to ensure popular support (except in cases where survival is at stake). Roughly speaking, there are three types of countries in the world today: poor, weak preindustrial states, which are often the chaotic remnants of collapsed empires; modernizing industrial states such as India or China; and the postindustrial societies that prevail in Europe, North America, and Japan. The use of force is common in the first type of country, still accepted in the second, but less tolerated in the third. In the words of British diplomat Robert Cooper, "A large number of the most powerful states no longer want to fight or to conquer."[20] War remains possible, but it is much less acceptable now than it was a century or even half a century ago.[21]

Finally, for most of today's great powers, the use of force would jeopardize their economic objectives. Even nondemocratic countries that feel fewer popular moral constraints on the use of force have to consider its effects on their economic objectives. As Thomas Friedman has put it, countries are disciplined by an "electronic herd" of investors who control their access to capital in a globalized economy.[22] And Richard Rosecrance writes, "In the past, it was cheaper to seize another state's territory by force than to develop the sophisticated economic and trading apparatus needed to derive benefit from commercial exchange with it."[23] Imperial Japan used the former approach when it created the Greater East Asia Co-prosperity Sphere in the 1930s, but Japan's post–World War II role as a trading state turned out to be far more successful, leading it to become the second largest national economy in the world. It is difficult now to imagine a scenario in which Japan would try to colonize its neighbors, or succeed in doing so.

As mentioned above, none of this is to suggest that military force plays no role in international politics today. For one thing, the information revolution has yet to transform most of the world. Many states are unconstrained by democratic societal forces, as Kuwait learned from its neighbor Iraq, and terrorist groups pay little heed to the normal constraints of liberal societies. Civil wars are rife in many parts of the world where collapsed empires left power vacuums. Moreover, throughout history, the rise of new great powers has been accompanied by anxieties that have sometimes precipitated military crises. In Thucydides's immortal description, the Peloponnesian War in ancient Greece was caused by the rise to power of Athens and the fear it created in Sparta.[24] World War I owed much to the rise of the kaiser's Germany and the fear that created in Britain.[25] Some foretell a similar dynamic in this century arising from the rise of China and the fear it creates in the United States.

Geoeconomics has not replaced geopolitics, although in the early twenty-first century there has clearly been a blurring of the traditional boundaries between the two. To ignore the role of force and the centrality of security would be like ignoring oxygen. Under normal circumstances, oxygen is plentiful and we pay it little attention. But once those conditions change and we begin to miss it, we can focus on nothing else.[26] Even in those areas where the direct employment of force falls out of use among countries—for instance, within Western Europe or between the United States and Japan—nonstate actors such as terrorists may use force. Moreover, military force can still play an important political role among advanced nations. For example, most countries in East Asia welcome the presence of American troops as an insurance policy against uncertain neighbors. Moreover, deterring threats or ensuring access to a crucial resource such as oil in the Persian Gulf increases America's influence with its allies. Sometimes the linkages may be direct; more often they are present in the back of statesmen's minds. As the Defense Department describes it, one of the missions of American troops based overseas is to "shape the environment."

With that said, economic power *has* become more important than in the past, both because of the relative increase in the costliness of force and because economic objectives loom large in the values of postindustrial societies.[27] In a world of economic globalization, all countries are to some extent dependent on market forces beyond their direct control. When President Clinton was struggling to balance the federal budget in 1993, one of his advisors stated in exasperation that if he were to be reborn, he would like to come back as "the market" because that was clearly the most powerful player.[28] But markets constrain different countries to different degrees. Because the United States constitutes such a large part of the market in trade and finance, it is better placed to set its own terms than is Argentina or Thailand. And if small countries are willing to pay the price of opting out of the market, they can reduce the power that other countries have over them. Thus American economic sanctions have had little effect, for example, on improving human rights in isolated Myanmar. Saddam Hussein's strong preference for his own survival rather than the welfare of the Iraqi people meant that crippling sanctions failed for more than a decade to remove him from power. And economic sanctions may disrupt but not deter non-state terrorists. But the exceptions prove the rule. Military power remains crucial in certain situations, but it is a mistake to focus too narrowly on the military dimensions of American power.

SOFT POWER

In my view, if the United States wants to remain strong, Americans need also to pay attention to our soft power. What precisely do I mean by soft power? Military power and economic power are both examples of hard command power that can be used to induce others to change their position. Hard power can rest on inducements (carrots) or threats (sticks). But there is also an indirect way to exercise power. A country may obtain the outcomes it wants in world politics because other countries want to follow it, admiring its values, emulating its example, aspiring to its level of prosperity and openness. In this sense, it is just as important to set the agenda in world politics and attract others as it is to force them to change through the threat or use of military or economic weapons. This aspect of power—getting others to want what you want—I call soft power.[29] It co-opts people rather than coerces them.

Soft power rests on the ability to set the political agenda in a way that shapes the preferences of others. At the personal level, wise parents know that if they have brought up their children with the right beliefs and values, their power will be greater and will last longer than if they have relied only on spankings, cutting off allowances, or taking away the car keys. Similarly, political leaders and thinkers such as Antonio Gramsci have long understood the power that comes from setting the agenda and determining the framework of a debate. The ability to establish preferences tends to be associated with intangible power resources such as an attractive culture, ideology, and institutions. If I can get you to *want* to do what I want, then I do not have to force you to do what you do *not* want to do. If the United States represents values that others want to follow, it will cost us less to lead. Soft power is not merely the same as influence, though it is one source of influence. After all, I can also influence you by threats or rewards. Soft power is also more than persuasion or the ability to move people by argument. It is the ability to entice and attract. And attraction often leads to acquiescence or imitation.

Soft power arises in large part from our values. These values are expressed in our culture, in the policies we follow inside our country, and in the way we handle ourselves internationally. As we will see in the next chapter, the government sometimes finds it difficult to control and employ soft power. Like love, it is hard to measure and to handle, and does not touch everyone, but that does not diminish its importance. As Hubert Védrine laments, Americans are so powerful because they can "inspire the dreams and desires of others, thanks to the mastery of global images through film and television and because, for these same reasons, large numbers of students from other countries come to the United States to finish their studies."[30] Soft power is an important reality.

Of course, hard and soft power are related and can reinforce each other. Both are aspects of the ability to achieve our purposes by affecting the behavior of others. Sometimes the same power resources can affect the entire spectrum of behavior from coercion to attraction.[31] A country that suffers economic and military decline is likely to lose its ability to shape the international agenda as well as its attractiveness. And some countries may be attracted to others with hard power by the myth of invincibility or inevitability. Both Hitler and Stalin tried to develop such myths. Hard power can also be used to establish empires and institutions that set the agenda for smaller states—witness Soviet rule over the countries of Eastern Europe. But soft power is not simply the reflection of hard power. The Vatican did not lose its soft power when it lost the Papal States in Italy in the nineteenth century. Conversely, the Soviet Union lost much of its soft power after it invaded Hungary and Czechoslovakia, even though its economic and military resources continued to grow. Imperious policies that utilized Soviet hard power actually undercut its soft power. And some countries such as Canada, the Netherlands, and the Scandinavian states have political clout that is greater than their military and economic weight, because of the incorporation of attractive causes such as economic aid or peacekeeping into their definitions of national interest. These are lessons that the unilateralists forget at their and our peril.

Britain in the nineteenth century and America in the second half of the twentieth century enhanced their power by creating liberal international economic rules and institutions that were consistent with the liberal and democratic structures of British and American capitalism—free trade and the gold standard in the case of Britain, the International Monetary Fund, World Trade Organization, and other institutions in the case of the United States. If a country can make its power legitimate in the eyes of others, it will encounter less resistance to its wishes. If its culture and ideology are attractive, others more willingly follow. If it can establish international rules that are consistent with its society, it will be less likely to have to change. If it can help support institutions that encourage other countries to channel or limit their activities in ways it prefers, it may not need as many costly carrots and sticks.

In short, the universality of a country's culture and its ability to establish a set of favorable rules and institutions that govern areas of international activity are critical sources of power. The values of democracy, personal freedom, upward mobility, and openness that are often expressed in American popular culture, higher education, and foreign policy contribute to American power in many areas. In the view of German journalist Josef Joffe, America's soft power "looms even larger than its economic and military assets. U.S. culture, low-brow or high, radiates outward with an intensity last seen in the days of the Roman Empire—but with a novel twist. Rome's and Soviet Russia's cultural sway stopped exactly at their military borders. America's soft power, though, rules over an empire on which the sun never sets."[32]

Of course, soft power is more than just cultural power. The values our government champions in its behavior at home (for example, democracy), in international institutions (listening to others), and in foreign policy (promoting peace and human rights) also affect the preferences of others. We can attract (or repel) others by the influence of our example. But soft power does not belong to the government in the same degree that hard power does. Some hard power assets (such as armed forces) are strictly governmental, others are inherently national (such as our oil and gas reserves), and many can be transferred to collective control (such as industrial assets that can be mobilized in an emergency). In contrast, many soft power resources are separate from American government and only partly responsive to its purposes. In the Vietnam era, for example, American government policy and popular culture worked at cross-purposes. Today popular U.S. firms or nongovernmental groups develop soft power of their own that may coincide or be at odds with official foreign policy goals. That is all the more reason for our government to make sure that its own actions reinforce rather than undercut American soft power. As I shall show in the next chapter, all these sources of soft power are likely to become increasingly important in the global information age of this new century. And, at the same time, the arrogance, indifference to the opinions of others, and narrow approach to our national interests advocated by the new unilateralists are a sure way to undermine our soft power.

Power in the global information age is becoming less tangible and less coercive, particularly among the advanced countries, but most of the world does not consist of postindustrial societies, and that limits the transformation of power. Much of Africa and the Middle East remains locked in preindustrial agricultural societies with weak institutions and authoritarian rulers. Other countries, such as China, India, and Brazil, are industrial economies analogous to parts of the West in the mid-twentieth century.[33] In such a variegated world, all three sources of power—military, economic, and soft—remain relevant, although to different degrees in different relationships. However, if current economic and social trends continue, leadership in the information revolution and soft power will become more important in the mix. Table 1.1 provides a simplified description of the evolution of power resources over the past few centuries.

Power in the twenty-first century will rest on a mix of hard and soft resources. No country is better endowed than the United States in all three dimensions—military, economic, and soft power. Our greatest mistake in such a world would be to fall into one-dimensional analysis and to believe that investing in military power alone will ensure our strength.

BALANCE OR HEGEMONY?

America's power—hard and soft—is only part of the story. How others react to American power is equally important to the question of stability and governance in this global information age. Many realists extol the virtues of the classic nineteenth-century European balance of power, in which constantly shifting coalitions contained the ambitions of any especially aggressive power. They urge the United States to rediscover the virtues of a balance of power at the global level today. Already in the 1970s, Richard Nixon argued that "the only time in the history of the world that we have had any extended periods of peace is when there has been a balance of power. It is when one nation becomes infinitely more powerful in relation to its potential competitors that the danger of war arises."[34] But whether such multipolarity would be good or bad for the United States and for the world is debatable. I am skeptical.

Table 1.1   *Leading States and Their Power Resources, 1500–2000*

Period	State	Major Resources
Sixteenth century	Spain	Gold bullion, colonial trade, mercenary armies, dynastic ties
Seventeenth century	Netherlands	Trade, capital markets, navy
Eighteenth century	France	Population, rural industry, public administration, army, culture (soft power)
Nineteenth century	Britain	Industry, political cohesion, finance and credit, navy, liberal norms (soft power), island location (easy to defend)
Twentieth century	United States	Economic scale, scientific and technical leadership, location, military forces and alliances, universalistic culture and liberal international regimes (soft power)
Twenty-first century	United States	Technological leadership, military and economic scale, soft power, hub of transnational communications

War was the constant companion and crucial instrument of the multipolar balance of power. The classic European balance provided stability in the sense of maintaining the independence of most countries, but there were wars among the great powers for 60 percent of the years since 1500.[35] Rote adherence to the balance of power and multipolarity may prove to be a dangerous approach to global governance in a world where war could turn nuclear.

Many regions of the world and periods in history have seen stability under hegemony—when one power has been preeminent. Margaret Thatcher warned against drifting toward "an Orwellian future of Oceania, Eurasia, and Eastasia—three mercantilist world empires on increasingly hostile terms . . . In other words, 2095 might look like 1914 played on a somewhat larger stage."[36] Both the Nixon and Thatcher views are too mechanical because they ignore soft power. America is an exception, says Josef Joffe, "because the 'hyperpower' is also the most alluring and seductive society in history. Napoleon had to rely on bayonets to spread France's revolutionary creed. In the American case, Munichers and Muscovites *want* what the avatar of ultra-modernity has to offer."[37]

The term "balance of power" is sometimes used in contradictory ways. The most interesting use of the term is as a predictor about how countries will behave; that is, will they pursue policies that will prevent any other country from developing power that could threaten their independence? By the evidence of history, many believe, the current preponderance of the United States will call forth a countervailing coalition that will eventually limit American power. In the words of the self-styled realist political scientist Kenneth Waltz, "both friends and foes will react as countries always have to threatened or real predominance of one among them: they will work to right the balance. The present condition of international politics is unnatural."[38]

In my view, such a mechanical prediction misses the mark. For one thing, countries sometimes react to the rise of a single power by "bandwagoning"—that is, joining the seemingly stronger rather than weaker side—much as Mussolini did when he decided, after several years of hesitation, to ally with Hitler. Proximity to and perceptions of threat also affect the way in which countries react.[39] The United States benefits from its geographical separation from Europe and Asia in that it often appears as a less proximate threat than neighboring countries inside those regions. Indeed, in 1945, the United States was by far the strongest nation on earth, and a mechanical application of balancing theory would have predicted an alliance against it. Instead, Europe and Japan allied with the Americans because the Soviet

Union, while weaker in overall power, posed a greater military threat because of its geographical proximity and its lingering revolutionary ambitions. Today, Iraq and Iran both dislike the United States and might be expected to work together to balance American power in the Persian Gulf, but they worry even more about each other. Nationalism can also complicate predictions. For example, if North Korea and South Korea are reunited, they should have a strong incentive to maintain an alliance with a distant power such as the United States in order to balance their two giant neighbors, China and Japan. But intense nationalism resulting in opposition to an American presence could change this if American diplomacy is heavy-handed. Non-state actors can also have an effect, as witnessed by the way cooperation against terrorists changed some states' behavior after September 2001.

A good case can be made that inequality of power can be a source of peace and stability. No matter how power is measured, some theorists argue, an equal distribution of power among major states has been relatively rare in history, and efforts to maintain a balance have often led to war. On the other hand, inequality of power has often led to peace and stability because there was little point in declaring war on a dominant state. The political scientist Robert Gilpin has argued that "*Pax Britannica* and *Pax Americana,* like the *Pax Romana,* ensured an international system of relative peace and security." And the economist Charles Kindleberger claimed that "for the world economy to be stabilized, there has to be a stabilizer, one stabilizer."[40] Global governance requires a large state to take the lead. But how much and what kind of inequality of power is necessary—or tolerable—and for how long? If the leading country possesses soft power and behaves in a manner that benefits others, effective countercoalitions may be slow to arise. If, on the other hand, the leading country defines its interests narrowly and uses its weight arrogantly, it increases the incentives for others to coordinate to escape its hegemony.

Some countries chafe under the weight of American power more than others. *Hegemony* is sometimes used as a term of opprobrium by political leaders in Russia, China, the Middle East, France, and others. The term is used less often or less negatively in countries where American soft power is strong. If hegemony means being able to dictate, or at least dominate, the rules and arrangements by which international relations are conducted, as Joshua Goldstein argues, then the United States is hardly a hegemon today.[41] It does have a predominant voice and vote in the International Monetary Fund, but it cannot alone choose the director. It has not been able to prevail over Europe and Japan in the World Trade Organization. It opposed the Land Mines Treaty but could not prevent it from coming into existence. Saddam Hussein remained in power for more than a decade despite American efforts to drive him out. The U.S. opposed Russia's war in Chechnya and civil war in Colombia, but to no avail. If hegemony is defined more modestly as a situation where one country has significantly more power resources or capabilities than others, then it simply signifies American preponderance, not necessarily dominance or control.[42] Even after World War II, when the United States controlled half the world's economic production (because all other countries had been devastated by the war), it was not able to prevail in all of its objectives.[43]

Pax Britannica in the nineteenth century is often cited as an example of successful hegemony, even though Britain ranked behind the United States and Russia in GNP. Britain was never as superior in productivity to the rest of the world as the United States has been since 1945, but as we shall see in chapter 5, Britain also had a degree of soft power. Victorian culture was influential around the globe, and Britain gained in reputation when it defined its interests in ways that benefited other nations (for example, opening its markets to imports or eradicating piracy). America lacks a global territorial empire like Britain's, but instead possesses a large, continental-scale home economy and has greater soft power. These differences between Britain and America suggest a greater staying power for American hegemony. Political scientist William Wohlforth argues that the United States is so far ahead that potential rivals find it dangerous to invite America's focused enmity, and allied states can feel confident that they can continue to rely on American protection.[44] Thus the usual balancing forces are weakened.

Nonetheless, if American diplomacy is unilateral and arrogant, our preponderance would not prevent other states and non-state actors from taking actions that complicate American calculations and constrain our freedom of action.[45] For example, some allies may follow the

American bandwagon on the largest security issues but form coalitions to balance American behavior in other areas such as trade or the environment. And diplomatic maneuvering short of alliance can have political effects. As William Safire observed when presidents Vladimir Putin and George W. Bush first met, "Well aware of the weakness of his hand, Putin is emulating Nixon's strategy by playing the China card. Pointedly, just before meeting with Bush, Putin traveled to Shanghai to set up a regional cooperation semi-alliance with Jiang Zemin and some of his Asian fellow travelers."[46] Putin's tactics, according to one reporter, "put Mr. Bush on the defensive, and Mr. Bush was at pains to assert that America is not about to go it alone in international affairs."[47]

Pax Americana is likely to last not only because of unmatched American hard power but also to the extent that the United States "is uniquely capable of engaging in 'strategic restraint,' reassuring partners and facilitating cooperation."[48] The open and pluralistic way in which our foreign policy is made can often reduce surprises, allow others to have a voice, and contribute to our soft power. Moreover, the impact of American preponderance is softened when it is embodied in a web of multilateral institutions that allow others to participate in decisions and that act as a sort of world constitution to limit the capriciousness of American power. That was the lesson we learned as we struggled to create an antiterrorist coalition in the wake of the September 2001 attacks. When the society and culture of the hegemon are attractive, the sense of threat and need to balance it are reduced.[49] Whether other countries will unite to balance American power will depend on how the United States behaves as well as the power resources of potential challengers.

NEW CHALLENGERS?

Periods of unequal power can produce stability, but if rising countries chafe at the policies imposed by the largest, they may challenge the leading state and form alliances to overcome its strength. So who are the potential candidates that might challenge the United States, and how much of a threat do they represent?

China

Many view China, the world's most populous country, as the leading candidate.[50] "Almost every commentator has for some years been regarding China as the likeliest of the usual suspects for future 'peer competitor' status."[51] Polls show that half the American public thinks China will pose the biggest challenge to U.S. world power status in the next hundred years (compared with 8 percent for Japan and 6 percent for Russia and Europe).[52] Some observers compare the rise of authoritarian China to that of the kaiser's Germany in the period preceding World War I. Sinologist Arthur Waldron, for example, argues that "sooner or later, if present trends continue, war is probable in Asia . . . China today is actively seeking to scare the United States away from East Asia rather as Germany sought to frighten Britain before World War I." Similarly, the columnist Robert Kagan claims "the Chinese leadership views the world in much the same way Kaiser Wilhelm II did a century ago. . . . Chinese leaders chafe at the constraints on them and worry that they must change the rules of the international system before the international system changes them."[53] Chinese leaders have often complained about U.S. "gunboat diplomacy" and invited Russia, France, and others to join it in resisting U.S. "hegemonism."[54] Moreover, "in government pronouncements, stories in the state-run press, books and interviews, the United States is now routinely portrayed as Enemy No. 1."[55] As two sober analysts put it, "It is hardly inevitable that China will be a threat to American interests, but the United States is much more likely to go to war with China than it is with any other major power."[56]

We should be skeptical, however, about drawing conclusions solely from current rhetoric, military contingency plans, and badly flawed historical analogies. In both China and the United States, perceptions of the other country are heavily colored by domestic political struggles, and there are people in both countries who want to see the other as an enemy. Even without such distortions, the military on both sides would be seen by its countrymen as derelict in its duties if it did not plan for all contingencies. As for history, it is important to remember that by 1900, Germany had surpassed Britain in industrial power and the kaiser was pursuing an adventurous, globally oriented foreign policy that was bound to bring about a clash with other great powers. In contrast, China lags far behind the United States economically and has focused its policies primarily on its region and on its economic development; its official communist ideology holds little appeal. Nonetheless, the rise of China recalls Thucydides's warning that belief in the inevitability of conflict can become one of its main causes.[57] Each side, believing it will end up at war with the other, makes reasonable military preparations, which then are read by the other side as confirmation of its worst fears.

In fact, the "rise of China" is a misnomer. "Reemergence" would be more accurate, since by size and history the Middle Kingdom has long been a major power in East Asia. Technically and economically, China was the world's leader (though without global reach) from 500 to 1500. Only in the last half millennium was it overtaken by Europe and America. The Asian Development Bank has calculated that in 1820, at the beginning of the industrial age, Asia made up an estimated three-fifths of world product. By 1940, this had fallen to one-fifth, even though the region was home to three-fifths of the world's population. Rapid economic growth has brought that back to two-fifths today, and the bank speculates that Asia could return to its historical levels by 2025.[58] Asia, of course, includes Japan, India, Korea, and others, but China will eventually play the largest role. Its high annual growth rate of 8 to 9 percent led to a remarkable tripling of its GNP in the last two decades of the twentieth century. This dramatic economic performance, along with its Confucian culture, enhanced China's soft power in the region.

Nonetheless, China has a long way to go and faces many obstacles to its development. At the beginning of the twenty-first century, the American economy is about twice the size of China's. If the American economy grows at a 2 percent rate and China's grows at 6 percent, the two economies would be equal in size sometime around 2020. Even so, the two economies would be equivalent in size but not equal in composition. China would still have a vast underdeveloped countryside—indeed, assuming 6 percent Chinese growth and only 2 percent American growth, China would not equal the United States in per capita income until somewhere between 2056 and 2095 (depending on the measures of comparison).[59] In terms of political power, per capita income provides a more accurate measure of the sophistication of an economy. The Asian Development Bank projects Chinese per capita income will reach 38 percent of that of the United States by 2025, about the same level relative to the United States that South Korea reached in 1990.[60] That is impressive growth, but it is a long way from equality. And since the United States is unlikely to be standing still during that period, China is a long way from posing the kind of challenge to American preponderance that the kaiser's Germany posed when it passed Britain at the beginning of the last century.

Moreover, linear projections of economic growth trends can be misleading. Countries tend to pick the low-hanging fruit as they benefit from imported technologies in the early stages of economic takeoff, and growth rates generally slow as economies reach higher levels of development. In addition, the Chinese economy faces serious obstacles of transition from inefficient state-owned enterprises, a shaky financial system, and inadequate infrastructure. Growing inequality, massive internal migration, an inadequate social safety net, corruption, and inadequate institutions could foster political instability. Coping with greatly increasing flows of information at a time when restrictions can hinder economic growth presents a sharp dilemma for Chinese leaders. As the Harvard economist Dwight Perkins points out, "Much of the early success of market reforms . . . resulted from the basic simplicity of the task." The process of creating a rule of law and adequate institutions in the economic area will be "measured in decades, not years or months."[61] Indeed, some observers fear instability caused by a collapsing rather than rising China.[62] A China that cannot control population growth, flows of migration, environmental effects on the global climate, and internal conflict poses another set of problems. Politics has a way of confounding economic projections.

As long as China's economy does grow, it is likely that its military power will increase, thus making China appear more dangerous to its neighbors and complicating America's commitments in the region. A RAND study projects that by 2015, China's military expenditure will be more than six times higher than Japan's and its accumulated military capital stock would be some five times that of Japan (measured at purchasing power parity).[63] The Gulf War of 1991, the tensions over Taiwan in 1995–96, and the Kosovo campaign of 1999 showed Chinese leaders how far China lagged behind in modern military capabilities, and as a result they nearly doubled military expenditures over the course of the 1990s. Nonetheless, China's total military budget actually declined from 2.5 to 2 percent of GDP in the last decades of the twentieth century, and the weakness of its political system makes it inefficient at converting economic resources into military capacity.[64] Some observers think that by 2005 China might achieve a military capability similar to that of a European country in the early 1980s. Others, citing imported technology from Russia, are more concerned.[65] In any event, growing Chinese military capacity would mean that any American military role in the region will require more resources.

Whatever the accuracy of such assessments of China's military growth, the most useful tool for our purposes is comparative assessment, and that depends on what the United States (and other countries) will be doing over the next decades. The key to military power in the information age depends on the ability to collect, process, disseminate, and integrate data from complex systems of space-based surveillance, high-speed computers, and "smart" weapons. China (and others) will develop some of these capabilities, but according to the Australian analyst Paul Dibb and colleagues, the revolution in military affairs (RMA) "will continue to favor heavily American military predominance. It is not likely that China will, in any meaningful way, close the RMA gap with the U.S."[66]

Robert Kagan believes that China aims "in the near term to replace the United States as the dominant power in East Asia and in the long term to challenge America's position as the dominant power in the world."[67] Even if this is an accurate assessment of China's intentions (and that is debated by experts), it is doubtful that China will have the capability. Every country has a wish list that reads like a menu without prices. Left to itself, China might like to force the return of Taiwan, dominate the South China Sea, and be recognized as the primary state in the East Asian region, but Chinese leaders will have to contend with the prices imposed by other countries as well as the constraints created by their own objectives of economic growth and the need for external markets and resources. Moreover, too aggressive a Chinese posture could produce a countervailing coalition among its neighbors in the region that would weaken both its hard and soft power.

The fact that China is not likely to become a peer competitor to the United States on a global basis does not mean that it could not challenge the United States in East Asia or that war over Taiwan is not possible. Weaker countries sometimes attack when they feel backed into a corner, such as Japan did at Pearl Harbor or China did when it entered the Korean War in 1950. "Under certain conditions Beijing will likely be fully undeterrable. If, for example, Taiwan were to declare independence, it is hard to imagine that China would forgo the use of force against Taiwan, regardless of the perceived economic or military costs, the likely duration or intensity of American intervention, or the balance of forces in the region."[68] But it would be unlikely to win such a war.

The U.S.-Japan alliance, which the Clinton-Hashimoto declaration of 1996 reaffirmed as the basis for stability in post–Cold War East Asia, is an important impediment to Chinese ambitions. This means that in the triangular politics of the region, China cannot play Japan against the United States or try to expel the Americans from the area. From that position of strength, the United States and Japan can work to engage China as its power grows, and provide incentives for it to play a responsible role. How China will behave as its power increases is an open question, but as long as the United States remains present in the region, maintains its relationship with Japan, does not support independence for Taiwan, and exercises its power in a reasonable way, it is unlikely that any country or coalition will successfully challenge its role in the region, much less at the global level. If the United States and China stumble into war or a cold war in East Asia, it will more likely be caused by inept policy related to Taiwan's independence rather than China's success as a global challenger.

Japan

Japan's economy has recently been in the doldrums because of poor policy decisions, but it would be a mistake to sell Japan short. It pos-

sesses the world's second largest national economy, highly sophisticated industry, the largest number of Internet users after the United
States, and the most modern military in Asia. While China has nuclear weapons and more men under arms, Japan's military is better
equipped and better trained. It also has the technological capacity to
develop nuclear weapons very quickly if it chose to do so.

Only a decade ago Americans feared being overtaken by the Japanese. A 1989 *Newsweek* article put it succinctly: "In boardrooms and
government bureaus around the world, the uneasy question is
whether Japan is about to become a superpower, supplanting America as the colossus of the Pacific and perhaps even the world's No. 1
nation."[69] Books predicted a Japanese-led Pacific bloc that would exclude the United States, and even an eventual war between Japan and
the United States.[70] Futurologist Herman Kahn had forecast that
Japan would become a nuclear superpower and that the transition in
Japan's role would be like "the change brought about in European
and world affairs in the 1870s by the rise of Prussia."[71] These views
extrapolated from an impressive Japanese record.[72]

On the eve of World War II, Japan had accounted for 5 percent of
world industrial production. Devastated by the war, it did not regain
that level until 1964. From 1950 to 1974, Japan averaged a remarkable
10 percent annual growth rate, and by the 1980s it had become the
world second largest economy, with 15 percent of world product.[73] It
became the world's largest creditor and largest donor of foreign aid.
Its technology was roughly equal to that of the United States and even
slightly ahead in some areas of manufacturing. Japan armed only
lightly (restricting military expenditures to about 1 percent of GNP)
and focused on economic growth as a highly successful strategy.
Nonetheless, as mentioned above, it created the most modern and
best-equipped conventional military force in East Asia.

Japan has an impressive historical record of reinventing itself. A
century and a half ago, Japan became the first non-Western country
to successfully adapt to modern globalization.[74] After centuries of
isolation, Japan's Meiji Restoration chose selectively from the rest of
the world, and within half a century the country became strong
enough to defeat a European great power in the Russo-Japanese War.
After 1945, it rose from the ashes of World War II. Recently, a prime

minister's commission on Japan's goals in the twenty-first century has called for a new reinvention.[75] Given the weakness of the political process, the need for further deregulation, the aging of the population, and the resistance to immigration, such change will not be easy and may take more than a decade to complete.[76] But given the continuing skills of Japan's people, the stability of its society, areas of technological leadership (for instance, mobile Internet applications), and manufacturing skills, current assessments of Japan may be too depressed.

Could a revived Japan, a decade or two hence, become a global challenger to the United States, economically or militarily, as was predicted a decade ago? It seems unlikely. Roughly the size of California, Japan will never have the geographical or population scale of the United States. Its record of economic success and its popular culture provide Japan with soft power, but the nation's ethnocentric attitudes and policies undercut that. Japan does show some ambition to improve its status as a world power. It seeks a permanent seat on the United Nations Security Council, and polls show that many younger Japanese are interested in becoming a more "normal country" in terms of defense. Some politicians have started a movement to revise Article 9 of the country's constitution, which restricts Japan's forces to self-defense. If the United States were to drop its alliance with Japan and follow the advice of those who want us to stay "offshore" and shift our allegiance back and forth to balance China and Japan, we could produce the sense of insecurity that might lead Japan to decide it had to develop its own nuclear capacity.[77]

Alternatively, if Japan were to ally with China, the combined resources of the two countries would make a potent coalition. While not impossible, such an alliance seems unlikely unless the United States makes a serious diplomatic or military blunder. Not only have the wounds of the 1930s failed to heal completely, but China and Japan have conflicting visions of Japan's proper place in Asia and in the world.[78] China would want to constrain Japan, but Japan might not want to play second fiddle. In the highly unlikely prospect that the United States were to withdraw from the East Asian region, Japan might join a Chinese bandwagon. But given Japanese concerns about the rise of Chinese power, continued alliance with the United States is the most likely outcome. An allied East Asia is not a plausible candidate to be the challenger that displaces the United States.

Russia

If Japan is an unlikely ally for China, what about Russia? Balance-of-power politics might predict such an alliance as a response to the 1996 reaffirmation of the U.S.-Japan security treaty. And there is historical precedent for such a union: in the 1950s, China and the Soviet Union were allied against the United States. After Nixon's opening to China in 1972, the triangle worked the other way, with the United States and China cooperating to limit what both saw as a threatening Soviet power. That alliance ended with the collapse of the Soviet Union. In 1992, Russia and China declared their relations a "constructive partnership"; in 1996, they proclaimed a "strategic partnership"; and in July 2001 they signed a treaty of "friendship and cooperation." A theme of the partnership is common opposition to the present (U.S.-dominated) "unipolar world."[79] China and Russia each supported America's anti-terrorist campaign after September, but remained leery of American power.

Despite the rhetoric, there are serious obstacles to a military alliance between China and Russia. The demographic situation in the Far East, where the population on the Russian side of the border is 6 million to 8 million and on the China side is up to 120 million, creates a degree of anxiety in Moscow.[80] Russia's economic and military decline has increased its concern about the rise of Chinese power. Trade and investment between the two countries is minor, and both sides rely much more on access to Western (including American) markets in goods and finance. It would take very clumsy (but not impossible) American behavior to overcome these obstacles and drive Russia and China more fully into each other's arms. As one observer has commented, the "way for the United States to retain its overall influence is to exercise power in a restrained, predictable manner that disproves the charge of hegemonism."[81] The more heavy-handed we are, the more we help Russia and China overcome their differences.

While this might not lead to as full-fledged a military alliance as occurred in the 1950s, it could lead to a high degree of political coordination designed to frustrate American plans.

Russia alone still poses a threat to the United States, largely because it is the one country with enough missiles and nuclear war-
heads to destroy the United States, and its relative decline has made it
more reluctant to renounce its nuclear status. Russia also possesses
enormous scale, an educated population, skilled scientists and engineers, and vast natural resources. But while a turn toward a nationalistic repressive regime might make Russia a threat again, it would not
present the same sort of challenge to American power that the Soviet
Union presented during the four decades after World War II.

In the 1950s, many people in the West feared that the Soviet Union
would surpass the United States as the world's leading power. The
Soviet Union had the world's largest territory, third largest population, and second largest economy, and it produced more oil and gas
than Saudi Arabia. It possessed half the world's nuclear weapons,
more men under arms than the United States, and the highest number of people employed in research and development. It exploded a
hydrogen bomb in 1953, only one year after the United States, and was
the first to launch a satellite into space, in 1957. In terms of soft power,
following World War II, the Soviet Union's communist ideology and
transnational organization had gained prestige in Europe by resisting
Hitler, and in the Third World its identification with the popular
movement toward decolonization made it attractive. It actively fostered a myth of the inevitability of the triumph of communism.

Nikita Khrushchev famously boasted in 1959 that the Soviet Union
would overtake the United States by 1970 or 1980 by the latest. As late
as 1976, Leonid Brezhnev told the French president that communism
would dominate the world by 1995. Such predictions were bolstered
by reported annual economic growth rates ranging between 5 and 6
percent and an increase in the Soviet share of world product from 11
to 12.3 percent between 1950 and 1970. After that, however, the Soviet
growth rate and share of world product began a long decline. In 1986,
Mikhail Gorbachev described the Soviet economy as "very disor-
dered. We lag in all indices."[82] A year later, Foreign Minister Eduard

Shevardnadze told his officials that "you and I represent a great country that in the last 15 years has been more and more losing its position as one of the leading industrially developed nations."[83]

The collapse of the Soviet Union in 1991 left a Russia significantly shrunken in territory (76 percent of the USSR's), population (50 percent of the USSR's), economy (45 percent of the USSR's), and military personnel (33 percent of the USSR's). Moreover, the soft power of communist ideology had virtually disappeared. Russian economic statistics, like those of the USSR before it, are notoriously inaccurate, but at the turn of the century it appeared that the United States economy was roughly twenty-seven times larger than that of Russia, its spending on research and development over sixty times that of Russia, and its military expenditure more than nine times greater.[84] In relative numbers of personal computers and Internet hosts, the ratios were 11:1 and 150:1.

Nor does it look as though Russia will catch up for a long time. To be sure, there are signs of improvement since the decline of the Soviet Union. Russia is no longer shackled with communist ideology and a cumbersome central planning system. There is some degree of democracy and free expression, although the regime of Vladimir Putin has taken measures aimed at stifling dissent and reasserting central political control. The likelihood of ethnic fragmentation, though still a threat (as the wars in Chechnya showed), has been reduced. Whereas ethnic Russians were only half of the former Soviet Union, they are now 81 percent of the Russian Federation. The political system remains fragile, and the institutions for an effective market economy are largely missing. Russia's robber baron capitalism lacks the kind of effective regulation that creates trust in market relationships, and "even 5 percent growth will not bring Russian incomes to the level of Spain and Portugal for decades."[85] The public health system is in disarray, mortality rates have increased, and birthrates are declining. Midrange estimates by UN demographers suggest that Russia's population may decline from 145 million today to 121 million by midcentury.[86]

Many Russian futures are possible, and according to the American government's National Intelligence Council, the possibilities range

from political resurgence to dissolution. "The most likely outcome is a
Russia that remains internally weak and institutionally linked to the
international system primarily through its permanent seat on the UN
Security Council. . . . Even under a best case scenario of five percent
annual economic growth, Russia would attain an economy less than
one-fifth the size of that of the United States" by 2015.[87] Because of its
residual nuclear strength, its proximity to Europe, and the potential of
alliance with China or India, Russia can choose to cooperate or to
cause problems for the United States but not to be a global challenger.

India

India too is sometimes mentioned as a future great power, and its
population of a billion people is four times that of the United States.
For decades, India suffered from what some called the "Hindu rate of
economic growth," that is, a rate of 1 or 2 percent, but in the last
decade that has changed and growth rates have approached 5 to 6
percent. India has an emerging middle class of several hundred million, and English is an official language spoken by some 50 million to
100 million people. Building on that base, Indian information industries are beginning to play a transnational role. In addition, India is a
military power, with several dozen nuclear weapons, intermediate-
range missiles, 1.2 million military personnel, and an annual military
expenditure of nearly $11 billion. In terms of soft power, India has an
established democracy and was long regarded as a leader of non-
aligned countries during the Cold War. India has an influential diaspora, and its motion picture industry is the largest in the world in
terms of the number of films produced yearly, competing with Hollywood in parts of Asia and the Middle East.[88]

At the same time, India remains very much an underdeveloped
country, with hundreds of millions of illiterate citizens living in
poverty. Despite rapid economic growth, more than half a billion
Indians will remain in dire poverty. Harnessing technology to improve agriculture will be India's main challenge in alleviating poverty
by 2015. Moreover, the widening gulf between have and have-not regions and disagreements over the pace and nature of reforms could

be a source of domestic strife.[89] India's GDP of $1.7 trillion is less than half that of China and 20 percent of U.S. GDP. If the United States grows at 3 percent and India at 6 percent, it would take India until 2077 to reach the overall size of the American economy. And the gap in per capita income is even more dramatic, with the United States at $33,900 and India at $1,800. At a 3 percent difference in growth rates, it would take India until 2133 to reach parity with the American economy.[90] India's military capabilities are impressive in South Asia but not in the larger Asian context, where its equipment is less sophisticated and its expenditures only about half those attributed to China.[91] RAND projects that if Indian economic growth continues at 5.5 percent and it continues to spend 4 percent of GNP on defense, in fifteen years its military capital stock would reach $314 billion, or 62 percent of China's (compared with 48 percent today).[92]

India is unlikely alone to become a global challenge to the United States in this century, but it has considerable assets that could be added to the scales of a Sino-Russian-Indian coalition. And yet the likelihood that such a coalition would become a serious anti-American alliance is small. Just as there is lingering suspicion in the Sino-Russian relationship, so there is a similar rivalry between India and China. While the two countries signed agreements in 1993 and 1996 that promised peaceful settlement of the border dispute that led them to war in 1962, it is also worth noting that India's defense minister labeled China as India's "potential enemy number one" just prior to India's nuclear tests in March 1998. Rather than becoming an ally, India is more likely to become part of the group of Asian nations that will tend to balance China.

Europe

The closest thing to an equal that the United States faces at the beginning of the twenty-first century is the European Union (EU). Although the American economy is four times larger than that of Germany, the largest European country, the economy of the European Union is roughly equal to that of the United States; its population is

considerably larger, as is its share of world exports. These propor-
tions will increase if, as planned, the European Union gradually ex-
pands to include the states of Central Europe over the next decades.
Europe spends about two-thirds of what the United States does on
defense, has more men under arms, and includes two countries that
possess nuclear arsenals. In terms of soft power, European cultures
have long had a wide appeal in the rest of the world, and the sense of
a Europe uniting around Brussels has had a strong attraction to Eastern Europe as well as Turkey. Governments and peoples there have
begun to shape their policies to fit in with Brussels. Europeans have
been important pioneers and played central roles in international institutions. As Samuel Huntington argued a decade ago, a cohesive
Europe "would have the population resources, economic strength,
technology, and actual and potential military strength to be the preeminent power of the 21st century."[93] And some today see America
and Europe on the road to political conflict. A 1995 article in the *National Review* provides a good example of this, arguing that "a political bloc is emerging in the form of the European Union that likes to
see itself as a challenge to America."[94]

The key question in assessing the challenge presented by the EU is
whether it will develop enough political and social-cultural cohesion
to act as one unit on a wide range of international issues, or whether
it will remain a limited grouping of countries with strongly different
nationalisms and foreign policies. The uniting of Europe has been a
slow but steady process for half a century, and the pressures of globalization have added to the incentives to strengthen European regional institutions.

Already the European Union has effectively constrained American
power. On questions of trade and influence within the World Trade
Organization, Europe is the equal of the United States. European
countries successfully defied American trade sanctions against Cuba
and Iran. The creation of the European Monetary Union and the
launching of the euro at the beginning of 1999 was greeted by a number of observers as a major challenge to the United States and to the
role of the dollar as the dominant reserve currency.[95] While such
views overly discounted the unique depth and breadth of American

capital markets, which make countries willing to hold dollars, the European role in monetary affairs and the International Monetary Fund is nearly equal to that of the United States. The size and attraction of the European market has meant that American firms seeking to merge have had to seek approval from the European Commission as well as the U.S. Justice Department—as GE found out to its consternation in 2001 when the EU rejected its proposed takeover of Honeywell. And in the Internet age, American policy makers are concerned to make sure American practices do not contravene European regulations on privacy of information; "whether you like it or not, the EU is setting the standards for privacy protection for the rest of the world."[96] In short, for better or worse, Europe could be America's equal in power.

At the same time, Europe faces significant limits on its degree of unity. National identities remain stronger than a common European identity, despite fifty years of integration, and national interests, while subdued in comparison to the past, still matter.[97] Integration was driven for years by the engine of Franco-German cooperation. Europe was for Germany (in light of its history) both a goal and a substitute for a more assertive foreign policy. For France, there were few contradictions between Europe and an assertive French foreign policy so long as it had Germany "in its pocket." As Germany grew with reunification, developed a more "normal" foreign policy, and insisted on more weight in votes on European issues, French attitudes toward EU institutions became more cautious. As French prime minister Lionel Jospin put it, "I want Europe, but I remain attached to my nation. Making Europe without unmaking France, or any other European nation, that is my political choice."[98] Moreover, the continuing enlargement of the European Union to include Central Europeans means that European institutions are likely to remain sui generis, but tending toward the confederal rather than the federal end of the spectrum. The prospects for a strong federal Europe may have disappeared when the original six countries agreed upon expansion that included Britain and parts of Scandinavia. On the question of whether the EU is becoming a state, Harvard political scientist Andrew Moravscik summarizes succinctly: "Most informed observers prefer to speak of a 'postmodern polity' in which the EU rules along-side, rather than in place of, national governments."[99]

None of this is to belittle European institutions and what they have accomplished. Legal integration is increasing, with European Court verdicts compelling member countries to change practices, and the number of cases before the court has been growing by 10 percent per year.[100] On the other hand, legislative and executive branch integration has lagged. The European Parliament plays a use-ful but limited role, and turnout for its elections is lower than for na-tional elections. When the fifteen member countries held a summit in Nice in December 2000 to revamp institutions and prepare for the possible entry of twelve new countries, the members were reluctant to strengthen the European Commission or Parliament. While ma-jority voting was extended to cover additional issues in trade, tax and social security policy remained subject to national vetoes.

The integration of foreign and defense policy has been especially contentious. In 1999, the EU created a position for a high-ranking of-ficial to coordinate foreign policies, and agreed to create a force of sixty thousand troops for crisis intervention backed by the necessary command staff, intelligence, and decision-making authority. But French ambitions to create an independent force-planning structure that would have duplicated NATO capabilities were not accepted. Other European countries wanted to make sure that the new force did nothing to weaken NATO and the American commitment to Eu-rope. The idea of a modest European force that was "separable but not separate" from NATO could actually strengthen the alliance by allowing for a better sharing of burdens through improved European capacity to deal with minor intra-European conflicts. Some Ameri-can defense officials were skeptical of the new force, but even French attitudes were ambivalent. As Karl Kaiser, a German political scien-tist, noted, "The first to scream if American troops upped and left Germany would be the French because of their lingering fears of German hegemony."[101]

The other key to whether the EU becomes a global challenger to the United States rests on the nature of the linkages across the At-lantic.[102] Some foresee a progressive erosion of ties. Harvard's Stephen

Walt cites three serious reasons: the lack of a common threat reduces cohesion in the alliance; the United States now trades one and a half times as much with Asia as with Europe; and there are growing cultural differences among elites on both sides of the Atlantic as generations change.[103] In the words of an Italian editor, "A collective apprehension about the United States seems the only glue that binds Europeans together. Scathing stories about the United States' death penalty, shootings in high schools, unforgiving market, and lack of welfare abound in the European press. Cross the ocean and you will read about European gerontocracy, high unemployment, and very low defense budgets. There is no sign of a community forming between the two entities that the world insists on branding together as the West."[104]

On the other hand, reports of transatlantic differences are often overstated. A decade ago, some realists proclaimed that NATO was finished. They predicted that Germany would weaken its ties with Europe and ally with Russia.[105] Lord Ismay, the alliance's first secretary-general, famously quipped that the purpose of NATO was "to keep the Americans in, the Russians out, and the Germans down." Today, NATO still provides an insurance policy against Russia becoming an authoritarian threat, ensures German integration into a larger defense domain that appeals to Germans themselves, and remains a popular institutional connection to Europe in the United States. In addition, NATO provides insurance against new threats in the Balkans, the Mediterranean, and the Middle East that would be beyond the modest capacities of the European Rapid Reaction Force. As *The Economist* speculates, it is possible that "by about 2030, both Europe and America will be having the same trouble with some other part of the world." It cites Russia, China, and Muslim southwest Asia as likely suspects.[106] At the same time, such projections could be disrupted by inept American policies that fail to manage the Russian relationship while antagonizing Europeans. After September 2001, relations with Russia improved in the context of the coalition to combat terrorism. "Although Russia will continue to recede in importance to the European governments, they will use U.S. handling of Russia as a barometer of how well or poorly Washington is exerting leadership and defending European interests."[107]

Nor is economic divorce likely. New technology, flexibility in labor markets, strong venture capital, and an entrepreneurial culture make the American market attractive to European investors. Direct investment in both directions is higher than with Asia and helps knit the economies together. Nearly a third of trade occurs *within* transnational corporations. Moreover, while trade inevitably produces some degree of friction in the domestic politics of democracies, it is a game from which both sides can profit if there is a will to cooperate, and U.S.-European trade is more balanced than U.S. trade with Asia. While there will be conflicts over economic policy, and a need for compromise, Europe is not likely to be in a position to dictate to the United States. Lingering labor market rigidity and state regulation will hamper restructuring, retooling, and reinvestment strategies. Europe will trail the United States in entrepreneurship and innovation as governments seek ways to balance encouragement of these factors against social effects. Thus the National Intelligence Council predicts that Europe will not achieve fully "the dreams of parity with the United States as a shaper of the global economic system."[108] Cooperation will continue, though again, much will depend on avoiding heavy-handed policies.

At the cultural level, Americans and Europeans have sniped at and admired each other for more than two centuries. For all the complaints about McDonald's, no one forces the French (and other Europeans) to eat there, though millions do each year. In some ways, the inevitable frictions show a closeness rather than a distance. As Karsten Voigt, a senior German politician, put it, "The distinction between foreign and domestic policy has blurred as our societies have interwoven. That is why emotional issues like genetically altered food or the way we treat the children of international divorces rise to the surface. In a way foreign policy was easier when it dealt with interests rather than emotions and morals."[109] Yet it is also true that American consumers can benefit from European efforts to raise standards in antitrust actions or Internet privacy. And in a larger sense, Americans and Europeans share the values of democracy and human rights more thoroughly with each other than with any other region of the world. As Ambassador Robert Blackwill has written, at the deepest level, neither the United States nor Europe threatens the vital or important interests of the other side.[110]

Whether these deeper values or the surface frictions that accompany cultural change will prevail will depend in large part on how the United States plays its hand. Despite the concern and unity expressed by many Europeans in the wake of the terrorist attacks in the United States in September 2001—the French newspaper *Le Monde,* often critical of American policy, proclaimed, "We are all Americans"—many of America's European friends continue to worry about recent American behavior. The specter of U.S. isolationism that haunted Europe during the Cold War has been replaced by the specter of U.S. unilateralism. "Perceptions prevail that the United States is increasingly tempted to pursue unilaterally defined policies with little regard for the interests and viewpoints of other nations, as if the United States confuses its national interest with a global interest."[111] Such frictions are more likely to lead to a drifting apart rather than a sharp divorce that would create a hostile challenger, but the loss would nonetheless be great. Not only will Europeans conspire more often to frustrate American political objectives, but the United States will lose important opportunities for cooperation in the solution of global problems such as terrorism and its best partner for promoting the values of democracy and human rights. Europe remains the part of the world that is closest to us in basic values. As Samuel Huntington has put it, "Healthy co-operation with Europe is the prime antidote for the loneliness of U.S. superpowerdom."[112] American unilateralism may not produce a hostile European challenger in the military sense, but it would certainly reduce some of our best opportunities for friendship and partnership.

THE DISTRIBUTION OF POWER IN THE GLOBAL INFORMATION AGE

How great is the disparity between our power and that of the rest of the world? In military power, we are the only country with both nuclear weapons and conventional forces with global reach. Our military expenditures are greater than those of the next eight countries combined, and we lead in the information-based "revolution in military affairs."[113] Economically, we have a 27 percent share of world product, which (at market prices) was equal to that of the next three countries combined (Japan, Germany, France). We are the home of fifty-nine of the hundred largest companies in the world by market value (compared to thirty-one for Europe and seven for Japan.) Of the *Financial Times*' listing of the 500 largest global companies, 219 were American, 158 European, and 77 Japanese.[114] In direct foreign investment, we invested and received nearly twice as much as the next ranking country (Britain) and accounted for half of the top ten investment banks. American e-commerce was three times that of Europe, and we are the home of seven of the top ten software vendors. Forty-two of the top seventy-five brands were American, as well as nine of the top ten business schools.[115] In terms of soft power, the United States is far and away the number one film and television exporter in the world, although India's "Bollywood" actually produces more movies per year.[116] We also attract the most foreign students each year to our institutions of higher education, followed by Britain and Australia. In addition to students, over 500,000 foreign scholars were in residence at American educational institutions in 2000.[117] In the words of the *Financial Times,* "the U.S. is the dominant economic model for the rest of the developed world and much of the developing world."[118]

The United States had already become the world's largest economy by the end of the nineteenth century. America's economic domination reached its peak (at between a third and a half of world product, depending on the calculation) soon after 1945.[120] For the next twenty-five years, the American share declined to its long-term average as others recovered and developed.[121] Before World War I and again before World War II, the United States accounted for about a quarter of world product, and it remains slightly above or below that level today (depending on whether market prices or purchasing parity prices are used in the calculation). The American share of the GDP of the seven largest economies that hold annual economic summits was 48.7 percent in 1970, 46.8 percent in 1980, and 45.2 percent at the end of the century. "What has appeared to keep the U.S. safely

Table 1.2 *Power Resources c. 2000*[119]

	United States	Japan	Germany (EU)	France (EU)	Britain (EU)	Russia	China	India
Basic								
Territory in thousands of km²	9,269	378	357	547	245	17,075	9,597	3,288
Population in millions (1999)	276	127	83	59	60	146	1,262	1,014
Literacy rate	97	99	99	99	99	98	81.5	52
Military								
Nuclear warheads (1999)	12070	0	0	450	192	22,500	>40	85–90
Budget in billions of dollars (1999)	288.8	41.1	24.7	29.5	34.6	31	12.6	10.7
Personnel	1,371,500	236,300	332,800	317,300	212,400	1,004,100	2,480,000	1,173,000
Economic								
GDP in billions of dollars in purchasing power parity (1999)	9,255	2,950	1,864	1,373	1,290	620	4,800	1,805
Per capita GDP, in purchasing power parity (1999)	33,900	23,400	22,700	23,300	21,800	4,200	3,800	1,800
Manufacturing value added, in billions of dollars (1996)	1,344	1,117	556	290	214	NA	309	63
High-tech exports, in billions of dollars (1997)	637	420	112	69	96	87	183	32
Number of personal computers per thousand population	570.5	286.9	297	221.8	302.5	37.4	12.2	3.3

at the top of the league has been its traditional strengths—a huge single market fostering competition, a stable currency and a sound financial system—allied to rapid technological progress in its information technology sector."[122]

Can this degree of economic dominance continue? Probably not. As globalization stimulates economic growth in poor countries that are able to take advantage of new technology and world markets, their share of world product should increase, much as did that of East Asian countries over the past few decades. If the United States and other wealthy countries grow at about 2.5 percent per year but the fifteen largest underdeveloped countries grow between 4 and 5.5 percent per year, "over half of world gross output 30 years hence will be in countries that are poor today whereas 1990s rich ones, the current members of the OECD, will see their share fall from 70% of the world total to about 45%. The United States share falls from about 23% to 15%."[123] The United States would still have the largest economy, but its lead would be more modest than it is today. Of course, such linear projections can be foiled by political change and historical surprises, and growth in developing countries may not be this fast. Nonetheless, it would be surprising if the U.S. share did *not* shrink over the course of the century. As a Canadian political scientist concludes, "Unless the United States suffers a major catastrophe (and one, moreover, that does not also affect other major powers), there is only one way that the relative balance of power capabilities between the United States and the other major powers extant at the turn of the millennium will change: very slowly, and over many decades."[124] Although the September 2001 tragedy was terrible, it would take a series of much larger catastrophes to really reduce the American lead.

Even in the likely event that the United States remains the largest country well into the century as measured by the power resources summarized in Table 1.2, there are other changes occurring in the distribution of power. After the collapse of the Soviet Union, some have described the resulting world as unipolar, some as multipolar. Both groups are right and both are wrong, because each is referring to a different dimension of power that can no longer be assumed to be homogenized by military dominance. Unipolarity is misleading because it exaggerates the degree to which the United States is able to get the results it wants in some dimensions of world politics, but multipolarity is misleading because it implies several roughly equal countries.

Instead, power today is distributed among countries in a pattern that resembles a complex three-dimensional chess game.[125] On the top chessboard, military power is largely unipolar. As we have seen, the United States is the only country with both intercontinental nuclear weapons and large, state-of-the-art air, naval, and ground forces capable of global deployment. But on the middle chessboard, economic power is multipolar, with the United States, Europe, and Japan representing two-thirds of world product, and with China's dramatic growth likely to make it a major player early in the century. As we have seen, on this economic board, the United States is not a hegemon and often must bargain as an equal with Europe. This has led some observers to call it a hybrid uni-multipolar world.[126] But the situation is even more complicated and difficult for the traditional terminology of the balance of power among states to capture. The bottom chessboard is the realm of transnational relations that cross borders outside of government control. This realm includes non-state actors as diverse as bankers electronically transferring sums larger than most national budgets, at one extreme, and terrorists carrying out attacks and hackers disrupting Internet operations, at the other. On this bottom board, power is widely dispersed, and it makes no sense to speak of unipolarity, multipolarity, or hegemony. Those who recommend a hegemonic American foreign policy based on such traditional descriptions of American power are relying on woefully inadequate analysis. When you are in a three-dimensional game, you will lose if you focus only on the interstate military board and fail to notice the other boards and the vertical connections among them.

Because of its leading edge in the information revolution and its past investment in traditional power resources, the good news for Americans is that the United States will likely remain the world's single most powerful country well into this new century. While potential coalitions to check American power could be created, as we have seen above, it is unlikely that they would become firm alliances unless the United States handles its hard power in an overbearing, unilateral manner that undermines its soft power. As Joseph Joffe has written, "Unlike centuries past, when war was the great arbiter, today the most interesting types of power do not come out of the barrel of a gun. . . . Today there is a much bigger payoff in 'getting others to want what you want,' and that has to do with cultural attraction and ideology and agenda setting and holding out big prizes for cooperation, like the vastness and sophistication of the American market. On that gaming table, China, Russia and Japan, even the West Europeans, cannot match the pile of chips held by the United States."[127] The United States could squander this soft power by heavy-handed unilateralism. As Richard Haass, the director of policy planning at the State Department in George W. Bush's administration, has warned, any attempt to dominate "would lack domestic support and stimulate international resistance, which in turn would make the costs of hegemony all the greater and its benefits all the smaller."[128] Much will depend on the evolution of American public opinion, congressional attitudes, and administration policies. That part of the answer is largely in American hands.

The bad news for Americans in this more complex distribution of power in the twenty-first century is that there are more and more things outside the control of even the most powerful state. September 11, 2001, should have sounded a wake-up call. Although the United States does well on the traditional measures, there is increasingly more going on in the world that those measures fail to capture. Under the influence of the information revolution and globalization, world politics is changing in a way that means Americans cannot achieve all their international goals acting alone. The United States lacks both the international and domestic prerequisites to resolve conflicts that are internal to other societies, and to monitor and control transnational transactions that threaten Americans at home. We must mobilize international coalitions to address shared threats and challenges. We will have to learn better how to share as well as lead. As a British observer has written, "The paradox of American power at the end of this millennium is that it is too great to be challenged by any other state, yet not great enough to solve problems such as global terrorism and nuclear proliferation. America needs the help and respect of other nations."[129] We will be in trouble if we do not get it. For reasons we shall see in the next two chapters, that part of the answer will increasingly be in others' hands.

2

THE INFORMATION REVOLUTION

In 1997, Jodie Williams, then a Vermont-based grassroots activist, won the Nobel peace prize for helping to create a treaty banning antipersonnel land mines despite the opposition of the Pentagon, the strongest bureaucracy in the strongest country in the world. She organized her campaign largely on the Internet. In 1999, fifteen hundred groups and individuals met in Seattle and disrupted an important meeting of the World Trade Organization. Again, much of their campaign was planned on the Internet. The next year, a young hacker in the Philippines launched a virus that spread round the world and may have caused $4 billion to $15 billion in damage in the United States alone. Unknown hackers have stolen information from the Pentagon, NASA, and major corporations such as Microsoft. The hard drives of computers seized from terrorists have revealed sophisticated networks of communication. On the other hand, young Iranians and Chinese use the Internet surreptitiously to plug into Western web sites and to discuss democracy. An information revolution is dramatically altering the world of American foreign policy, making it harder for officials to manage policy. At the same time, by promoting decentralization and democracy, the information revolution is creating conditions that are consistent with American values and serve our long-term interests—if we learn how to take advantage of them.

Four centuries ago, the English statesman-philosopher Francis Bacon wrote that information is power. At the start of the twenty-first century, a much larger part of the population both within and among countries has access to this power. Governments have always worried about the flow and control of information, and the current period is not the first to be strongly affected by changes in information technology. Gutenberg's invention of movable type, which allowed printing of the Bible and its accessibility to large portions of the European population, is often credited with playing a major role in the onset of the Reformation. Pamphlets and committees of correspondence paved the way for the American Revolution. In the tightly censored world of eighteenth-century France, news that circulated through several media and modes outside the law—oral, manuscript, and print—helped lay the foundation for the French Revolution. As Princeton historian Robert Darnton argues, "Every age was an information age, each in its own way."[1] But not even Bacon could have imagined the present-day information revolution.

The current information revolution is based on rapid technological advances in computers, communications, and software that in turn have led to dramatic decreases in the cost of processing and transmitting information. The price of a new computer has dropped by nearly a fifth every year since 1954. Information technologies have risen from 7 percent to nearly 50 percent of new investment in the United States. Computing power has doubled every eighteen months for the last thirty years and even more rapidly in recent times, and it now costs less than 1 percent of what it did in the early 1970s. If the price of automobiles had fallen as quickly as the price of semiconductors, a car today would cost $5.

Traffic on the Internet has been doubling every hundred days for the past few years. In 1993, there were about fifty web sites in the world; by the end of decade, that number had surpassed five million.[2] Communications bandwidths are expanding rapidly, and communications costs continue to fall even more rapidly than computing power. As late as 1980, phone calls over copper wire could carry only one page of information per second; today a thin strand of optical fiber can transmit ninety thousand *volumes* in a second.[3] In terms of 1990 dollars, the cost of a three-minute transatlantic phone call has fallen from $250 in 1930 to considerably less than $1 at the end of the century.[4] In 1980, a gigabyte of storage occupied a room's worth of space; now it can fit on a credit-card-sized device in your pocket.[5]

The key characteristic of the information revolution is not the *speed* of communications between the wealthy and powerful—for more than 130 years, virtually instantaneous communication has been possible between Europe and North America. The crucial change is the enormous reduction in the *cost* of transmitting information. For all practical purposes, the actual transmission costs have become negligible; hence the amount of information that can be transmitted worldwide is effectively infinite. The result is an explosion of information, of which documents are a tiny fraction. By one estimate, there are 1.5 billion gigabytes of magnetically stored digital information (or 250 megabytes for each inhabitant of the earth), and shipments of such information are doubling each year. At the turn of the twenty-first century, there were 610 billion e-mail messages and 2.1 billion static pages on the World Wide Web, with the number of pages growing at a rate of 100 percent annually.[6] This dramatic change in the linked technologies of computing and communications, sometimes called the third industrial revolution, is changing the nature of governments and sovereignty, increasing the role of non-state actors, and enhancing the importance of soft power in foreign policy.[7]

LESSONS FROM THE PAST

We can get some idea of where we are heading by looking back at the past. In the first industrial revolution, around the turn of the nineteenth century, the application of steam to mills and transportation had a powerful effect on the economy, society, and government. Patterns of production, work, living conditions, social class, and political power were transformed. Public education arose to satisfy the need for literate, trained workers to work in increasingly complex and potentially dangerous factories. Police forces such as London's bobbies were created to deal with urbanization. Subsidies were provided for the necessary infrastructure of canals and railroads.[8]

The second industrial revolution, around the turn of the twentieth century, introduced electricity, synthetics, and the internal combustion engine and brought similar economic and social changes. The United States went from a predominantly agrarian nation to a primarily industrial and urban one. In the 1890s, most Americans still worked on farms or as servants. A few decades later, the majority lived in cities and worked in factories.[9] Social class and political cleavages were altered as urban labor and trade unions become more important. And again, with lags, the role of government changed. The bipartisan Progressive movement ushered in antitrust legislation; early consumer protection regulation was implemented by the forerunner of the Food and Drug Administration, and economic stabilization measures by the Federal Reserve Board.[10] The United States rose to the status of a great power in world politics. Some expect the third industrial revolution to produce analogous transformations in economy, society, government, and world politics.[11]

These historical analogies help us understand some of the forces that will shape world politics in the twenty-first century. Economies and information networks have changed more rapidly than governments have, with their scale having grown much faster than that of sovereignty and authority. "If there is a single overriding sociological problem in post-industrial society—particularly in the management of transition—it is the management of scale."[12] Put more simply, the building blocks of world politics are being transformed by the new technology, and our policies will have to adjust accordingly. If we focus solely on the hard power of nation-states, we will miss the new reality and fail to advance our interests and our values.

CENTRALIZATION OR DIFFUSION?

Six decades ago, the eminent sociologist William Ogburn predicted that new technologies would result in greater political centralization and strengthening of states in the twentieth century. In 1937, Ogburn argued that "government in the United States will probably tend toward greater centralization because of the airplane, the bus, the truck, the Diesel engine, the radio, the telephone, and the various uses to which the wire and wireless may be placed. The same inventions operate to influence industries to spread across state lines. . . . The centralizing tendency of government seems to be world-wide, wherever modern transportation and communication exist."[13] By and large, he was right about the twentieth century, but this trend is likely to be reversed in the twenty-first century.

Questions of appropriate degrees of centralization of government are not new. As the economist Charles Kindleberger pointed out, "how the line should be altered at a given time—toward or away from the center—can stay unresolved for long periods, typically fraught with tension."[14] If the nation-state has "become too small for the big problems of life and too big for the small problems,"[15] we may find not centralization or decentralization but a diffusion of governance activities in several directions at the same time. The following table illustrates the possible diffusion of activities away from central governments—vertically to other levels of government and horizontally to market and private nonmarket actors, the so-called third sector. Nonprofit institutions have grown rapidly in the United States, now accounting for 7 percent of paid employment (more than the number of federal and state government employees) and United States–based international nongovernmental organizations expanded tenfold between 1970 and the early 1990s.[16] If the twentieth century saw a predominance of the centripetal forces predicted by Ogburn, the twenty-first may see a greater role of centrifugal forces.

The height of twentieth-century centralization was the totalitarian state perfected by Josef Stalin in the Soviet Union.[17] It aptly fit—indeed, was made possible by—industrial society, and it was ultimately undermined by the information revolution. Stalin's economic model was based on central planning, which made quantity rather than profits the main criterion of a manager's success. Prices were set by planners rather than by markets. Consumers as customers played little role. The Stalinist economy was successful in mastering relatively

Table 2.1   *The Diffusion of Governance in the Twenty-first Century*

	Private	*Public*	*Third Sector*
Supranational	Transnational corporations (e.g., IBM, Shell)	International governmental organizations (e.g., UN, WTO)	Nongovernmental organizations (e.g., Oxfam, Greenpeace)
National	National corporations (e.g., American Airlines)	↖ ↑ ↗ *Twentieth-Century central government* ↙ ↓ ↘	National non-profits (e.g., American Red Cross)
Subnational	Local businesses	Local government	Local groups

unsophisticated technologies and producing basic goods such as steel and electricity on a massive scale. It was effective in extracting capital from the agricultural sector in the 1930s and using it to build heavy industry. It was also effective in postwar reconstruction, when labor was plentiful. However, with a diminishing birthrate and scarce capital, Stalin's model of central planning ran out of steam.[18]

In addition, Soviet central planners lacked the flexibility to keep up with the quickened pace of technological change in the increasingly information-based global economy; they did not come to terms with the third industrial revolution. As Russian specialist Marshall Goldman once put it, "Stalin's growth model eventually became a fetter rather than a facilitator."[19] As computers and microchips became not merely tools of production but imbedded in products, the life cycles of products shortened, sometimes dramatically. Many products were now becoming obsolete in only a few years or even sooner, even though a rigid planning system might take much longer to react or simply continue toward obsolete goals. The Soviet bureaucracy was far less flexible than markets in responding to rapid change, and for years the very word *market* was practically forbidden.[20]

Stalin's political legacy was yet another hindrance to the Soviet Union. An information-based society required broadly shared and freely flowing information to reap maximum gains. Horizontal communication among computers became more important than top-down vertical communication. But horizontal communication involved political risks, in that computers could become the equivalent of printing presses. Moreover, telephones multiplied these risks by providing instant communication among computers. For political reasons, Soviet leaders were reluctant to foster the widespread and free use of computers. Two simple statistics demonstrate the Soviet disadvantage in the expanding information economy of the 1980s: by the middle of the decade, there were only fifty thousand personal computers in the USSR (compared to thirty million in the United States), and only 23 percent of urban homes and 7 percent of rural homes had telephones.[21] Although this situation made political control easier, it had disastrous economic effects. In the mid-1980s, the Soviets failed to produce personal computers on a large scale. At the end of the decade, Soviet officials reluctantly admitted that their computer technology lagged seven to ten years behind that of the West. Further, lack of freedom for hackers and other informal innovators severely handicapped the development of software. The Soviets paid a heavy price for central control.[22]

Governments of all kinds will find their control slipping during the twenty-first century as information technology gradually spreads to the large majority of the world that still lacks phones, computers, and electricity. Even the U.S. government will find some taxes harder to collect and some regulations (for example, concerning gambling or prescription drugs) harder to enforce. Many governments today control the access of their citizens to the Internet by controlling Internet service providers. It is possible, but costly, for skilled individuals to route around such restrictions, and control does not have to be complete to be effective for political purposes. But as societies develop, they face dilemmas in trying to protect their sovereign control over information. When they reach levels of development where their knowledge workers want free access to the Internet, they run the risk of losing their scarcest resource for competing in the information economy. Thus Singapore today is wrestling with the dilemma of reshaping its educational system to encourage the individual creativity that the information economy demands, and at the same time maintain some existing social controls over the flow of information. In the words of Singapore's prime minister, Goh Chok Tong, "We have to reinvent ourselves. We have to go beyond being efficient and productive to create and attract new enterprise."[23] When asked how Singapore could control the Internet after its schools educated a new generation in how to work around the controls, the senior minister, Lee Kuan Yew, replied that at that stage it would not matter anymore.[24] Closed systems become more costly, and openness becomes worth the price.

China is a more complicated case than Singapore because of its size and lower level of economic development. The Chinese government has traditionally doled out information depending on bureaucratic rank and discouraged the flow of information among individuals. As Sinologist Tony Saich has described, "Under such a system the real basis of exchange is secrets and privileged access to information."[25] Now the Chinese government is trying to profit from the economic benefits of the Internet without letting it unravel their system of political control. They do this by authorizing only four networks for international access, blocking web sites, and forbidding Chinese web sites to use news from web sites outside the country. The Internet is censored via the service providers and the portals that host bulletin boards.

Use of the Internet in China has grown dramatically, from a million users in 1998 to about twenty million two years later. Nonetheless, those users represent only about 1.3 percent of the population and are mostly relatively well-off city dwellers, not the majority rural population. Some sites and topics are quickly suppressed, but general critiques of communist leaders and the party's monopoly on power are common, as are debates about the growing divide between rich and poor in China.[26] Underground dissident journals are sent to hundreds of thousands of Chinese e-mail accounts from the safety of overseas. The *New York Times* reported recently that the influence of "shadow media is growing exponentially, along with China's Internet, as articles from even the most obscure newspapers quickly find their way onto web sites and into chat rooms."[27]

Some of the articles are radical and chauvinistic rather than liberal and democratic. During the crisis following the spring 2001 midair collision between a U.S. surveillance aircraft and a Chinese fighter plane, the Chinese government toughened its public position after monitoring the nationalistic responses on the Internet.[28] The Internet is not necessarily a fast path to liberal democracy. The Chinese leadership is aware that it cannot control completely the flow of information or access to foreign sites by its citizens. Its intention is to lay down warnings about limits.[29] In a sense, Chinese leaders are betting that they can have the Internet à la carte, picking out the economic plums and avoiding the political costs that come with the whole menu. In the near term, they are probably correct in their bet, but the long run remains more doubtful. In the opinion of Singapore's Lee Kuan Yew, "Over the next 30 to 40 years there is going to be a drift into all the cities and the small towns will become big ones, all with access to the Internet, access to information. There is no way you can govern a well informed, large managerial/professional class without taking their views into account."[30]

One political effect of increased information flows through new media is already clear: governments have lost some of their traditional control over information about their own societies. In 2001, for example, the Indian government lost several ministers and nearly collapsed after reports of corruption appeared on an Internet news site. Scandals that were once more easily contained in New Delhi proved impossible to control. "Not only did Tehelka.com reveal the corrupt underbelly of the Indian military: it also helped fan the controversy by serving as a bulletin board for readers and politicians to air their views."[31] In the Philippines, hundreds of thousands of protesters working successfully to oust President Joseph Estrada "were able to call meetings at short notice by sending text messages on their mobile phones."[32] Corruption remains a problem in many countries, but it is no longer solely a domestic affair, as nongovernmental organizations now publicize corruption rankings of countries on the Internet. Countries that seek to develop need foreign capital and the technology and organization that go with it. Increasingly, foreign capital demands transparency. Governments that are not transparent are less credible, since the information they offer is seen as biased and selective. Moreover, as economic development progresses and middle-class societies develop, repressive measures become more expensive not merely at home but also in terms of international reputation. Both Taiwan and South Korea discovered in the late 1980s that repression of rising demands for democracy would be too expensive in terms of their reputation and soft power.

Countries will vary in how far and how fast the information revolution will push decentralization. Some states are weaker than the private forces within them, others not. Private armies have played a key role in Sierra Leone; drug cartels are a major force in Colombia. Ecuador and Haiti have far weaker bureaucracies than South Africa and Singapore. Even in the postindustrial world, most European countries have a tradition of stronger central government than the United States does. Total government spending is about half of gross national product in Europe, while it has held steady at around a third of the economy in the United States and Japan and declined in New Zealand.[33]

Two other trends are closely related to the information revolution and reinforce the prospect that this century will see a shift in the locus of collective activities away from central governments. As we shall see in the next chapter, globalization preceded the information revolution but has been greatly enhanced by it, opening up opportunities for private transnational actors such as corporations and nonprofits to establish standards and strategies that strongly affect public policies that were once the domain of central governments. Similarly, the information revolution has enhanced the role of markets. The balance between states and markets shifted after the 1970s in a way that made the state just one source of authority among several.[34] Even in Sweden and France, not to mention Eastern Europe and the less economically developed countries, significant privatizations have expanded market forces in the past two decades. The causes of marketization involved more than just the information revolution. They include the failure of planned economies to adapt to the information revolution, the inflation that followed the oil crises of the 1970s, the early success of the East Asian economies, and changes in political and ideological coalitions (the Thatcher-Reagan revolution) inside wealthy democracies. The net effect, however, is to accelerate the diffusion of power away from governments to private actors, and that, in turn, presents new challenges and opportunities for American foreign policy.

AS THE REVOLUTION PROGRESSES

We are still at an early stage of the current information revolution, and its effects on economics and politics are uneven. As with steam in the late eighteenth century and electricity in the late nineteenth, productivity growth lagged as society had to learn to fully utilize the new technologies.[35] Social institutions change more slowly than technology. For example, the electric motor was invented in 1881, but it was nearly four decades before Henry Ford pioneered the reorganization of factories to take full advantage of electric power. Computers today account for 2 percent of America's total capital stock, but "add in all the equipment used for gathering, processing and transmitting information, and the total accounts for 12% of America's capital stock, exactly the same as the railways at the peak of their development in the late nineteenth century. . . . Three-quarters of all computers are used in the service sector such as finance and health where output is notoriously hard to measure."[36] As we will see in chapter 4, the increase in productivity of the American economy began to show up only as recently as the mid-1990s.[37]

The advent of truly mass communications and broadcasting a century ago, which was facilitated by newly cheap electricity, provides some lessons about possible social and political effects today. It ushered in the age of mass popular culture.[38] The effects of mass communication and broadcasting, though not the telephone, tended to have a centralizing political effect. While information was more widespread, it was more centrally influenced even in democratic countries than in the age of the local press. Roosevelt's use of radio in the 1930s worked a dramatic shift in American politics. These effects were particularly pronounced in countries where they were combined with the rise of totalitarian governments, which were able to suppress competing sources of information. Indeed, some scholars believe that totalitarianism could not have been possible without the mass communications that accompanied the second industrial revolution.[39]

In the middle of the twentieth century, people feared that the computers and communications of the current information revolution would create the central governmental control dramatized in George Orwell's vision of *1984*. Mainframe computers seemed set to enhance central planning and increase the surveillance powers of those at the top of a pyramid of control. Government television would dominate the news. Through central databases, computers can make government identification and surveillance easier, and commercialization has already altered the early libertarian culture and code of the Internet.[40] Nonetheless, the technology of encryption is evolving, and programs such as Gnutella and Freenet enable users to trade digital information anonymously.[41] They promise greater space for individuals than the early pessimists envisioned, and the Internet is more difficult for governments to control than the technology of the second information revolution was. On balance, the communication theorist Ithiel de Sola Pool was correct in his characterization of "technologies of freedom."[42]

As computing power has decreased in cost and computers have shrunk in size and become more widely distributed, their decentralizing effects have outweighed their centralizing effects. The Internet creates a system in which power over information is much more widely distributed. Compared with radio, television, and newspapers, controlled by editors and broadcasters, the Internet creates unlimited communication one-to-one (e.g., via e-mail), one-to-many (e.g., via a personal home page or electronic conference), many-to-one (e.g., via electronic broadcast), and, perhaps most important, many-to-many (e.g., an online chat room). "Internet messages have the capacity to flow farther, faster, and with fewer intermediaries."[43]

Central surveillance is possible, but governments that aspire to control information flows through control of the Internet face high costs and ultimate frustration. Rather than reinforcing centralization and bureaucracy, the new information technologies have tended to foster network organizations, new types of community, and demands for different roles for government.[44]

What this means is that foreign policy will not be the sole province of governments. Both individuals and private organizations, here and abroad, will be empowered to play direct roles in world politics. The spread of information will mean that power will be more widely distributed and informal networks, such as those mentioned at the beginning of this chapter, will undercut the monopoly of traditional bureaucracy. The speed of Internet time means that all governments, both here and overseas, will have less control of their agendas. Political leaders will enjoy fewer degrees of freedom before they must respond to events, and then will have to share the stage with more actors. Privatization and public-private partnerships will increase. As we shape our foreign policy in the information age, we will have to avoid being mesmerized by terms such as *unipolarity* and *hegemony* and by measures of strength that compare only the hard power of states run by centralized governments. The old images of sovereign states balancing and bouncing off each other like billiard balls will blind us to the new complexity of world politics.

A NEW WORLD POLITICS

The effects on central governments of the third industrial revolution are still in their early stages. Management expert Peter Drucker and the futurists Heidi Toffler and Alvin Toffler argue that the information revolution is bringing an end to the hierarchical bureaucratic organizations that typified the age of the first two industrial revolutions.[45] In civil societies, as decentralized organizations and virtual communities develop on the Internet, they cut across territorial jurisdictions and develop their own patterns of governance. Internet guru Esther Dyson refers to the "disintermediation of government" and portrays a global society of the connected being overlaid on traditional local geographical communities.[46]

If these prophets are right, the result would be a new cyberfeudalism, with overlapping communities and jurisdictions laying claims to multiple layers of citizens' identities and loyalties. In short, these transformations suggest the reversal of the modern centralized state that has dominated world politics for the past three and a half centuries. A medieval European might have owed equal loyalty to a local lord, a duke, a king, and the pope. A future European might owe loyalty to Brittany, Paris, and Brussels, as well as to several cybercommunities concerned with religion, work, and various hobbies.

While the system of sovereign states is still the dominant pattern in international relations, one can begin to discern a pattern of crosscutting communities and governance that bears some resemblance to the situation before the Peace of Westphalia formalized the state system in 1648. Transnational contacts across political borders were typical in the feudal era but gradually became constrained by the rise of centralized nation-states. Now sovereignty is changing. Three decades ago, transnational contacts were already growing, but they involved relatively small numbers of elites involved in multinational corporations, scientific groups, and academic institutions.[47] Now the Internet, because of its low costs, is opening transnational communications to many millions of people.

The issue of sovereignty is hotly contested in American foreign policy today. The sovereigntists, closely allied with the new unilateralists, resist anything that seems to diminish American autonomy.[48] They worry about the political role of the United Nations in limiting the use of force, the economic decisions handed down by the World Trade Organization, and efforts to develop environmental institutions and treaties. In their eyes, the notion of an international community of opinion is illusory.

But even excluding the fringe groups that believe the United Nations has black helicopters ready to swoop into American territory, the debate over the fate of the sovereign state has been poorly framed. As a former UN official put it, "There is an extraordinarily impoverished mind-set at work here, one that is able to visualize long-term challenges to the system of states only in terms of entities that are institutionally substitutable for the state."[49] A better historical analogy is the development of markets and town life in the early feudal period. Medieval trade fairs were not substitutes for the institutions of feudal authority. They did not tear down the castle walls or remove the local lord. But they did bring new wealth, new coalitions, and new attitudes summarized by the maxim "Town air brings freedom."

Medieval merchants developed the *lex mercatoria,* which governed their relations, largely as a private set of rules for conducting business.[50] Similarly today, a range of individuals and entities, from hackers to large corporations, are developing the code and norms of the Internet partly outside the control of formal political institutions. The development of transnational corporate intranets behind firewalls and encryption "represent private appropriations of a public space."[51] Private systems, such as corporate intranets or worldwide newsgroups devoted to specific issues like the environment, do not frontally challenge the governments of sovereign states; they simply add a layer of relations that sovereign states do not effectively control. Americans will participate in transnational Internet communities without ceasing to be loyal Americans, but their perspectives will be broader than those typical of loyal Americans before the Internet came into existence.

Or consider the shape of the world economy, in which a nation's strength is usually measured by its imports and exports from other sovereign nations. Such trade flows and balances still matter, but the decisions on what to produce and whether to produce it at home or overseas are increasingly made within the domains of transnational corporations. Some American companies, such as Nike, produce virtually none of their products inside this country, though intangible (and valuable) design and marketing work is done here. In the 1990s, declining information and telecommunications costs allowed firms to broaden the geographic dispersion of their operations. Thus imports and exports provide a very incomplete picture of global economic linkages. For example, overseas production by American transnational corporations was more than twice the value of American exports; sales by foreign-owned companies inside the United

States were nearly twice the value of imports.[52] Microeconomic links "have created a nonterritorial 'region' in the world economy—a decentered yet integrated space-of-flows, operating in real time, which exists alongside the spaces-of-places that we call national economies."[53] If we restrict our images to billiard ball states, we miss this layer of reality.

Even in the age of the Internet, the changing roles of political institutions is likely to be a gradual process. After the rise of the territorial state, other successors to medieval rule such as the Italian city-states and the Hanseatic League persisted as viable alternatives, able to tax and fight for nearly two centuries.[54] Today, the Internet rests on servers located in specific nations, and various governments' laws affect access providers. The real issue is not the continued existence of the sovereign state, but how its centrality and functions are being altered. "The reach of the state has increased in some areas but contracted in others. Rulers have recognized that their effective control can be enhanced by walking away from some issues they cannot resolve."[55] All countries, including the United States, are facing a growing list of problems that are difficult to control within sovereign boundaries—financial flows, drug trade, climate change, AIDS, refugees, terrorism, cultural intrusions—to name a few. Complicating the task of national governance is not the same as undermining sovereignty. Governments adapt. However, in the process of adaptation they change the meaning of sovereign jurisdiction, control, and the role of private actors.

Take, for example, the problems of controlling U.S. borders. In one year, 475 million people, 125 million vehicles, and 21 million import shipments come into the country at 3,700 terminals in 301 ports of entry. It takes five hours to inspect a fully loaded forty-foot shipping container, and more than 5 million enter each year. In addition, more than 2.7 million undocumented immigrants have simply walked or ridden across the Mexican and Canadian borders in recent years. As we have seen, terrorists easily slip in, and it is easier to bring in a few pounds of a deadly biological or chemical agent than to smuggle in the tons of illegal heroin and cocaine that arrive annually. The only way for the Customs Service and the Immigration and Naturalization

Service to cope with such flows is to reach beyond the national borders through intelligence and cooperation inside the jurisdiction of other states, and to rely on private corporations to develop transparent systems for tracking international commercial flows so that enforcement officials can conduct virtual audits of inbound shipments before they arrive. Thus customs officers work throughout Latin America to assist businesses in the implementation of security programs that reduce the risk of being exploited by drug smugglers, and cooperative international mechanisms are being developed for policing trade flows.[56] The sovereign state adapts, but in doing so it transforms the meaning and exclusivity of governmental jurisdiction. Legal borders do not change, but they blur in practice.

National security—the absence of threat to our major values—is changing. Damage done by climate change or imported viruses can be larger in terms of money or lives lost than the effects of some wars. But even if one frames the definition of national security more narrowly, the nature of military security is changing. As the U.S. Commission on National Security in the Twenty-first Century pointed out, the country has not been invaded by foreign armies since 1814, and the military is designed to project force and fight wars far from our shores. But the military is not well equipped to protect us against an attack on our homeland by terrorists wielding weapons of mass destruction or mass disruption or even hijacked civil aircraft.[57] Thus in July 2001, the secretary of defense, Donald Rumsfeld, dropped from the Pentagon's planning priorities the ability to fight two major regional conflicts and elevated homeland defense to a higher priority. But as we discovered only a few months later, military measures are not a sufficient solution to our vulnerabilities.

Today, attackers may be governments, groups, individuals, or some combination. They may be anonymous and not even come near the country. In 1998, when Washington complained about seven Moscow Internet addresses involved in the theft of Pentagon and NASA secrets, the Russian government replied that phone numbers from which the attacks originated were inoperative. We had no way of knowing whether the government had been involved or not. More than thirty nations have developed aggressive computer-warfare programs, but as anyone with a computer knows, any individual can also enter the game. With a few keystrokes, an anonymous source anywhere in the world might break into and disrupt the (private) power grids of American cities or the (public) emergency response systems.[58] And U.S. government firewalls are not enough. Every night American software companies send work electronically to India, where software engineers can work while Americans sleep and send it back the next morning. Someone outside our borders could also embed trap-doors deep in computer code for use at a later date. Nuclear deterrence, border patrols, and stationing troops overseas to shape regional power balances will continue to matter in the information age, but they will not be sufficient to provide national security.

Competing interpretations of sovereignty arise even in the domain of law. Since 1945, human rights provisions have coexisted in the charter of the United Nations alongside provisions that protect the sovereignty of states. Article 2.7 says that nothing shall authorize the United Nations to intervene in matters within domestic jurisdictions. Yet the development of a global norm of antiracism and repugnance at the South African practice of apartheid led large majorities at the UN to abridge this principle. More recently, the NATO intervention in Kosovo was the subject of hot debate among international lawyers, with some claiming it was illegal because it was not explicitly authorized by the UN Security Council and others arguing that it was legal under the evolving body of international humanitarian law.[59] The 1998 detention of General Augusto Pinochet in Britain in response to a Spanish request for extradition based on human rights violations and crimes committed while he was president of Chile is another example of this complexity. In 2001, a magistrate in Paris tried to summon former U.S. Secretary of State Henry Kissinger to testify in a trial related to Chile.

Information technology, particularly the Internet, has eased the tasks of coordination and strengthened the hand of human rights activists, but political leaders, particularly in formerly colonized countries, cling to the protections that legal sovereignty provides against outside interventions. The world is likely to see these two partly contradictory bodies of international law continue to coexist for years to come, and as we shall see in chapter 5, Americans will have to wrestle with these contradictions as we decide how to promote human rights and when to intervene in conflicts for humanitarian reasons.

For many people, the national state provides a source of the political identity that is important to them. People are capable of multiple identities—family, village, ethnic group, religion, nationality, cosmopolitan—and which predominates often depends on the context.[60] At home, I am from Lexington; in Washington, I am from Massachusetts; overseas, I am an American. In many preindustrial countries, subnational identities (tribe or clan) prevail. In some postindustrial countries, including the United States, cosmopolitan identities such as "global citizen" or "custodian of planet Earth" are beginning to emerge. Since large identities (such as nationalism) are not directly experienced, they are "imagined communities" that depend very much on the effects of communication.[61] It is still too early to understand the full effects of the Internet, but the shaping of identities can move in contradictory directions at the same time—up to Brussels, down to Brittany, or fixed on Paris—as circumstances dictate.

The result may be greater volatility rather than consistent movement in any one direction. The many-to-many and one-to-many characteristics of the Internet seem "highly conducive to the irreverent, egalitarian, and libertarian character of the cyber-culture." One effect is "flash movements"—sudden surges of protest—triggered by particular issues or events, such as antiglobalization protests or the sudden rise of the anti-fuel-tax coalition that captured European politics in the autumn of 2000.[62] Politics becomes more theatrical and aimed at global audiences. The Zapatista rebels in Mexico's Chiapas state relied less on bullets than on transnational publicity, and, of course, terrorists seek theatrical effects as well as destruction. Television is as important as weapons to them. The political scientist James Rosenau has tried to summarize such trends by inventing a new word, *fragmegration,* to express the idea that both integration toward larger identities and fragmentation into smaller communities can occur at the same time. But one need not alter the English language to realize that apparently contradictory movements can occur simultaneously. They do not spell the end of the sovereign state, but they do make its politics more volatile and less self-contained within national shells.

Private organizations also increasingly cross national boundaries. Transnational religious organizations opposed to slavery date back to 1775, and the nineteenth century saw the founding of the Socialist International, the Red Cross, peace movements, women's suffrage organizations, and the International Law Association, among others. Before World War I, there were 176 international nongovernmental organizations. In 1956, they numbered nearly a thousand; in 1970, nearly two thousand. More recently, there has been an explosion in the number of NGOs, increasing from five to approximately twenty-seven thousand during the 1990s alone. And the numbers do not tell the full story, because they represent only formally constituted organizations.[63] Many claim to act as a "global conscience" representing broad public interests beyond the purview of individual states, or interests that states are wont to ignore. They develop new norms by directly pressing governments and business leaders to change policies, and indirectly by altering public perceptions of what governments and firms should be doing. In terms of power resources, these new groups rarely possess much hard power, but the information revolution has greatly enhanced their soft power.[64]

Not only is there a great increase in the number of transnational and governmental contacts, but there has also been a change in type. Earlier transnational flows were heavily controlled by large bureaucratic organizations such as multinational corporations or the Catholic Church that could profit from economies of scale. Such organizations remain important, but the lower costs of communication in the Internet era have opened the field to loosely structured network organizations with little headquarters staff, and even individuals. These nongovernmental organizations and networks are particularly effective in penetrating states without regard to borders. Because they often involve citizens who are well placed in the domestic politics of several countries, they are able to focus the attention of the media and governments on their preferred issues. The treaty banning land mines, mentioned above, was the result of an interesting coalition of Internet-based organizations working with middle-power governments, such as Canada, and some individual politicians and celebrities, including the late Princess Diana. Environmental issues are another example. The role of NGOs was important as a channel of communication across delegations in the global warming discussions at Kyoto in 1997. Industry, unions, and NGOs competed in Kyoto for the attention of media from major countries in a transnational struggle over the agenda of world politics. And NGOs sometimes compete with each other for media attention. The World Economic Forum, an NGO that invites top government and business leaders to Davos, Switzerland, each winter, included some NGOs in its 2001 programs, but that did not prevent other NGOs from staging local demonstrations and yet others from holding a counterforum in Porto Alegre, Brazil, designed to garner global attention.

A different type of transnational community, the scientific community of like-minded experts, is also becoming more prominent. By framing issues such as ozone depletion or global climate change, where scientific information is important, such "epistemic communities" create knowledge and consensus that provide the basis for effective cooperation.[65] The Montreal Protocol on ozone depletion was in part the product of such work. While not entirely new, these scientific communities have also grown as a result of the lowered costs of communications.

Geographical communities and sovereign states will continue to play the major role in world politics for a long time to come, but they will be less self-contained and more porous. They will have to share the stage with actors who can use information to enhance their soft power and press governments directly, or indirectly by mobilizing their publics. Governments that want to see rapid development will find that they have to give up some of the barriers to information flow that historically protected officials from outside scrutiny. No longer will governments that want high levels of development be able to afford the comfort of keeping their financial and political situations inside a black box, as Myanmar and North Korea have done. That form of sovereignty proves too expensive. Even large countries with hard power, such as the United States, find themselves sharing the stage with new actors and having more trouble controlling their borders. Cyberspace will not replace geographical space and will not abolish state sovereignty, but like the town markets in feudal times, it will coexist with them and greatly complicate what it means to be a sovereign state or a powerful country. As Americans shape foreign policy for the global information age, we will have to become more aware of the importance of the ways that information technology creates new communications, empowers individuals and nonstate actors, and increases the role of soft power.

POWER AMONG STATES

The information revolution is making world politics more complex by enabling transnational actors and reducing control by central governments, but it is also affecting power among states. Here the United States benefits, and many poorer countries lag behind.[66] While some poorer countries such as China, India, and Malaysia have made significant progress in entering the information economy, 87 percent of people online live in postindustrial societies.[67] The world in the information age remains a mixture of agricultural, industrial, and service-dominated economies. The postindustrial societies and governments most heavily affected by the information age coexist and interact with countries thus far little affected by the information revolution.

Will this digital divide persist for a long time? Decreasing costs may allow poor countries to leapfrog or skip over certain stages of development. For instance, wireless communications are already replacing costly land lines, and voice recognition technologies can give illiterates access to computer communications. The Internet may help poor farmers better understand weather and market conditions before they plant crops, and more information may diminish the role of predatory middlemen. Distance learning and Internet connections may help isolated doctors and scientists in poor countries. But what poor countries need most is basic education and infrastructure. As an editorial in the *Far East Economic Review* put it succinctly: "Closing the digital divide would be good, but right now most of Asia's poor are still looking forward to home electricity."[68]

Technology spreads over time, and many countries are keen to develop their own Silicon Valleys. But it is easier to identify the virtual keys to the high-tech kingdom than to open the actual gates. Well-developed communications infrastructure, secure property rights, sound government policies, an environment that encourages new business formation, deep capital markets, and a skilled workforce, many of whom understand English (the language of 80 percent of all web pages), will come to some poor countries in time, but not quickly. Even in India, which meets some of the criteria, software companies employ about 340,000 people, while half of India's population of one billion remains illiterate.[69]

The information revolution has an overall decentralizing and leveling effect, but will it also equalize power among nations? As it reduces costs and barriers of entry into markets, it should reduce the power of large states and enhance the power of small states and nonstate actors. But in practice, international relations are more complex than such technological determinism implies. Some aspects of the information revolution help the small, but some help the already large and powerful. There are several reasons why.

First, size still matters. What economists call barriers to entry and economies of scale remain in some of the aspects of power that are related to information. For example, soft power is strongly affected by the cultural content of what is broadcast or appears in movies and television programs. Large established entertainment industries often enjoy considerable economies of scale in content production and distribution. The dominant American market share in films and television programs in world markets is a case in point. It is hard for newcomers to compete with Hollywood. Moreover, in the information economy, there are network effects, with increasing returns to scale. One telephone is useless. The second adds value, and so forth as the network grows. In other words, "to those who hath a network, shall be given."

Second, even where it is now cheap to disseminate existing information, the collection and production of new information often requires major investment. In many competitive situations, it is *new* information that matters most. In some dimensions, information is a nonrivalrous public good: one person's consumption does not diminish that of another. Thomas Jefferson used the analogy of a candle—if I give you a light, it does not diminish my light. But in a competitive situation, it may make a big difference if I have the light first and see things before you do. Intelligence collection is a good example. America, Russia, Britain, and France have capabilities for collection and production that dwarf those of other nations.[70] Published accounts suggest that the United States spends some $30 billion a year on intelligence. In some commercial situations, a fast follower can do better than a first mover, but in terms of power among states, it is usually better to be a first mover than a fast follower. It is ironic, but no accident, that for all the discussion of how the Internet shrinks distance, information technology firms still cluster in a congested little area south of San Francisco because of what is called the "cocktail party effect." What makes for success is informal access to new information before it becomes public. "In an industry where new technology is perpetually on the verge of obsolescence, firms must recognize demand, secure capital and bring a product to market quickly or else be beaten by a competitor."[71] Market size and proximity to competitors, suppliers, and customers still matter in an information economy.

Third, first movers are often the creators of the standards and architecture of information systems. As described in Robert Frost's great poem, once the paths diverge in the wood and one is taken, it is difficult to get back to the other. Sometimes crude, low-cost technologies will open shortcuts that make it possible to overtake the first mover, but in many instances the path-dependent development of information systems reflects the advantage of the first mover.[72] The use of the English language and the pattern of top-level domain names on the Internet is a case in point. Partly because of the transformation of the American economy in the 1980s, and partly because of large investments driven by Cold War military competition, the United States was often the first mover and still enjoys a lead in the application of a wide variety of information technologies.

Fourth, as argued in chapter 1, military power remains important in some critical domains of international relations. Information technology has some effects on the use of force that benefit the small and some that favor the already powerful. The off-the-shelf commercial availability of formerly costly military technologies benefits small states and nongovernmental actors and increases the vulnerability of large states. For example, today anyone can order from commercial companies inexpensive one-meter-resolution satellite images of what goes on in military bases. Commercial firms and individuals (including terrorists) can go to the Internet and get access to satellite photographs that were top-secret and cost governments billions of dollars just a few years ago.[73] When a nongovernmental group felt that American policy toward North Korea was too alarmist a few years ago, it published private satellite pictures of North Korean rocket launch pads. Obviously, other countries can purchase similar pictures of American bases.

Global positioning devices that provide precise locations, once the property of the military alone, are readily available at local electronics stores. What's more, information systems create vulnerabilities for rich states by adding lucrative targets for terrorists who engage in asymmetrical warfare. Former House Speaker Newt Gingrich, who has looked deeply into the subject, believes that "there's a real danger that a powerful nation will believe it can create the cyberspace equivalent of a Pearl Harbor sneak attack. It's conceivable in the next 25 years that a sophisticated adversary (such as a small country with cyberwarfare resources) will decide it can blackmail the United States."[74] There is also the prospect of freelance cyberattacks. For example, after the collision between the U.S. surveillance plane and the Chinese fighter, both Chinese and American hackers engaged in a spate of attacks on both government and private web sites in each other's countries.

Other trends, however, strengthen the already powerful. As I argued in chapter 1, information technology has produced a revolution in military affairs. Space-based sensors, direct broadcasting, high-speed computers, and complex software provide the ability to gather, sort, process, transfer, and disseminate information about complex events that occur over a wide geographic area. This dominant battle space awareness along with precision guided weapons produces a powerful advantage. As the Gulf War showed, traditional assessments of balance-of-weapons platforms such as tanks or planes become irrelevant unless they include the ability to integrate information with those weapons. That was the mistake that Saddam Hussein made (as well as those in Congress who predicted massive American casualties). Many of the relevant technologies are available in commercial markets, and weaker states can be expected to purchase many of them. The key, however, will be not possession of fancy hardware or advanced systems but the ability to integrate a "system of systems." In this dimension, the United States is likely to keep its lead. In information warfare, a small edge makes all the difference. The revolution in military affairs will not diminish and may, in some circumstances, even increase the American lead over other countries.[75]

THREE DIMENSIONS OF INFORMATION

In understanding the relation of information to power in world politics, it helps if one distinguishes three different dimensions of information that are sometimes lumped together.[76] The first dimension is flows of data such as news or statistics. There has been a tremendous and measurable increase in the amount of information flowing across international borders. The average cost of that information has been declining, and much of it is virtually free. Declining costs and added points of access help small states and non-state actors. On the other hand, the vast scale of free flows puts a premium on the capacities of editors and systems integrators, which is a benefit to the large and powerful.

A second dimension is information that is used for advantage in competitive situations. With competitive information, as mentioned above, the most important effects are often at the margin. Here going first matters most, and that usually favors the more powerful. Much competitive information is associated with commerce, but as discussed above, the effect of information on military power can also be thought of as a subset of competitive information.

The third dimension is strategic information—knowledge of your competitor's game plan. Strategic information is virtually priceless. It is as old as espionage. Any country or group can hire spies, and to the extent that commercial technologies and market research provide technical capabilities that were previously available only at the cost of large investment, there is an equalizing effect. But to the extent that large investments in intelligence gathering produce more and better strategic information, the large and powerful will benefit. While it is true that fewer of the interesting intelligence questions in a post–Cold War world are secrets (which can be stolen) than mysteries (to which no one knows the answer), large intelligence collection capabilities still provide important strategic advantages.

One of the most interesting aspects of power in relation to increasing flows of information is the "paradox of plenty."[77] A plenitude of information leads to a poverty of attention. When we are overwhelmed with the volume of information confronting us, it is hard to know what to focus on. Attention rather than information becomes the scarce resource, and those who can distinguish valuable signals from white noise gain power. Editors, filters, and cue givers become more in demand, and this is a source of power for those who can tell us where to focus our attention. Power does not necessarily flow to those who can produce or withhold information. Unlike asymmetrical interdependence in trade, where power goes to those who can afford to hold back or break trade ties, power in information flows goes to those who can edit and authoritatively validate information, sorting out what is both correct and important. Because of our free press, this generally benefits the United States.

Among editors and cue givers, credibility is the crucial resource and an important source of soft power. Reputation becomes even more important than in the past, and political struggles occur over the creation and destruction of credibility. Communities tend to cluster around credible cue givers, and, in turn, perceived credibility tends to reinforce communities. Internet users tend to frequent web sites that that provide information they find both interesting and credible. Governments compete for credibility not only with other governments but with a broad range of alternatives including news media, corporations, nongovernmental organizations, intergovernmental organizations, and networks of scientific communities.

Thinking counterfactually, Iraq might have found it easier to have won acceptance for its view of the invasion of Kuwait as a postcolonial vindication, analogous to India's 1961 capture of Goa, if CNN had framed the issue from Baghdad rather than from Atlanta (from which Saddam was portrayed as analogous to Hitler in the 1930s). Soft power allowed the United States to frame the issue. Nongovernmental organizations can mount public relations campaigns that impose significant costs and alter the decisions of large corporations, as Greenpeace did in the case of Royal Dutch Shell's disposal of its Brentspar drilling rig. The sequel is equally illustrative, for Greenpeace lost credibility when it later had to admit that some of its factual statements had been inaccurate.

Politics then becomes a contest of competitive credibility. Governments compete with each other and with other organizations to enhance their own credibility and weaken that of their opponents— witness the struggle between Serbia and NATO to frame the interpretation of events in Kosovo in 1999. Reputation has always mattered in world politics, but the role of credibility becomes an even more important power resource because of the deluge of free information and the "paradox of plenty" in an information age. The BBC, for example, was an important soft power resource for Britain in Eastern Europe during the Cold War. Now it (and other government broadcasts) has more competitors, but to the extent that it maintains credibility in an era of white noise, its value as a power resource may increase. As we shall see in chapter 5, if the U.S. goverment thought in these terms, it would invest far more than it now does in the instruments of soft power (such as information and cultural exchange programs) and be less likely to try to constrain the Voice of America as it did in September 2001. We would be more concerned about how the policies we follow at home and unilateralist foreign policies sometimes undermine our credibility.

SOFT POWER IN THE GLOBAL INFORMATION AGE

One implication of the increasing importance of editors and cue givers in this global information age is that the relative importance of soft power will increase, because soft power rests on credibility. Countries that are well placed in terms of soft power do better.[78] The countries that are likely to gain soft power in an information age are (1) those whose dominant culture and ideas are closer to prevailing global norms (which now emphasize liberalism, pluralism, and autonomy), (2) those with the most access to multiple channels of communication and thus more influence over how issues are framed, and (3) those whose credibility is enhanced by their domestic and international performance. These dimensions of power in an information age suggest the growing importance of soft power in the mix of power resources, and a strong advantage to the United States.

Of course, soft power is not brand-new, nor was the United States the first government to try to utilize its culture to create soft power. After its defeat in the Franco-Prussian War, the French government sought to repair the nation's shattered prestige by promoting its language and literature through the Alliance Française, created in 1883. "The projection of French culture abroad thus became a significant component of French diplomacy."[79] Italy, Germany, and others soon followed suit. The advent of radio in the 1920s led many governments into the area of foreign language broadcasting, and in the 1930s, Nazi Germany perfected the propaganda film. The American government was a latecomer to the idea of using American culture for the purposes of diplomacy. It established a Committee on Public Information during World War I but abolished it with the return of peace. By the late 1930s, the Roosevelt administration became convinced that "America's security depended on its ability to speak to and to win the support of people in other countries." With World War II and the Cold War, the government became more active, with official efforts such as the United States Information Agency, the Voice of America, the Fulbright program, American libraries, lectures, and other programs. But much soft power arises from societal forces outside government control. Even before the Cold War, "American corporate and advertising executives, as well as the heads of Hollywood studios, were selling not only their products but also America's culture and values, the secrets of its success, to the rest of the world."[80] Soft power is created partly by governments and partly in spite of them.

A decade ago some observers thought the close collaboration of government and industry in Japan would give it a lead in soft power in the information age. Japan could develop an ability to manipulate perceptions worldwide instantaneously and "destroy those that impede Japanese economic prosperity and cultural acceptance."[81] When Matsushita purchased MCA, its president said that movies critical of Japan would not be produced.[82] Japanese media tried to break into world markets, and the government-owned NHK network began satellite broadcasts in English. The venture failed, however, as NHK's reports seemed to lag behind those of commercial news organizations, and the network had to rely on CNN and ABC.[83] This does not mean that Japan lacks soft power. On the contrary, its pop culture has great appeal to teenagers in Asia.[84] But Japan's culture remains much more inward-oriented than that of the United States, and its government's unwillingness to deal frankly with the history of the 1930s undercuts its soft power.

To be sure, there are areas, such as the Middle East, where ambivalence about American culture limits our soft power. All television in the Arab world used to be state-run until tiny Qatar allowed a new station, Al-Jazeera, to broadcast freely, and it proved wildly popular in the Middle East.[85] Its uncensored images ranging from Osama bin Laden to Tony Blair had a powerful political influence after September 2001. Bin Laden's ability to project a Robin Hood image enhanced his soft power with some Muslims around the globe. As an Arab journalist described the situation earlier, "Al-Jazeera has been for this intifada what CNN was to the Gulf War."[86] In fundamentalist Iran, people are ambivalent. Pirated videos are widely available, and a government ban "has only enhanced the lure of both the best and the worst of Western secular culture."[87]

There are, of course, tensions even within Western secular culture that limit American soft power. In the mid-1990s, 61 percent of

French, 45 percent of Germans, and 32 percent of Italians perceived American culture as a threat to their own. Majorities in Spain, France, Germany, and Italy thought there were too many American-made films and television programs on national TV.[88] And both Canada and the European Union place restrictions on the amount of American content that can be shown.

But such attitudes reflect ambivalence rather than rejection. In the 1920s, the Germans were the cinematographic pacesetters, as were the French and the Italians in the 1950s and 1960s. India produces many more films than does Hollywood, but all the distribution channels in the world couldn't turn Indian movies into global blockbusters. In the eyes of German journalist Josef Joffe, the explanation is obvious: "America has the world's most open culture, and therefore the world is most open to it."[89] Or as a perceptive French critic notes, "Nothing symbolizes more the triumph of American culture than the quintessential art form of the 20th century: the cinema. . . . This triumph of the individual motivated by compassion or a noble ambition is universal . . . the message is based on the openness of America and the continuing success of its multicultural society." But he also notes that "the more the French embrace America, the more they resent it."[90] Or as a Norwegian observed, "American culture is becoming everyone's *second* culture. It doesn't necessarily supplant local traditions, but it does activate a certain cultural bilingualism."[91] And like many second languages, it is spoken with imperfections and different meanings. The wonder, however, is that it is spoken at all.

Of course, Serbs wearing Levi's and eating at McDonald's not only supported repression in Kosovo, but used a Hollywood film, *Wag the Dog,* to mock the United States during the war. Child soldiers in Sierra Leone committed atrocities such as lopping off the hands of civilians while wearing American sports team T-shirts. Osama bin Laden despised American culture as do some of his fundamentalist sympathizers. For better or worse, the U.S. is "exciting, exotic, rich, powerful, trend-setting—the cutting edge of modernity and innovation."[92] Despite vulgarity, sex, and violence, "our pictures and music exalt icons of freedom, celebrating a society conducive to upward mobility, informality, egalitarian irreverence, and vital life-force. This exaltation has its appeals in an age when people want to partake of the good life American style, even if as political citizens, they are aware of the downside for ecology, community, and equality."[93] For example, in explaining a new movement toward using lawsuits to assert rights in China, a young Chinese activist explained, "We've seen a lot of Hollywood movies—they feature weddings, funerals and going to court. So now we think it's only natural to go to court a few times in your life."[94] At the same time, such images of a liberal society can create a backlash among conservative fundamentalists.

Ambivalence sets limits on popular culture as a source of American soft power, and marketing by American corporations can create both attraction and resistance. As historian Walter LaFeber puts it, transnational corporations "not only change buying habits in a society, but modify the composition of the society itself. For the society that receives it, soft power can have hard effects."[95] Protest is often directed at McDonald's and Coca-Cola. For better and worse, there is not much the U.S. government can do about these negative impacts of American cultural exports. Efforts to balance the scene by supporting exports of American high culture—libraries and art exhibits—are at best a useful palliative. Many aspects of soft power are more a byproduct of American society than of deliberate government actions, and they may increase or decrease government power. The background attraction (and repulsion) of American popular culture in different regions and among different groups may make it easier or more difficult for American officials to promote their policies. In some cases, such as Iran, American culture may produce rejection (at least for ruling elites); in others, including China, the attraction and rejection among different groups may cancel each other. In still other cases, such as Argentina, American human rights policies that were rejected by the military government of the 1970s produced considerable soft power for the United States two decades later when those who were earlier imprisoned subsequently came to power.

The Argentine example reminds us not to exaggerate the role of popular culture and that soft power is more than just cultural power. As we saw in chapter 1, soft power rests on agenda setting as well as attraction, and popular culture is only one aspect of attraction (and not always that). The high cultural ideas that the United States exports in the minds of the half a million foreign students who study every year in American universities, or in the minds of the Asian entrepreneurs who return home after succeeding in Silicon Valley, are more closely related to elites with power. Most of China's leaders have a son or daughter educated in the United States who portray a realistic view of the United States that is often at odds with the caricatures in official Chinese propaganda.

Government polices at home and abroad can enhance or curtail our soft power. For example, in the 1950s, racial segregation at home undercut our soft power in Africa, and today, our practice of capital punishment and weak gun control laws undercut our soft power in Europe. Similarly, foreign policies strongly affect our soft power. Jimmy Carter's human rights policies are a case in point, but so also are government efforts to promote democracy during the Reagan and Clinton administrations. Conversely, foreign policies that appear arrogant and unilateral in the eyes of others diminish our soft power, as we will explore further in chapter 5.

The soft power that is becoming more important in the information age is in part a social and economic by-product rather than solely a result of official government action. NGOs with soft power of their own can complicate and obstruct government efforts to obtain the outcomes it wants, and purveyors of popular culture sometimes hinder government agents in achieving their objectives. But the larger long-term trends are in our favor. To the extent that official policies at home and abroad are consistent with democracy, human rights, openness, and respect for the opinions of others, the United States will benefit from the trends of this global information age, even though pockets of reaction and fundamentalism will persist and react in some countries. But there is a danger that we may obscure the deeper message of our values through arrogance and unilateralism. Our culture, high and low, helps produce soft power in an information age, but government actions also matter—not only through programs such as the Voice of America and Fulbright scholarships but, even more important, when our policies avoid arrogance and stand for values that others admire. The trends of the information age are in our favor, but only if we avoid stepping on our own message.

CONCLUSION

A century ago, at the height of the industrial age, the great German sociologist Max Weber identified a monopoly on the legitimate use of force as a defining characteristic of the modern state. That still remains true, but in the information age, governments are less securely in control of the major sources of power than in the past century. Large states still have overwhelming military advantages, but the spread of technologies of mass destruction opens opportunities for terrorists and creates vulnerabilities in postindustrial societies. And for preindustrial societies, private armies and criminal groups in some instances have forces that can overwhelm governments.

In terms of economic power, transnational corporations operate on a scale that is larger than that of many countries. At least a dozen transnational corporations have annual sales that are larger than the gross national products of more than half the states in the world. For example, the sales of Mitsubishi are larger than the GNP of Vietnam; the sales of Shell are three times the GNP of Guatemala; those of Siemens are six times the GNP of Jamaica.[96] And with soft power, while large countries such as the United States have a lead, the government is often unable to control it. Moreover, as soft power becomes more important in an information age, it is worth remembering that it is the domain where nongovernmental organizations and networks are poised to compete because it is their major power resource. The state remains sovereign, but its powers, even for the United States, are not what they once were. As two perceptive foreign observers put it, "If the state remains at the centre of governance in the world, what has changed? In a word everything. Never have so many different nonstate actors competed for the authority and influence that once belonged to the states alone."[97]

What conclusions can we draw in this early phase of the global information age? Predictions of the equalizing effect of the information and communications revolutions on the distribution of power among states are wrong. In part this is because economies of scale and barriers to entry persist in regard to commercial and strategic information, and in part because with respect to free information, the larger states will often be well placed in the competition for the credibility that creates soft power. Second, cheap flows of information have created an enormous change in channels of contact across state borders. Nongovernmental actors and individuals operating transnationally have much greater opportunities to organize and to propagate their views. States are more easily penetrated and less like black boxes. Our political leaders will find it more difficult to maintain a coherent ordering of foreign policy issues.

Third, the Internet is creating a new transnational domain that is superimposed on sovereign states in the same way newly created medieval markets were centuries ago, and it promises an equally significant evolution of attitudes and identities. Fourth, the information revolution is changing political processes in such a way that open democratic societies like the United States will compete more successfully than authoritarian states for the key power resource of credibility, but democratization will not be rapid in much of the preindustrial world. Fifth, soft power is becoming more important in relation to hard coercive power than it was in the past, as credibility becomes a key power resource for both governments and nongovernmental groups. Although the United States is better placed in terms of credibility and soft power than many countries, the coherence of government policies is likely to diminish. Finally, geographically based sovereign states will continue to structure politics in an information age, but the processes of world politics within that structure are undergoing profound change. The power of the sovereign state will still matter, but it will not be what it used to be.

What this means is that many of the traditional measures of American preeminence that we saw in chapter 1 will prove to be illusory. Talk about unipolarity and hegemony will begin to sound increasingly hollow. If all we had to do in a global information age was fend off new military challengers, the tasks of American foreign policy would be relatively straightforward and our hard power would suffice.

By traditional measures, no sovereign state is likely to surpass us, and terrorists cannot defeat us. But an information revolution is posing more subtle challenges by changing the very nature of states, sovereignty, and control—and the role of soft power. Fewer issues that we care about will prove susceptible to solution through our dominant military power. Policy makers will have to pay more attention to the politics of credibility and the importance of soft power. And they will have to share a stage crowded with newly empowered nongovernmental actors and individuals. As we shall see in the next chapter, all this will occur in a very diverse world in which globalization is shrinking the distances that provided protection in the past.

3

GLOBALIZATION

Americans feel their lives affected more and more by events originating outside the country. Terrorists from halfway around the world wrought havoc in New York and Washington. Or to take an economic example, who would have thought that imprudent banking practices in a small economy such as Thailand in 1997 would lead to the collapse of the Russian ruble, massive loans to stave off crisis in Brazil, and the New York Federal Reserve Bank's intervention to prevent the collapse of a hedge fund from harming the American economy? In an ecological example, helicopters recently fumigated many American cities in an attempt to eradicate the potentially lethal West Nile virus, which might have arrived in the blood of a traveler, via a bird smuggled through customs, or in the gut of a mosquito that flitted into a jet.[1] Fears of "bioinvasion" led some environmental groups to place full-page ads in the *New York Times* calling for a reduction in global trade and travel.[2] And as the twenty-first century began, rioters protesting globalization filled the streets of Washington, Prague, Quebec, Genoa, and other cities where leaders met.

MADE IN AMERICA?

Globalization—the growth of worldwide networks of interdependence—is virtually as old as human history. What's new is that the networks are thicker and more complex, involving people from more regions and social classes.[3] The ancient Silk Road that linked medieval Europe and Asia is an example of the "thin" globalization that involved small amounts of luxury goods and elite customers (though a broader part of the European population suffered from the imported viruses that accompanied the traders). Economic globalization increased dramatically in the nineteenth century. In their 1848 Communist Manifesto, Karl Marx and Friedrich Engels argued that "all old-established national industries have been destroyed or are being destroyed. . . . In place of the old local and national seclusion and self-sufficiency, we have intercourse in every direction, universal interdependence of nations."[4]

The idea that globalization equals Americanization is common but simplistic. The United States itself is the product of seventeenth- and eighteenth-century globalization. As Adam Smith wrote in 1776, "the discovery of America, and that of a passage to the East Indies by the Cape of Good Hope, are the two greatest and most important events recorded in the history of mankind . . . by uniting, in some measure, the most distant parts of the world."[5] But it is also true that the United States is a giant in the contemporary phase of globalization. In the words of French foreign minister Hubert Vedrine, "The United States is a very big fish that swims easily and rules supreme in the waters of globalization. Americans get great benefits from this for a large number of reasons: because of their economic size; because globalization takes place in their language; because it is organized along neoliberal economic principles; because they impose their legal, accounting, and technical practices; and because they're advocates of individualism."[6]

It is understandable, and probably inevitable, that those who resent American power and popular culture use nationalism to fight it. In the 1940s, French officials sought to ban Coca-Cola, and it was not finally approved for sale in France until 1953.[7] In a well-publicized

1999 case, José Bové, a French sheep farmer (who incidentally spent the early years of his life in Berkeley, California), became a French hero and earned global press coverage by protecting "culinary sovereignty" through destroying a McDonald's restaurant.[8] No one forces the French public to enter the golden arches, but Bové's success with the media spoke to the cultural ambivalence toward things American. As Iran's president complained in 1999, "The new world order and globalization that certain powers are trying to make us accept, in which the culture of the entire world is ignored, looks like a kind of neo-colonialism."[9]

Several dimensions of globalization are indeed dominated today by activities based in Wall Street, Silicon Valley, and Hollywood. However, the intercontinental spread of Christianity preceded by many centuries Hollywood's discovery of how to market films about the Bible. And the global spread of Islam, continuing to this day, is not "made in USA." The English language, which is spoken by about 5 percent of the world's people, was originally spread by Britain, not the United States.[10] Ties between Japan and its Latin American diaspora have nothing to do with the United States, nor do ties between French-, Spanish-, and Portuguese-speaking countries, respectively. Nor does the contemporary spread of AIDS in Africa and Asia. Nor European banks lending to emerging markets in Asia and Latin America. The most popular sports team in the world is not American: it is Manchester United, with two hundred fan clubs in twenty-four countries. Three of the leading "American" music labels have British, German, and Japanese owners. Some of the most popular video games come from Japan and Britain.[11] The rise of reality programming, which has enlivened or debased the standards of television entertainment in recent years, spread from Europe to the United States, not vice versa.

As British sociologist Anthony Giddens observes, "Globalization is not just the dominance of the West over the rest; it affects the United States as it does other countries."[12] Or in the words of Singapore diplomat Kishore Mahbubani: "The West will increasingly absorb good minds from other cultures. And as it does so, the West will undergo a major transformation: it will become within itself a microcosm of the new interdependent world with many thriving cultures and ideas."[13] Globalization is not intrinsically American, even if much of its current content is heavily influenced by what happens in the United States.

Several distinctive qualities of the United States make it uniquely adapted to serve as a center of globalization. American culture is produced by and geared toward a multiethnic society whose demographics are constantly altered by immigration. America has always had a syncretic culture, borrowing freely from a variety of traditions and continuously open to the rest of the world. And European concerns over American influence are not new. A number of books were published on the subject a century ago—for example, a British author, W. T. Stead, wrote *The Americanization of the World* in 1902. The United States is also a great laboratory for cultural experimentation, the largest marketplace to test whether a given film or song resonates with one subpopulation or another, or perhaps with people in general. Ideas flow into the United States freely and flow out with equal ease—often in commercialized form, backed by entrepreneurs drawing on deep pools of capital and talent. A Pizza Hut in Asia looks American, though the food, of course, is originally Italian. There seems to be an affinity between opportunities for globalization and these characteristics of American society.[14]

American culture does not always flow into other societies unchanged, nor does it always have political effects. The ideas and information that enter global networks are "downloaded" in the context of national politics and local cultures, which act as selective filters and modifiers of what arrives. McDonald's menus are different in China, and American movies are dubbed in varying Chinese accents to reflect Chinese perceptions of the message being delivered.[15] Political institutions are often more resistant to transnational transmission than popular culture. Although the Chinese students in Tiananmen Square in 1989 built a replica of the Statue of Liberty, China has emphatically not adopted American political institutions.[16]

Globalization today is America-centric, in that much of the information revolution comes from the United States and a large part of the content of global information networks is currently created in the United States and enhances American "soft power." French culture

minister Jack Lang warned that soft power "moved mostly in one direction because Americans were so closed-minded and provincial, if
not grossly ignorant of other cultures."[17] But Lang misses the openness of American society, which accepts and recycles culture from the
rest of the world. Moreover, some U.S. practices are very attractive to
other countries: honest regulation of drugs, as by the Food and Drug
Administration (FDA); transparent securities laws and practices that
limit fraudulent dealing, monitored by the Securities and Exchange
Commission (SEC). U.S.-made standards are sometimes hard to
avoid, as in the rules governing the Internet itself. But other U.S. standards and practices—from pounds and feet (rather than the metric
system) to capital punishment and the right to bear arms—have encountered puzzlement or even outright hostility in other nations. Soft
power is a reality, but it does not accrue to the United States in all areas
of activity, nor is the United States the only country to possess it. Globalization is more than just Americanization.

THE NATURE OF THE BEAST

Globalization—worldwide networks of interdependence—does not
imply universality.[18] As we saw in the last chapter, at the beginning of
the twenty-first century almost one-half of the American population
used the World Wide Web, compared to 0.01 percent of the population of South Asia. Most people in the world today do not have telephones; hundreds of millions of people live as peasants in remote
villages with only slight connections to world markets or the global
flow of ideas. Indeed, globalization is accompanied by increasing
gaps, in many respects, between the rich and the poor. It does not
imply either homogenization or equity.[19]

Even among rich countries, there is a lot less globalization than
meets the eye.[20] A truly globalized world market would mean free
flows of goods, people, and capital, and similar interest rates. In fact
we have a long way to go.[21] For example, even in the local NAFTA
market, Toronto trades ten times as much with Vancouver as with
Seattle, though the distance is the same and tariffs are minimal.

Globalization has made national boundaries more porous but not ir-relevant.[22] Nor does globalization mean the creation of a universal community. In social terms, contacts among people with different religious beliefs and other deeply held values have often led to con-flict: witness the great crusades of medieval times or the current no-tion of the United States as "the Great Satan," held by some Islamic fundamentalists.[23] Clearly, in social as well as economic terms, ho-mogenization does not follow necessarily from globalization.

Globalization has a number of dimensions, though all too often economists write as if it and the world economy were one and the same. But other forms of globalization have significant effects on our day-to-day lives. The oldest form of globalization is environmental interdependence. For example, the first smallpox epidemic is recorded in Egypt in 1350 B.C. The disease reached China in A.D. 49, Europe af-ter 700, the Americas in 1520, and Australia in 1789.[24] The plague or black death originated in Asia, but its spread killed a quarter to a third of the population of Europe in the fourteenth century. Euro-peans carried diseases to the Americas in the fifteenth and sixteenth centuries that destroyed up to 95 percent of the indigenous popula-tion.[25] Since 1973, thirty previously unknown infectious diseases have emerged, and other familiar diseases have spread geographically in new drug-resistant forms.[26] The spread of foreign species of flora and fauna to new areas has wiped out native species, and efforts to control them may cost several hundred billion dollars a year.[27] On the other hand, not all effects of environmental globalization are ad-verse. For instance, nutrition and cuisine in both Europe and Asia benefited from the importation of such New World crops as pota-toes, corn, and tomatoes, and the green revolution agricultural tech-nology of the past few decades has helped poor farmers throughout the world.[28]

Global climate change will affect not only Americans but the lives of people everywhere. Thousands of scientists from over a hundred countries recently reported that there is new and strong evidence that most of the warming observed over the last fifty years is attributable to human activities, and average global temperatures in the twenty-first century are projected to increase between 2.5 and 10 degrees

Fahrenheit. The result could be increasingly severe variations in climate, with too much water in some regions and not enough in others. The effects in North America will include stronger storms, floods, droughts, and landslides. Rising temperatures have lengthened the freeze-free season in many regions and cut snow cover since the 1960s by 10 percent. The rate at which the sea level rose in the last century was ten times faster than the average rate over the last three millennia.[29] As Harvard scientist James McCarthy notes, "What is different now is that Earth is populated with 6 billion people and the natural and human systems that provide us with food, fuel, and fiber are strongly influenced by climate." As climate change accelerates, "future change may not occur as smoothly as it has in the past."[30] It does not matter whether carbon dioxide is placed in the atmosphere from China or the United States; it affects global warming in the same way. And the impact on American policy was clear in the reactions of other countries in the early days of George W. Bush's administration. After foreign protests and a National Academy of Sciences report, President Bush had to reverse his early position that there was inadequate evidence of human effects on global warming.[31]

Military globalization consists of networks of interdependence in which force, or the threat of force, is employed. The world wars of the twentieth century are a case in point. During the Cold War, the global strategic interdependence between the United States and the Soviet Union was acute and well recognized. Not only did it produce world-straddling alliances, but either side could have used intercontinental missiles to destroy the other within the space of thirty minutes. Such interdependence was distinctive not because it was totally new, but because the scale and speed of the potential conflict were so enormous. Today, terrorist networks constitute a new form of military globalization.

Social globalization is the spread of peoples, cultures, images, and ideas. Migration is a concrete example. In the nineteenth century, some eighty million people crossed oceans to new homes—far more than in the twentieth century.[32] But ideas are an equally important aspect of social globalization. Four great religions of the world— Buddhism, Judaism, Christianity, and Islam—have spread across great distances over the last two millennia, as has the scientific method and worldview over the past few centuries. Political globalization (a part of social globalization) is manifest in the spread of constitutional arrangements, the increase in the number of countries that have become democratic, and the development of international rules and institutions. Those who think it is meaningless to speak of an international community ignore the importance of the global spread of political ideas such as the antislavery movement in the nineteenth century, anticolonialism after World War II, and the environmental and feminist movements today.

Changes in the various dimensions of globalization can move in opposite directions at the same time. Economic globalization fell dramatically between 1914 and 1945, while military globalization increased to new heights during the two world wars, as did many aspects of social globalization. (War disrupts existing societies and spreads new ideas.) So did globalization increase or decrease between 1914 and 1945? The economic deglobalization that characterized the first half of the twentieth century was so deep that the world economy did not reach the 1914 levels of international trade and investment again until the 1970s. This was in part a reflection of the enormous disruption of World War I, but there was another problem as well. The industrial world had not come to terms with the inequalities created by rapid economic globalization. Markets outran politics in Europe, and the great political movements of communism and fascism stemmed in part from popular reactions to the inequalities that accompanied laissez-faire world markets.[33]

Is such economic deglobalization and attendant political disruption likely in the years to come? It's possible, but less likely than it was a century ago. For one thing, after 1945 the creation of the welfare state put a safety net under poor people in most developed countries, which acted as a safety valve that made open economies and economic globalization more acceptable. There is a positive correlation between the strength of the welfare state and the openness of economies.[34] Globalization is not destroying (as opposed to constraining) the welfare state in Europe and the postmodern societies. While political reactions to economic globalization have been growing in postindustrial societies, they are not like the mass movements that overturned the political systems in Europe in the first half of the twentieth century. At the same time, international inequality has increased in some regions, including countries such as China. In much of the less developed world, the absence of safety nets could become a cause of political reaction against economic globalization.[35] International protest movements that include American citizens and organizations have increased and, as we shall see below, are raising difficult policy questions.

In short, globalization is the result of both technological progress and government policies that have reduced barriers to international exchange. The United States has been a major instigator and beneficiary of the contemporary phase of globalization, but we cannot control it. Moreover, if protests and government policies were to curtail the beneficial economic dimensions of globalization, we would still be left with the detrimental effects of military and environmental globalization. Globalization is a mixed blessing, but like it or not, it creates new challenges for American foreign policy.

TWENTY-FIRST-CENTURY GLOBALIZATION: WHAT'S NEW?

While globalization has been going on for centuries, its contemporary form has distinct characteristics. In a phrase, it is "thicker and quicker." Globalization today is different from how it was in the nineteenth century, when European imperialism provided much of its political structure, and higher transport and communications costs meant fewer people were involved directly with people and ideas from other cultures. But many of the most important differences are closely related to the information revolution. As Thomas Friedman argues, contemporary globalization goes "farther, faster, cheaper and deeper."[36]

Economists use the term "network effects" to refer to situations where a product becomes more valuable once many other people also use it. As we saw in the last chapter, one telephone is useless, but its value increases as the network grows. This is why the Internet is causing such rapid change.[37] A knowledge-based economy generates "powerful spillover effects, often spreading like fire and triggering further innovation and setting off chain reactions of new inventions . . . But goods—as opposed to knowledge—do not always spread like fire."[38] Moreover, as interdependence has become thicker and quicker, the relationships among different networks have become more important. There are more interconnections among the networks. As a result, system effects—where small perturbations in one area can spread throughout a whole system—become more important.[39]

Financial markets are a good example of system effects. As mentioned above, the 1997 Asian financial crisis affected markets on several continents. The relative magnitude of foreign investment in 1997 was not unprecedented. The net outflow of capital from Britain in the four decades before 1914 averaged 5 percent of its gross domestic product, compared to 2 to 3 percent for rich countries today.[40] The fact that the financial crisis of 1997 was global in scale also had precursors: Black Monday on Wall Street in 1929 and the collapse of Austria's Credit Anstalt bank in 1930 triggered a worldwide financial crisis and global depression.

But today's gross financial flows are much larger. Daily foreign exchange flows increased from $15 billion in 1973 to $1.5 trillion by 1995, and the 1997 crisis was sparked by a currency collapse in a small emerging market economy, not by Wall Street. Further, the 1997 crisis caught most economists, governments, and international financial institutions by surprise, and complex new financial instruments made it difficult to understand. In December 1998 Federal Reserve Board chairman Alan Greenspan said: "I have learned more about how this new international financial system works in the last twelve months than in the previous twenty years."[41] Sheer magnitude, complexity, and speed distinguish contemporary economic globalization from earlier periods and increase the challenges it presents to American foreign policy.[42]

Military globalization also became more complex. The end of the Cold War brought military deglobalization—that is, distant disputes between the superpowers became less relevant to the balance of power. But the increase in social globalization over the past several decades had the opposite effect and introduced new dimensions of military globalism: humanitarian intervention and terrorism. Humanitarian concerns interacting with global communications led to pressure for military interventions in places such as Somalia, Bosnia, and Kosovo. And fundamentalist reactions to modern culture interacted with technology to create new options for terrorism and for asymmetrical warfare. For example, in devising a strategy to stand up to the United States, some Chinese midlevel officers proposed terrorism, drug trafficking, environmental degradation, and computer virus propagation. They argued that the more complicated the combination—for example, terrorism plus a media war plus a financial war—the better the results. "From that perspective, 'Unrestricted War' marries the Chinese classic, *The Art of War* by Sun Tzu, with modern military technology and economic globalization."[43]

As American officials fashion foreign policies, they encounter the increasing thickness of globalism—the density of the networks of interdependence—which means that the effects of events in one geographical area or in the economic or ecological dimension can have profound effects in other geographical areas or on the military or social dimension. These international networks are increasingly complex, and their effects are therefore increasingly unpredictable. Moreover, in human systems, people are often hard at work trying to outwit each other, to gain an economic, social, or military advantage precisely by acting in an unpredictable way. As a result, globalization is accompanied by pervasive uncertainty. There will be a continual competition between increased complexity and uncertainty, on one hand, and efforts by governments, corporations, and others to comprehend and manipulate to their benefit these increasingly complex interconnected systems. Frequent financial crises or sharp increases in unemployment could lead to popular movements to limit interdependence and to a reversal of economic globalization. Chaotic uncertainty is too high a price for most people to pay for somewhat higher average levels of prosperity. Unless some aspects of globalization can be effectively governed, as we shall see below, it may not be sustainable in its current form.

Quickness also adds to uncertainty and the difficulties of shaping policy responses. As mentioned at the outset, modern globalization operates at a much more rapid pace than its earlier forms. Smallpox took nearly three millennia to conquer all inhabited continents, finally reaching Australia in 1775. AIDS took little more than three decades to spread from Africa all around the world. And to switch to a metaphorical virus, in 2000 the Love Bug computer virus needed only three days to straddle the globe. From three millennia to three decades to three days: that is the measure of the quickening of globalization.

Sometimes globalization's challenges are viewed solely in terms of the speed of information flow, but that is too simple.[44] The velocity of individual messages has not changed very significantly since the telegraph became more or less universal toward the end of the nineteenth century. But institutional velocity—how rapidly a system and the units within it change—reflects the thickness of globalism. Markets react more quickly than before, since information diffuses so much more rapidly and huge sums of capital can respond at a moment's notice. An NGO can report an event from the Brazilian rain forest and spread it around the world on the Internet in a matter of minutes. Individual news items do not travel much faster from Sarajevo to New York than they did in 1914, but the institutions and economics of cable television and the Internet made news cycles shorter and have put a larger premium on small advantages in speed. In 1914, one newspaper did not normally scoop another by receiving and processing information an hour earlier than another; as long as the information could be processed before the next day's issue was put to bed, it was timely. But today, an hour—or even a few minutes—makes the critical difference whether a cable television network is on top of a story or behind the curve. Sometimes CNN scoops official reporting, and I have often entered the office of a Pentagon or State Department official and found CNN tuned in on a television set in the corner.

Direct public participation in global affairs has also increased in rich countries. Ordinary people invest in foreign mutual funds, gamble on offshore Internet sites, travel, and sample exotic cuisine that used to be the preserve of the rich. Friedman termed this change the "democratization" of technology, finance, and information, because diminished costs have made what previously were luxuries available to a much broader range of society.[45] *Democratization* is probably the wrong word, however, since in markets, money votes, and people start out with unequal stakes. There is no equality, for example, in capital markets, despite the new financial instruments that permit more people to participate. A million dollars or more is often the entry price for hedge fund investors. *Pluralization* might be more accurate, suggesting the vast increase in the number and variety of participants in global networks. In 1914, according to John Maynard Keynes, "the inhabitant of London could order by telephone, sipping his morning tea in bed, the various products of the whole earth, in such quantity as he might see fit, and reasonably expect their early delivery upon his doorstep."[46] But Keynes's Englishman had to be wealthy to be a global consumer. Today virtually any American can do the same thing. Supermarkets and Internet retailers extend that capacity to the vast majority of the people in postindustrial societies.

As we saw in the last chapter, nongovernmental organizations—whether large ones such as Greenpeace or Amnesty International, or the proverbial three kooks with a fax machine and a modem—can now raise their voices, worldwide, as never before. Whether they establish the credibility to get and hold anyone's attention has become the key political question.

This vast expansion of transnational channels of contact at multicontinental distances, generated by the media and a profusion of nongovernmental organizations, means that more issues are up for grabs internationally, including regulations and practices (ranging from pharmaceutical testing to accounting and product standards to banking regulation) that were formerly regarded as the prerogatives of national governments. Large areas of the governance of transnational life are being handled by private actors, whether it be the creation of the code that governs the Internet or the establishment of safety standards in the chemical industry.

Some observers go so far as to argue that communications costs have erased the significance of distance. In some domains, such as financial markets, this is largely true, but as a generalization, it is a half-truth. First, participation in global interdependence has increased, but many people are only tenuously connected to any communications networks that transcend their states, or even their localities. Most people in the world, as we have noted, do not own telephones, and many peasant villages in Asia, Africa, and Latin America are linked to the world as a whole only through slow and often thin economic, social, and political links. Furthermore, even for those people tied closely into global communications networks, the significance of distance varies greatly by issue—economic, ecological, military, and so forth. If globalization implies the shrinking of distance, those distances have shrunk at different rates for different people and different issues.[47]

Distance is indeed irrelevant if a stock can be sold instantaneously in New York or Hong Kong by an investor in Abidjan to one in Moscow. But physical goods move more slowly than capital, since automobiles and textiles cannot be transformed into digits on a computer. Orders for them can be sent without regard to distance, but the cars or clothes have to move physically from Japan or Guatemala to Johannesburg or Rome. Such movement is faster than it once was—flowers and shoes are now sent thousands of miles by jet aircraft—but is by no means instantaneous or inexpensive. Even more constrained by distance are personal services: people who desire facelifts cannot get them online.

Variability by distance applies to other dimensions of globalism as well. The actual movement of ideas and information is virtually instantaneous, but their comprehension and acceptance depend on cultural differences. UN secretary general Kofi Annan can talk about human rights and sovereignty simultaneously to people in Boston, Belgrade, Buenos Aires, Beijing, Beirut, Bombay, and Bujumbura— but the same words are heard very differently in these seven cities. Likewise, American popular culture may be interpreted by young people in some cultures as validating fundamentally new values and lifestyles, but in other settings it may be viewed merely as essentially trivial symbols, expressed only in baseball caps, T-shirts, and music. Cultural distances resist homogenization. Finally, elements of social globalization that rely on the migration of people are highly constrained by distance and by legal jurisdictions, since travel remains costly for most people in the world, and governments everywhere seek to control and limit migration.

What the information revolution has added to contemporary globalization is a quickness and thickness in the network of interconnections that make them more complex. But such "thick globalism" is not uniform: it varies by region and locality, and by issue. As we shape our foreign policy for this new century, we will have to respond to issues that involve greater complexity, more uncertainty, shorter response times, broader participation by groups and individuals, and an uneven shrinkage of distance. The world is more upon us, but in terms of our policy responses, one size will not fit all.

GLOBALIZATION AND AMERICAN POWER

With the end of the Cold War, the United States became more powerful than any state in recent history. Globalization contributed to that position, but it may not continue to do so throughout the century. Today globalization reinforces American power; over time it may dilute that power. Globalization is the child of both technology and policy. American policy deliberately promoted norms and institutions such as GATT, the World Bank, and the IMF that created an open international economic system after 1945. For forty-five years, the extent of economic globalization was limited by the autarkic policies of the communist governments. The end of the Cold War reduced such barriers, and American economic and soft power benefited both from the related ascendance of market ideology and the reduction of protectionism.

The United States plays a central role in all dimensions of contemporary globalization. Globalization at its core refers to worldwide networks of interdependence. A network is simply a series of connections of points in a system, but networks can take a surprising number of shapes and architectures. An airline hub and spokes, a spiderweb, an electricity grid, a metropolitan bus system, and the Internet are all networks, though they vary in terms of centralization and complexity of connections. Theorists of networks argue that under most conditions, centrality in networks conveys power—that is, the hub controls the spokes.[48] Some see globalism as a network with an American hub and spokes reaching out to the rest of the world. There is some truth in this picture, as the United States is central to all four forms of globalization: economic (the United States has the largest capital market), military (it is the only country with global reach), social (it is the heart of pop culture), and environmental (the United States is the biggest polluter, and its political support is necessary for effective action on environmental issues). As argued above, the United States has played a central role in the current phase of globalization for a variety of reasons, including its syncretic culture, market size, the effectiveness of some of its institutions, and its military force. And this centrality has in turn benefited American hard and soft power. In this view, being the hub conveys hegemony.

Those who advocate a hegemonic or unilateralist foreign policy are attracted to this image of global networks. Yet there are at least four reasons it would be a mistake to envisage contemporary networks of globalism simply in terms of the hub and spokes of an American empire that creates dependency for smaller countries. This metaphor is useful as one perspective on globalization, but it does not provide the whole picture.

First, the architecture of networks of interdependence varies according to the different dimensions of globalization. The hub-and-spokes metaphor fits military globalism more closely than economic, environmental, or social globalism because American dominance is so much greater in that domain. Even in the military area, most states are more concerned about threats from neighbors than from the United States, a fact that leads many to call in American global power to redress local balances. The American presence is welcome in most of East Asia as a balance to rising Chinese power. That is, the hub-and-spokes metaphor fits power relations better than it portrays threat relations, and as we saw in chapter 1, balancing behavior is heavily influenced by perceptions of threat. If instead of the role of welcome balancer, the United States came to be seen as a threat, it would lose the influence that comes from providing military protection to balance others. At the same time, in economic networks a hub-and-spokes image is inaccurate. In trade, for example, Europe and Japan are significant alternative nodes in the global network.

Environmental globalization—the future of endangered species in Africa or the Amazonian rain forest in Brazil—is also less centered around the United States. And where the United States is viewed as a major ecological threat, as in production of carbon dioxide, it is less welcome, and there is often resistance to American policies.

Second, the hub-and-spokes image may mislead us about an apparent absence of reciprocity or two-way vulnerability. Even militarily, the ability of the United States to strike any place in the world does not make it invulnerable, as we learned at high cost on September 11, 2001. Other states and groups and even individuals can employ unconventional uses of force or, in the long term, develop weapons of mass destruction with delivery systems that would enable them to threaten the United States. Terrorism is a real threat, and nuclear or mass biological attacks would be more lethal than hijacked aircraft. As we saw in the last chapter, global economic and social transactions are making it increasingly difficult to control our borders. When we open ourselves to economic flows, we simultaneously open ourselves to a new type of military danger. And while the United States has the largest economy, it is both sensitive and potentially vulnerable to the spread of contagions in global capital markets, as we discovered in the 1997 "Asian" financial crisis. In the social dimension, the United States may export more popular culture than any other country, but it also imports more ideas and immigrants than most countries. Managing immigration turns out to be an extremely sensitive and important aspect of the response to globalism. Finally, the United States is environmentally sensitive and vulnerable to actions abroad that it cannot control. Even if the United States took costly measures to reduce emissions of carbon dioxide at home, it would still be vulnerable to climate change induced by coal-fired power plants in China.

A third problem with the simple hub-and-spokes dependency image that is popular with the hegemonists is that it fails to identify other important connections and nodes in global networks. New York is important in the flows of capital to emerging markets, but so are London, Frankfurt, and Tokyo. In terms of social and political globalization, Paris is more important to Gabon than Washington is;

Moscow is more important in Central Asia. Our influence is often limited in such situations. The Maldive Islands, only a few feet above sea level in the Indian Ocean, are particularly sensitive to the potential effects of producing carbon dioxide in the rest of the world. They are also completely vulnerable, since their sensitivity has to do with geography, not policy. At some time in the future, China will become more relevant to the Maldives than the United States is, because they will eventually outstrip us in the production of greenhouse gases. For many countries, we will not be the center of the world.

Finally, as the prior example suggests, the hub-and-spokes model may blind us to changes that are taking place in the architecture of the global networks. Network theorists argue that central players gain power most when there are structural holes—gaps in communications—between other participants. When the spokes cannot communicate with each other without going through the hub, the central position of the hub provides power. When the spokes can communicate and coordinate directly with each other, the hub becomes less powerful. The growth of the Internet provides these inexpensive alternative connections that fill the gaps.[49]

As the architecture of global networks evolves from a hub-and-spokes model to a widely distributed form like that of the Internet, the structural holes shrink and the structural power of the central state is reduced. It is true, for now, that Americans are central to the Internet; at the beginning of the twenty-first century, they comprise more than half of all Internet users. But by 2003, projections suggest, the United States will have 180 million Internet users, and there will be 240 million abroad.[50] This will be even more pronounced two decades hence, as Internet usage continues to spread. English is the most prevalent language on the Internet today, but by 2010, Chinese Internet users are likely to outnumber American users.[51] The fact that Chinese web sites will be read primarily by ethnic Chinese nationals and expatriates will not dethrone English as the web's lingua franca, but it will increase Chinese power in Asia by allowing Beijing "to shape a Chinese political culture that stretches well beyond its physical boundaries."[52] And China will not be alone. With the inevitable spread of technological capabilities, more-distributed network architectures will evolve. At some time in the future, when there are a billion Internet users in Asia and 250 million in the United States, more web sites, capital, entrepreneurs, and advertisers will be attracted to the Asian market.

The United States now seems to bestride the world like a colossus, to use *The Economist*'s phrase.[53] Looking more closely, we see that American dominance varies across realms and that many relationships of interdependence go both ways. Large states such as the United States—or, to a lesser extent, China—have more freedom than do small states, but they are rarely exempt from the effects of globalization. And states are not alone. As we saw in the last chapter, organizations, groups, and even individuals are becoming players. For both better and worse, technology is putting capabilities within the reach of individuals that were solely the preserve of government in the past.[54] Falling costs are increasing the thickness and complexity of global networks of interdependence. The United States promotes and benefits from economic globalization. But over the longer term, we can expect globalization itself to spread technological and economic capabilities and thus reduce the extent of American dominance.

GLOBALIZATION AND LOCAL CULTURES

Local culture and local politics also set significant limits on the extent to which globalization enhances American power. Contrary to conventional wisdom, globalization is not homogenizing the cultures of the world.

Although they are related, globalization and modernization are not the same. People sometimes attribute changes to globalization that are caused in large part simply by modernization.[55] The modernity of the industrial revolution transformed British society and culture in the nineteenth century. The global spread of industrialization and the development of alternative centers of industrial power eventually undercut Britain's relative position. And while the modernity of the new industrial centers altered their local cultures so that in some ways they looked more like Britain than before, the cause was modernization, not Anglicization. Moreover, while modernity produced some common traits such as urbanization and factories, the residual local cultures were by no means erased. Convergence toward similar institutions to deal with similar problems is not surprising, but it does not lead to homogeneity.[56] There were some similarities in the industrial societies of Britain, Germany, America, and Japan in the first half of the twentieth century, but there were also important differences. When China, India, and Brazil complete their current process of industrialization, we should not expect them to be replicas of Japan, Germany, or the United States.

In the same vein, though the United States is widely perceived as being at the forefront of the information revolution, and though the information revolution results in many similarities in social and cultural habits (such as television viewing or Internet use), it is incorrect to attribute those similarities to Americanization. Correlation is not causation. If one imagines a thought experiment in which a country introduces computers and communications at a rapid rate in a world in which the United States did not exist, one would expect major social and cultural changes to occur from the modernization (or, as some say, postmodernity). Of course, since the United States exists and is at the forefront of the information revolution, there is a current degree of Americanization, but it is likely to diminish over the course of the century as technology spreads and local cultures modernize in their own ways.

Evidence of historical proof that globalization does not necessarily mean homogenization can be seen in the case of Japan, a country that deliberately isolated itself from an earlier wave of globalization carried by seventeenth-century European seafarers. In the middle of the nineteenth century it became the first Asian country to embrace globalization and to borrow successfully from the world without losing its uniqueness. During the Meiji Restoration Japan searched broadly for tools and innovations that would allow it to become a major power rather than a victim of Western imperialism. It sent young people to the West for education. Its delegations scoured the world for ideas in science, technology, and industry. In the political realm, Meiji reformers were well aware of Anglo-American ideas and institutions but deliberately turned to German models because they were deemed more suitable to a country with an emperor.

The lesson that Japan has to teach the rest of the world is not simply that an Asian country can compete in military and economic power, but rather that after a century and a half of globalization, it is possible to adapt while preserving a unique culture. Of course, there are American influences in contemporary Japan (and Japanese influences such as Pokémon in the United States). Thousands of Japanese youth are co-opting the music, dress, and style of urban black America. But some of the groups dress up like samurai warriors onstage. As one claims, "We're trying to make a whole new culture and mix the music."[57] One can applaud or deplore or simply be amused by any particular cultural transfers, but one should not doubt the persistence of Japan's cultural uniqueness.

The image of American homogenization also reflects a mistakenly static view of culture. Few cultures are static, and efforts to portray them as unchanging often reflect conservative political strategies rather than descriptions of reality. The Peruvian writer Mario Vargas Llosa put it well in saying that arguments in favor of cultural identity and against globalization "betray a stagnant attitude towards culture that is not borne out by historical fact. Do we know of any cultures that have remained unchanged through time? To find any of them one has to travel to the small, primitive, magico-religious communities made up of people . . . who due to their primitive condition, become progressively more vulnerable to exploitation and extermination."[58] Vibrant cultures are constantly changing and borrowing from other cultures. And the borrowing is not always from the United States. For example, as mentioned above, many more countries turned to Canada than to the United States as an example for constitution building in the aftermath of the Cold War. Canadian views of how to deal with hate crimes were more congenial to South Africa and the countries of Eastern Europe than were American First Amendment practices.[59]

And as mentioned above, globalization is a two-edged sword. In some areas, there is not only a backlash against American cultural imports but an effort to change American culture itself. American policies toward capital punishment may now have majority support inside the United States, but they are regarded as egregious violations of human rights in much of Europe and have been the focus of transnational campaigns led by human rights groups. American environmental attitudes toward climate change or genetic modification of food bring similar criticism. As the British author Jonathan Freedlund says, "In the past, anti-Americans saved their bile for two separate areas of U.S. misconduct. They were appalled, first, by America's antics abroad. They were disgusted, second, by the way Americans behaved inside their own country. . . . Now thanks to globalization, the two older forms of hostility have converged."[60]

Finally, there is some evidence that globalization and the information revolution may reinforce rather than reduce cultural diversity. In one British view, "globalization is the reason for the revival of local culture in different parts of the world. . . . Globalization not only pulls upwards, but also pushes downwards, creating new pressures for local autonomy."[61] Some French commentators express fear that in a world of global Internet marketing, there will no longer be room for a culture that cherishes some 250 different types of cheese. But on the contrary, the Internet allows dispersed customers to come together in a way that encourages niche markets, including many sites dedicated only to cheese. The information revolution also allows people to establish a more diverse set of political communities. The use of the Welsh language in Britain and Gaelic in Ireland is greater today than fifty years ago.[62] Britain, Belgium, and Spain, among others in Europe, have devolved more power to local regions. The global information age may strengthen rather than weaken many local cultures.

As technology spreads, less powerful actors become empowered. Terrorism is the recent dramatic example, but consider also the relations between transnational corporations and poor countries.[63] In the early stages, the multinational company, with its access to the global resources of finance, technology, and markets, holds all the high cards and gets the best of the bargain with the poor country. With time, as the poor country develops skilled personnel, learns new technologies, and opens its own channels to global finance and markets, it successfully renegotiates the bargain and captures more of the benefits. When the multinational oil companies first went into Saudi Arabia, they claimed the lion's share of the gains from the oil; today the Saudis do. Of course, there has been some change in Saudi culture as engineers and financiers have been trained abroad, incomes have risen, and some degree of urbanization has occurred, but Saudi culture today certainly does not look like that of the United States.

Skeptics might argue that modern transnational corporations will escape the fate that befell the giant oil companies because many are virtual companies that design products and market them but farm out manufacturing to dozens of suppliers in poor countries. The big companies play small suppliers against each other, seeking ever lower labor costs. But as the technology of cheap communications allows NGOs to conduct campaigns of "naming and shaming" that threaten their market brands in rich countries, such multinationals become vulnerable as well. As we saw in the previous chapter, some technological change benefits the stronger parties, but some helps the weak.

Economic and social globalization are not producing cultural homogeneity. The rest of the world will not someday look just like the United States. American culture is very prominent at this stage in global history, and it contributes to American soft power in many, but not all, areas. At the same time, immigrants as well as ideas and events outside our borders are changing our own culture, and that adds to our appeal. We have an interest in preserving that soft power. We should use it now to build a world congenial to our basic values in preparation for a time in the future when we may be less influential. As globalization spreads technical capabilities and information technology allows broader participation in global communications, American economic and cultural preponderance may diminish over the course of the century. This in turn has mixed results for American soft power. A little less dominance may mean a little less anxiety about Americanization, fewer complaints about American arrogance, and a little less intensity in the anti-American backlash. We may have less control in the future, but we may find ourselves living in a world somewhat more congenial to our basic values of democracy, free markets, and human rights. In any case, the political reactions to globalization will be far more diverse than a unified reaction against American cultural hegemony.

POLITICAL REACTIONS TO GLOBALIZATION

Political protests against globalization have increased in recent years. The 1999 "battle of Seattle" inaugurated a long string of street protests against the effects of globalization.

Global effects are powerful, but they do not enter societies in an unmediated way. On the contrary, they are filtered through domestic political alignments. How global information is downloaded in different countries is a function of domestic politics. In that sense, even in an age of globalization, all politics remains local. The protesters do not represent some undifferentiated mass of civil society, notwithstanding their frequent claims to do so. For example, José Bové, a star of the poor peoples' economic forum at Porto Alegre in 2001, staunchly defends Europe's common agricultural policy, which damages farmers in poor countries. Away from the protests, the reality is that different political systems have different capacities to shape the economic, sociological, environmental, and military forces that impinge on them; their people have different values relative to those forces; and their political institutions react differently with those values to produce policies of response.

Domestic institutions channel responses to change. Some countries imitate success, as exemplified by democratizing capitalist societies from South Korea to Eastern Europe. Some accommodate in distinctive and ingenious ways: for instance, small European states such as the Netherlands or Scandinavia have maintained relatively large governments and emphasized compensation for disadvantaged sectors, while the Anglo-American industrialized countries have, in general, emphasized markets, competition, and deregulation. Capitalism is far from monolithic, with significant differences between Europe, Japan, and the United States. There is more than one way to respond to global markets and to run a capitalist economy.

In other societies such as Iran, Afghanistan, and Sudan, conservative groups resist globalization strongly, even violently. Reactions to globalization help stimulate fundamentalism.[64] In some ways, the Al Qaeda terrorists represent a civil war within Islam, which seeks to transform into a global clash of civilization. Global forces can reformulate ethnic and political identities in profound and often unanticipated ways. In Bosnia, political entrepreneurs appealed to traditional identities of people in rural areas in order to overwhelm and dissolve the cosmopolitan identities that had begun to develop in the cities with devastating results. And Iran has seen struggles between Islamic fundamentalists and their more liberal opponents—who are also Islamic but more sympathetic to Western ideas.

As mentioned earlier, rising inequality was a major cause of the political reactions that halted an earlier wave of economic globalization early in the twentieth century. The recent period of globalization, like the half century before World War I, has also been associated with increasing inequality among and within some countries. The ratio of incomes of the 20 percent of people in the world living in the richest countries to those of the 20 percent living in the poorest countries increased from 30:1 in 1960 to 74:1 in 1997. By comparison, it increased between 1870 and 1913 from 7:1 to 11:1.[65] In any case, inequality can have political effects even if it is not increasing. "The result is a lot of angry young people, to whom new information technologies have given the means to threaten the stability of the societies they live in and even to threaten social stability in countries of the wealthy zone."[66] As increasing flows of information make people more aware of inequality, it is not surprising that some choose to protest.

Whatever the facts of inequality, there is even less clarity concerning its causation or the most effective remedies to it. In part, increases in inequality by country are a straightforward result of rapid economic growth in some but not all parts of the world. They demonstrate that movement out of poverty is possible, although often hindered by political factors as well as resource constraints. Most of the poorest countries in the world—whether in Africa or the Middle East—have suffered from misrule, corruption, and inept macroeconomic policies. The weakness of their political systems can be blamed in part on colonialism and nineteenth-century globalization, but the sources of their recent poor performance are more complex.[67] Several countries in East Asia that were equally poor in the 1950s used networks of globalization to greatly increase their wealth and status in the world economy. It is difficult to find any countries that have prospered while closing themselves off from globalization, but openness alone is not sufficient to overcome inequality.[68]

Equally striking is the uneven distribution of the benefits of globalization among individuals within and across countries. For instance, in Brazil in 1995, the richest tenth of the population received almost half of the national income, and the richest fifth had 64 percent, while the poorest fifth had only 2.5 percent and the poorest tenth less than 1 percent. In the United States, the richest tenth received 28 percent of income, and the richest fifth had 45 percent, while the poorest fifth had almost 5 percent and the poorest tenth 1.5 percent.[69] Across countries, inequalities are even more dramatic: the richest three billionaires in the world in 1998 had combined assets greater than the combined incomes of the six hundred million people in the world's least developed countries.[70]

Consider also China, a poor country that has been growing very fast since its leaders decided to open their economy in the 1980s, thus exposing their society to the forces of globalization. China's "human development index" as calculated by the United Nations—reflecting life expectancy, educational attainment, and GDP per capita—showed dramatic gains.[71] Hundreds of millions of Chinese were made better off by market reforms and globalization, but hundreds of millions of others, particularly in the western parts of the country, saw little or no gain. And some will be made worse off, particularly as China exposes inefficient state-owned enterprises to international composition under the terms of its accession to the World Trade Organization (WTO). How China handles the resulting politics of inequality will be a key question in its future.[72]

Will this inequality create problems for American foreign policy? In the late nineteenth century, inequality rose in rich countries and fell in poor countries; up to half of the rise in inequality could be attributed to the effects of globalization. Many of those changes were due to mass migration, which explained about 70 percent of the real wage convergence in the late nineteenth century.[73] The political consequences of these shifts in inequality are complex, but the historian Karl Polanyi argued powerfully in his classic study *The Great Transformation* that the market forces unleashed by the industrial revolution and globalization in the nineteenth century produced not only great economic gains but also great social disruptions and political reactions.[74] There is no *automatic* relationship between inequality and political reaction, but the former can give rise to the latter. Particularly when inequality is combined with instability, such as financial crises and recessions that throw people out of work, such reactions could eventually lead to restrictions on economic globalization.

The recent surge in protests against globalization is, in part, a reaction to the changes produced by economic integration. From an economist's view, imperfect markets are inefficient, but from a political view, some imperfections in international markets can be considered "useful inefficiencies" because they slow down and buffer political change. As globalization removes such inefficiencies, it removes the buffers and becomes the political victim of its economic successes. In addition, as described above, as global networks become more complex there are more linkages among issues that can create friction—witness the various cases of trade and the environment that have proved contentious at the WTO. But a large part of the current protest movement is the result of social globalization, increased communication across borders, reduced costs, and greater ease in coordinating protests among individuals and NGOs. In 1997, even before the so-called battle of Seattle, NGOs used the Internet to coordinate protests that helped scuttle a multilateral agreement on investment being negotiated in Paris.

Unlike the mass working-class movements of socialism in the nineteenth and early twentieth centuries, the current protests tend to be elite rather than mass movements. While their leaders often claim to speak on behalf of the poor and to represent global civil society, they tend to be relatively well-off self-selected groups from wealthy countries. The groups that protested at meetings of the WTO, the International Monetary Fund, the World Bank, and the Group of Eight in Seattle, Washington, Prague, Genoa, and elsewhere were odd coalitions. Among them were old leftist opponents of capitalism, trade unionists trying to protect well-paid jobs against competition from poor countries, environmentalists wishing for stronger international regulation, young idealists wishing to show solidarity with the poor, and young anarchists rioting for fun and profit. As one young Scandinavian protester told a *New York Times* reporter in Genoa, "Globalization is fashionable at the moment, just the way the environment or health care were in recent years, but we are targeting the system and globalization is one chapter."[75]

Some protesters wanted more international regulation that would intrude on national sovereignty; others wanted less infringement of sovereignty. But whatever the incoherence of the coalitions, they were able to capture global attention from media and governments. Their concerns about corporate domination of "neoliberal" globalization, about growing inequality, about cultural homogenization, and about absence of democratic accountability managed to touch responsive chords, if not to ignite a mass movement.[76] To the extent that the United States wants to see economic globalization continue, it will have to think more clearly about the responses to such charges and about the governance of globalism, as we shall see below and in chapter 5.

THE GOVERNANCE OF GLOBALISM

If laissez-faire economics has built-in instability, and networks of interdependence are stretching beyond the boundaries of the nation-state, how is globalism to be governed? A world government is not the answer. Some writers draw an analogy from American history, asking today's nation-states to join together as the thirteen colonies did. Just as the development of a national economy in the late nineteenth century led to the growth of federal government power in Washington, so the development of a global economy will require federal power at the global level.[77] Some see the United Nations as the incipient core.[78] But the American analogy is misleading. The thirteen original colonies shared far more in English language and culture than the more than two hundred nations of the world share today, and even the Americans did not avoid a bloody civil war. By the time a continental economy developed, the framework of the American federation was firmly in place. Rather than thinking of a hierarchical world government, we should think of networks of governance crisscrossing and coexisting with a world divided formally into sovereign states.

Many countries' first response to global forces is to take internal action to decrease their vulnerability to outside influences—they resort to protectionism when they can do so at reasonable cost. Sometimes they are limited by costly retaliation, as in recent trade cases between the United States and the European Union. In agriculture and textiles, however, the rich countries' protective responses impose costs on poor countries who are ill placed to retaliate. On the other hand, some unilateral responses can be positive. In the 1980s, United States firms reacted to Japanese and European competition in automobiles by implementing internal changes that increased their efficiency. In some instances, such as general accounting procedures or transparent regulation of security markets, companies and governments unilaterally adopted external standards to enhance their access to capital. Competition in standards need not lead to a race to the bottom, as countries may unilaterally decide to race to the top. For example, Israel decided to adopt the European Union's pesticide standards, and a number of Latin American countries have espoused U.S. standards.[79]

These examples reinforce a relatively obvious point: for now, the key institution for global governance is going to remain the nation-state.[80] In the face of globalization, however, even countries as strong as the United States will find that unilateral measures will often be insufficient, will fail, or will generate reactions. Countries facing increased globalization will become, therefore, increasingly willing to sacrifice some of their own legal freedom of action in order to constrain, and make more predictable, others' actions toward themselves. They will find, like Molière's character who discovered that he had been speaking prose all his life, that the world has long had cooperative institutions for managing common affairs. Hundreds of organizations and legal regimes exist to manage the global dimensions of trade, telecommunications, civil aviation, health, environment, meteorology, and many other issues.

To achieve what they want, most countries, including the United States, find that they have to coordinate their activities. Unilateral action simply cannot produce the right results on what are inherently multilateral issues. Cooperation may take the form of bilateral and multilateral treaties, informal agreements among bureaucracies, and delegation to formal intergovernmental institutions. Regulation of global flows will often grow by layers of accretion rather than by a single treaty and will long remain imperfect. Some cases are easier than others. For example, cooperation on prosecution of child pornography on the Internet is proving easier than regulation of hate mail, as there are more shared norms in the former case than in the latter.[81]

Finally, some attempts at governance will not involve states as coherent units but rather will be either transgovernmental (meaning that components of states engage with one another) or transnational (involving nongovernmental actors). That is, alongside the necessary but imperfect interstate institutional framework, there is developing an informal political process that supplements the formal process of cooperative relations among states. In the public sector, different components of governments have informal contact.[82] Rare is the embassy of a large democratic country today in which foreign-service personnel form a majority of those stationed abroad. Instead, the majority of officers in American embassies come from agencies such as agriculture, transportation, commerce, energy, NASA, defense, intelligence, and the FBI.

On the private side, transnational corporations and offshore fund managers are playing a larger-than-ever role in creating rules and standards. Their practices often create de facto governance. International commercial arbitration is basically a private justice system and credit rating agencies are private gate-keeping systems. They have emerged as important governance mechanisms whose authority is not centered in the state.[83] In the nonprofit sector, as we have seen, there has been an extraordinary growth of organizations—still largely Western, but increasingly transnational. For reasons discussed in chapter 2, these organizations and the multiple channels of access across borders are able to put increasing leverage on states and intergovernmental organizations as well as transnational corporations.

The soft power of these organizations is frequently seen in the mobilization of shame to impose costs on national or corporate reputations.[84] Transnational drug companies gave up lawsuits in South Africa over infringement of their patents on AIDS drugs because, in the words of the *Financial Times,* "demands for greater social responsibility from business are getting louder, better organised, and more popular. They cannot be ignored. The climbdown by the drug companies was the most significant event. It amounted to a recognition that their legal battle in South Africa was a public relations disaster."[85] Similar campaigns of naming and shaming have altered the investment and employment patterns of companies like Mattel and Nike in the toy and footwear industries. Some transnational corporations such as Shell have set up large staffs just to deal with NGOs. Jean-François Rischard of the World Bank, for instance, advocates "global issues networks" that would issue ratings that measure how well countries and private businesses are doing in meeting norms on the environment and other issues that affect the welfare of the planet. The process would be quick and nonbureaucratic, and the sanctions would be through imposing damage on reputations.[86]

The results may or may not be consistent with government preferences. For example, if transnational corporations were to respond to an NGO campaign by agreeing to raise the age of child labor in their factories, they might be countermanding the decision of the elected government of a sovereign country like India more effectively than any formal international vote taken in the World Trade Organization. The evolution of these civil and business networks has been largely uncoordinated, and it remains unclear how they could fit together in a representative form of global governance. Neither can claim to represent citizenry as a whole.[87] The networks of private and transnational actors are contributing to the governance of an incipient, albeit imperfect, civil society at the global level. Because these networks deal with partial perspectives of business and nonprofit advocates, some observers have suggested adding the input of governments or parts of governments to represent broader public interests. Global policy networks exist on such issues as corruption (led by Transparency International), the construction of large dams (led by the World Commission on Dams), debt relief for poor countries (led by Jubilee 2000), polio eradication (led by the World Health Organization), and numerous others.[88]

How should we react to these changes? Our democratic theory has not caught up with global practice.[89] Financial crises, climate change, migration, terrorism, and drug smuggling ignore borders but profoundly affect American citizens' lives. British sociologist Anthony Giddens believes that because they escape control by sovereign democratic processes, they are one of the main reasons for "the declining appeal of democracy where it is best established."[90] For some, such as undersecretary of state John Bolton, the solution is to strengthen U.S. democracy by pulling out of intrusive institutions and rejecting any constraints on sovereignty.[91] But even the unilateralists and sovereigntists will find that international institutions are necessary because many of the issues raised by globalization are inherently multilateral.

Antiglobalization protesters call into question the legitimacy of global institutions and networks on the grounds that they are undemocratic.[92] For example, Lori Wallach, one of the organizers of the coalition that disrupted the WTO in Seattle, attributed half of its success to "the notion that the democracy deficit in the global economy is neither necessary nor acceptable."[93] Institutional legitimacy can also rest on tradition and efficacy, but in today's world, consistency with democratic procedures has become increasingly important.

In fact, these global institutions are quite weak. Even the much-maligned WTO is a weak organization with a small budget and staff, hardly the stuff of world government. Moreover, unlike nonelected NGOs (some of which have larger budgets than the WTO), international institutions tend to be highly responsive to national governments, which are the real source of democratic legitimacy. Other defenders say that the question of democracy is irrelevant, since international institutions are merely instruments to facilitate interstate cooperation. Their legitimacy derives from the democratic governments that created them and from their effectiveness.

Except for the most technical organizations, which fall below the political radar, such defenses based on the weakness of international institutions are probably not enough to protect them from attacks on their legitimacy. In a world where the norm of democracy has become the touchstone of legitimacy, protesters will charge that they suffer from a democracy deficit. Even though the organizations are weak, their rules and resources can have powerful effects. Moreover, the protesters make three interesting points. First, not all the countries that are members of the organizations are democratic. Second, long lines of delegation from multiple governments and lack of transparency often weaken accountability. Third, although the organizations may be agents of states, they often represent only parts of states. For example, trade ministers attend the meetings of the WTO, finance ministers participate in the meetings of the IMF, and central bankers meet at the Bank for International Settlements in Basel. To functional outsiders, even in the same government, these institutions look like closed and secretive clubs. To develop the legitimacy of international governance will require three things: (1) greater clarity about democracy, (2) a richer understanding of accountability, and (3) a willingness to experiment.

Democracy is government by officials who are accountable and removable by the majority of people in a jurisdiction (albeit with provisions for protections of individuals and minorities). But who are "we the people" in a world where political identity at the global level is so weak? The principle of one state, one vote respects sovereignty, but it is not democratic. On that formula a citizen of Nauru, a UN member, would have ten thousand times more voting power than a citizen of China. On the other hand, treating the world as one global constituency implies the existence of a political community in which citizens of around two hundred states would be willing to be continually outvoted by more than a billion Chinese and a billion Indians. (Ironically, such a world would be a nightmare for many of the protesting NGOs that seek to promote international environmental and labor standards as well as democracy.)

Minorities acquiesce in the will of a majority when they feel they participate in a larger community. There is little evidence that a sufficiently strong sense of community exists at the global level or that it could soon be created.[94] In the absence of a much stronger sense of community than now exists, the extension of domestic voting procedures to the global level is neither practical nor just. A stronger European Parliament may reduce a sense of "democratic deficit" as the relatively homogeneous democratic states of the European Union evolve, but it is doubtful that the analogy or terminology (parliament) makes sense under the conditions of diversity that prevail on the global scale. Adding legislative assemblies to global institutions, except in a purely advisory or consultative role, might well produce an undemocratic body that would interfere with the delegated accountability that now links institutions to democracy. Those who argue for a global parliament are correct in stating that unelected interest groups cannot "speak for the citizenry as a whole," but they are wrong in thinking the only serious answer is "some type of popularly elected global body"—at least not until the world develops a widespread sense of identity as "a citizenry as a whole."[95] Alfred Lord Tennyson's "Parliament of Man" made great Victorian poetry, but it does not yet make good political analysis, even in a global information age.

We should not assume that globalization in its current form will inevitably continue as it has. Political reactions against globalization and its rudimentary institutions of governance are now commonplace. Concerns about instability, inequality, and cultural identity are justified, even if overstated. The fact that democratic accountability is difficult to achieve in a globalized world makes policies that foster globalization vulnerable to attack. The results are not likely to be the same as those seen in the period between the onset of World War I and the end of World War II, but the possibility of a protectionist setback for economic globalism cannot be excluded if there is great instability or a prolonged economic downturn. Ironically, if the current political backlash leads to a rash of unilateral protectionist policies, it might slow or reverse the world's economic integration even as global warming, transnational terrorism, or the spread of AIDS continues apace. It would be ironic if current protests curtailed the positive aspects of globalization while leaving the negative dimensions.

On balance, Americans have benefited from globalization. To the extent that we wish to continue to do so, we will need to deal with its discontents. This cannot be accomplished by resorting to slogans of sovereignty, unilateral policies, or drawing inward, as the unilateralists and sovereigntists suggest: "If we can't do it our way, then we just won't do it. But at least we the people, the American people, will remain masters of our ship." This prescription mistakes the abstractions of sovereignty for the realities of power.[96] The result would be to undermine our soft power and America's ability to influence others' responses to globalization. Instead, the United States should use its current preeminence to help shape institutions that will benefit both Americans and the rest of the world as globalization evolves. Americans will have to factor multilateral institutions and governance into a broader conception of our national interests, as we shall see in chapter 5.

4

THE HOME FRONT

How well will Americans respond to the challenges of this global information age? A nation can lose power as a result of being overtaken by rising nations, but as we saw in the first chapter, this is not the most likely challenge. The barbarians did not defeat Rome; rather, it rotted from within. People lost confidence in their culture and institutions, elites battled for control, corruption increased, and the economy failed to grow adequately.[1] Today terrorist barbarians cannot destroy American power unless we also rot from within. Are there similar signs of decay in the United States today? Could this nation lose its ability to influence world events positively because of domestic battles over culture, collapse of institutions, and economic stagnation? If our society and institutions appear to be collapsing, we will be less attractive to others. If our economy fails, we will lose the basis for our hard power as well as our soft power. Even if the United States continues to hold the high cards of military, economic, and soft power, could we lose our capacity to transform those resources into effective influence? After all, sometimes card players lose despite being dealt high hands.

Power conversion—translating power resources into effective influence—is a long-standing problem for the United States. The

United States was the world's most powerful country in the decade following World War I, but because of our internal preoccupations in the 1920s and economic failure in the 1930s, we failed to marshal our resources effectively on the international stage, and for this we paid the price in World War II. American foreign policy making is a messy process for reasons deeply rooted in our political culture and institutions. The Constitution is based on the eighteenth-century liberal view that power is best controlled by fragmentation and countervailing checks and balances. In foreign policy, the Constitution has always invited the president and Congress to struggle for control.[2] That struggle is complicated when the Congress and presidency are controlled by different political parties. Strong economic and ethnic pressure groups struggle for their self-interested definitions of the national interest, and a political culture of American exceptionalism complicates matters by making our foreign policy uniquely moralistic.[3] This has led some realists, such as former secretary of defense James Schlesinger, to despair that American foreign policy "lacks the steadiness that has been associated with great powers."[4]

Now, at a time when Americans need to adapt to a more complicated world, one in which foreign and domestic policies overlap more than ever, some observers believe these traditional inefficiencies in power conversion are being exacerbated by cultural conflict, institutional collapse, and economic problems. Each issue has spawned a vast literature. My interest here is not to settle such debates but rather to sample enough of their content to detect whether they provide evidence of a Roman fate for the United States. I will show that, at beginning of the new century, such evidence is slim.

MORAL DECAY AND CULTURAL DIVIDE

Some saw evidence of deep cleavage in the closely fought 2000 presidential election, where the electoral map showed "the interior heartland, home of the 'dutiful' people," supporting Bush, and "the godless coasts, the industrial mid-west," and the big cities voting for Gore. A county-by-county map portrays a more complex picture but confirms a rural-urban split and a difference between inner and outer suburbs.[5] Others go further and depict moral decay in the country as a whole. In the words of conservative historian Gertrude Himmelfarb, the United States is currently confronting "the collapse of ethical principles and habits, the loss of respect for authorities and institutions, the breakdown of the family, the decline of civility, the vulgarization of high culture, and the degradation of popular culture." The counterculture of the 1960s has become dominant, while the traditional culture of the 1950s has been relegated to dissident status.[6] Robert Bork also sees almost every aspect of our culture in decline, and Father Richard Neuhaus has compared America to Nazi Germany.[7]

If these divisions were as deep as portrayed, they could undercut our hard power by inhibiting our capacity to act collectively, and diminish our soft power by reducing the attractiveness of our society and culture. But neither is the case.

If middle-class America is as divided as these accounts imply, says sociologist Alan Wolfe, "our future as a nation will be marked by incessant conflicts between irreconcilable worldviews, raising the prospect that the democratic stability that has kept the country together since the Civil War will no longer be attainable." But he argues that ordinary Americans are not as engaged in culture wars as intellectuals believe they are. The message from the middle-class Americans he studied to those who worry that America might fall apart is a calming one. Mature patriotism and tolerance replaced the bitter divisions that accompanied the Vietnam War in the 1960s and 1970s, and, (with some exceptions) characterized the response to the September 2001 events.[8]

It is true that some cultural indicators such as crime, divorce rates, and teenage pregnancy are worse today than in the 1950s, but all three measures improved considerably in the 1990s. Even before September 2001, the nation had made tangible progress toward more than two-thirds of seventy or more significant domestic goals related to prosperity, quality of life, opportunity, personal security, and values. Contrary to views often expressed by the cultural pessimists, "there is no reliable evidence that American students are learning less in school, or that the American Dream is vanishing, or that the environment is more polluted."[9] Rates of homicide and drug use have decreased in the last decade, while health, environment, and safety have improved.[10] Most children still live with both natural parents, and the divorce rate has stabilized. American membership in religious organizations increased from 41 percent to 70 percent over the course of the twentieth century, although church attendance remained roughly level at 43 percent in 1939 and 40 percent in 1999.[11] While the United States has social problems—and always has had—it does not seem to be rushing to hell in a handbasket.

How, then, can one explain the cultural pessimism that existed before September 2001?[12] In part, it reflects the mass media's tendency to emphasize stories consistent with the bad-news theme. "If most Americans think the real world is like the world they see on TV, it is easy to see why they think the country is in deep trouble."[13] Reaction to national-level trends is a mediated phenomenon, with few people having direct experience. To the extent they do, the majority tell pollsters that their own lives, communities, schools, and congressmen are fine, though they worry about the national level. If everyone "knows" from the media that things are a mess at the national level and you have no direct experience at the national level but only a good personal experience, you tell the pollster the conventional wisdom about the national condition. The result is an optimism gap, but not convincing evidence of decline.

And in part, cultural pessimism is simply very American, extending back to our Puritan roots. Charles Dickens observed a century and a half ago that "if its individual citizens, to a man, are to be believed, [America] always is depressed, and always is stagnated, and always is at an alarming crisis, and never was otherwise."[14] Polls show that an optimism gap existed in the 1950s. Changing generations may also play a role in our perceptions. The generation that lived through the Depression and World War II had a more modest sense of entitlement and fewer expectations to be disappointed than today's generation.[15] And historical cultural battles over immigration, slavery, evolution, temperance, McCarthyism, and civil rights were arguably more serious than any of today's issues of contention. Polls show that people often attribute a golden glow to the past that they did not feel at the time. It is always easy to show decay by comparing the good in the past with the bad in the present (or progress by doing the converse).

For our purposes, the task is not to arbitrate intellectual battles over cultural change but to ask how such cultural judgments affect American national power and our ability to carry out an effective foreign policy. There are two possible connections. First, if Americans were so distracted or divided by internal battles over cultural issues that we lost the capacity to act collectively in foreign policy, we would undercut our hard power. That was the case in the early 1970s in the aftermath of our deep divisions over Vietnam, but it is simply not plausible in today's setting. As Himmelfarb herself concludes, "Americans can justly pride themselves on surviving both the cultural revolution and the culture war without paroxysms of persecution or bloodshed, without, indeed, serious social strife. For all their differences, the 'two cultures' remain firmly fixed within 'one nation.' "[16] We saw that amply demonstrated after September 11, 2001.

Then there's the connection between cultural divisions and our soft power. A decline in the quality of American cultural life could reduce our soft power if the bitterness of our family fights disgusted others, or if the overdramatization of our faults lead others to lower their respect for our national example. Certainly there are faults to report. Although the United States has made progress in many important respects over the past forty years, we lag behind Canada, France, Germany, Britain, and Japan in infant mortality, life expectancy, children in poverty, health insurance coverage, homicides, and births out of wedlock. "All too often, the areas in which we lead the industrial world are fields in which we would greatly prefer *not* to excel, such as rates of homicide and incarceration, percentages of the population in poverty, or per capita costs of health care."[17] Even though we are doing better than in the past, we are not doing as well as we could or as some others are. Such comparisons can be costly for American soft power, but doubly so if they are exaggerated and amplified by American politicians and intellectuals seeking to score points in domestic battles.

At the same time, the United States is not alone in many of the cultural changes that cause controversy. When such problems are shared, comparisons are less invidious and less damaging to our soft power. A Population Council report finds "trends like unwed motherhood, rising divorce rates, smaller households and the feminization of poverty are not unique to America, but are occurring worldwide."[18] Respect for authority and some standards of behavior have declined since 1960 throughout the Western world. But there is little indication that our levels of personal responsibility are much lower today than those of other advanced Western societies, and our levels of charitable giving and community service are generally higher.[19] As Himmelfarb admits, "In this international perspective, the American 'case' emerges clearly, not as an unprecedented anomaly, but as an all-too-common phenomenon."[20] Our soft power is eroded more by issues such as capital punishment or gun control, where we are the deviants in opinion among advanced countries, than by the cultural changes that we share with others. To the extent that social changes are similar in postmodern societies, culture battles become transnational rather than merely national. Those who applaud or deplore such changes find allies in other countries, and stark national comparisons become blurred. Such blurring limits the loss of soft power that accompanies inadequate (not declining) American performance.

IMMIGRATION AND AMERICAN VALUES

Fears over the effect of immigration on national values and on a coherent sense of American identity have been with us since the early years of the nation, and they have been accentuated by the September 2001 terrorist attacks. Benjamin Franklin worried about the stupidity of German immigrants, few of whom knew English, and whose presence might mean "great disorders may arise among us."[21] The nineteenth-century Know-Nothing party was built upon opposition to immigrants, particularly the Irish. Asians were singled out for exclusion from 1882 onward, and with the Immigration Restriction Act of 1924 the influx of immigrants slowed to a trickle for the next four decades. During the twentieth century, the nation recorded its highest percentage of foreign-born residents in 1910—14.7 percent of the population. Today, 10.4 percent are foreign born, but some people are worried not about two cultures but about too many cultures.[22]

Twice as many Americans are skeptical about immigration as are sympathetic to it. Various polls show that a plurality or majority want fewer immigrants coming into the country.[23] They fear the effects on wages and the costs to taxpayers, and above all they worry that the culture cannot assimilate large numbers of new immigrants. The rise of multiculturalism, a philosophy that rejects the melting-pot metaphor and instead celebrates ethnic differences, exacerbates such fears.[24] In response, states have enacted laws to restrict benefits for illegal immigrants and to reinforce English as the official language.

In the aftermath of the Immigration Act of 1965, which eliminated racial and ethnic restrictions, patterns of immigration changed, with the majority of new immigrants coming from less developed countries.[25] Half of the foreign-born residents today are from Latin America; a quarter are from Asia.[26] They have little to do with terrorism. This second great migration has seen a worsening economic performance by new immigrants partly due to a decline in their relative work skills. Immigration produced a small measurable net benefit (0.1 percent of GNP) for the country as a whole, but also harmed the economic opportunities of the least skilled workers and had a severe fiscal impact on the affected states, such as California.[27]

Both the numbers and the origins of the new immigrants have caused concerns about immigration's effects on American culture. Data from the 2000 census showed a soaring Hispanic population driven largely by waves of new immigrants, legal and illegal, with Hispanics about to replace blacks as the nation's largest minority.[28] Demographic projections portray a country in 2050 in which non-Hispanic whites will be only a slim majority. Hispanics will be 25 percent, blacks 14 percent, and Asians 8 percent.[29] For some, including author Peter Brimelow (himself an immigrant from Britain), the United States can no longer afford to be an immigrant country. "What is unusual in the current American immigration debate is that Americans are being urged to abandon the bonds of a common ethnicity so completely and to trust instead in ideology to hold together their state." A century ago, the last great wave of immigrants were met by an unflinching demand that they Americanize. He worries that today such a demand is weakened by multiculturalism taught in American schools.[30]

But Brimelow and others underestimate the continuing power of the melting pot. Communications and market forces still produce a powerful incentive for mastering the English language and accepting a degree of assimilation. According to the National Research Council, three-fifths of the immigrants who came in the 1980s spoke English well, and of those in the country thirty years or more, only 3 percent reported they could not speak English well.[31] Most of the evidence suggests that the latest immigrants are assimilating at least as quickly as their predecessors. Modern media help new immigrants to know more about their new country beforehand than immigrants did a century ago. A *Washington Post* poll of twenty-five hundred Latinos showed that nine out of ten who were newly arrived in America thought it important to change to fit in. But nine out of ten also thought it important to retain part of their ethnic culture.[32] Alan Wolfe finds this type of view acceptable to the middle-class Americans he interviewed. While they firmly oppose bilingualism in education, they tend to both accept a multiculturalism that reflects the diversity of the groups belonging to America and respect America at the same time.[33]

While the short-run economic benefits of immigration are modest, and too rapid a rate of immigration can cause social problems, over the long term immigration has strengthened the power of the United States and will continue to do so. For one thing, population is one of the sources of power, and most developed countries will experience a shortage of people as the century progresses. Some eighty-three countries and territories currently have fertility rates that are below the level necessary for a constant population level. To maintain its current population size, Japan would have to accept 350,000 newcomers a year for the next fifty years, which is difficult for a culture that historically has been hostile to immigration.[34]

For all of America's ambivalence, we are a country of immigration. The result is that by 2050, the United States will likely hold its rank in terms of population and will be the only developed country remaining among the world's twenty most populous nations.[35] Today the United States is the third largest country; fifty years from now it is still likely to be third (after only China and India). "Even if the current membership of the European Union were to form a single state, its projected 2050 population would be significantly smaller than America's."[36] Not only is this relevant to economic power, but given the fact that nearly all developed countries are aging and face a burden of providing for the older generation, immigration could help reduce the sharpness of the policy problem. In addition, even though the directly measurable short-term economic benefits at the national level are relatively small, some short-term economic benefits of skilled immigrants can be important to particular areas. For example, in 1998 Chinese- and Indian-born engineers were running one-quarter of Silicon Valley's high-technology businesses, which accounted for $17.8 billion in sales.[37] In its effects on population and the economy, immigration bolsters America's hard power.

Equally important are immigration's benefits for America's soft power. The fact that people want to come to the United States enhances our appeal, and the upward mobility of immigrants is attractive to people in other countries. America is a magnet, and many people can envisage themselves as Americans. Many successful Americans "look like" people in other countries. Moreover, connections between immigrants and their families and friends back home help to convey accurate and positive information about the United States. In addition, the presence of multiple cultures creates avenues of connection with other countries and helps create a necessary broadening of American attitudes in an era of globalization. While the September 2001 terrorist attacks pointed out the need to improve our immigration and naturalization system, it would be a mistake for Americans to reject immigration. Rather than diluting our hard and soft power, immigration enhances both.

CONFIDENCE IN OUR INSTITUTIONS

In 1964, three-quarters of the American public said they trusted the federal government to do the right thing most of the time. After 1970, roughly a quarter of the public admitted to such trust. Levels of trust sometimes spiked after dramatic events (as they did in 2001), but the long term trend after 1970 was decline.[38] Government was not alone.

Over the past three decades, public confidence dropped in half for many major institutions: 61 to 30 percent for universities, 55 to 21 percent for major companies, 73 to 29 percent for medicine, and 29 to 14 percent for journalism.[39] Could our hard or soft power erode because of loss of confidence in our institutions?

One possible interpretation is that the decline was a sign of health. The United States was founded in part on a mistrust of government; the Constitution was deliberately set up in such a way as to resist centralized power. Thomas Jefferson felt that the less government, the better, and a long Jeffersonian tradition says we should not worry too much about the level of confidence in government. If the polls reflect wariness, that may be a good thing. Moreover, when asked not about day-to-day government but about the underlying constitutional framework, the public is very positive. If you ask Americans what is the best place to live, 80 percent say the United States. If asked whether they like their democratic system of government, 90 percent say yes. Few people feel the system is rotten and must be overthrown.

Some aspects of mistrust are probably cyclical, while others represent discontent with bickering in the political process rather than deep disillusion with institutions. Compared with the 1950s, party politics became more polarized, but nasty politics is nothing new. In the 1884 presidential campaign, the two prevailing slogans were "Blaine, Blaine, James G. Blaine, the continental liar from the state of Maine," and "Ma, Ma, where's my pa? Gone to the White House, ha, ha, ha" (referring to Grover Cleveland's illegitimate child). Part of the problem is that faith in government became very high among the generation that survived the Depression and won World War II. In that case, over the long view of American history, the anomaly was overconfidence in government in the 1950s and early 1960s, not low levels thereafter.[40]

Moreover, much of the evidence for loss of trust in government comes from polling data, and responses are sensitive to the way questions are asked. One of the most important surveys, the National Election Study, has long asked whether people trust the government a great deal of the time. If the response "only some of the time" is added to "a great deal," then Congress and the executive branch of the federal government received approval from about 60 percent of the public.[41] What cannot be dismissed is that there was a downward trend to answers to the same questions over time, and the duration of the resurgence after September 2001 remains uncertain. The sharpest decline occurred in the late 1960s and early 1970s. According to a study in the 1970s, people "who had direct dealings with government agencies, both federal and state, were found to be satisfied with their bureaucratic encounters" but still reported a negative general view of government agencies.[42] Like the optimism gap noted above, there seems to be an "experience gap" in which people report to pollsters something other than their direct experience.

How do people get their information about government if not from direct personal experience? Seventy percent say they rely on the media rather than friends or personal experience. Confidence in institutions seems to be more a social than a personal judgment.[43] The role of the media changed over the same period during which the decline in confidence in institutions occurred. Both the press and television became more intrusive, editorial, and negative in their reporting.[44] In addition, television entertainment increasingly portrayed government figures in a negative light. In the 1970s, most government characters in sitcoms were seen in a positive light, but by the mid-1990s, most were portrayed in disparaging tones.[45] These effects were reinforced by changes in the political process that emphasized negative ads and a tendency for politicians to "run against Washington." The effect has been what advertisers call a "de-marketing" campaign against government. It is worth noting that two federal agencies that bucked the trend of declining confidence (as measured by answers to pollsters) are both large bureaucracies—the military and the postal service. What they also have in common is that both engaged in substantial positive advertising about themselves—for recruiting in the case of the military, and to compete with private companies in the case of the postal service. Marketing matters.

This does not imply that there are no problems with expressions of declining confidence in government. Whatever the reasons for the decline, if the public becomes unwilling to provide such crucial resources as tax dollars or to voluntarily comply with laws, or if bright young people refuse to go into government service, governmental capacity would be impaired and people would become more dissatisfied with it. Such a result could impair both American hard and soft power. As yet, however, these results do not seem to have materialized. The General Accounting Office reports that federal agencies are "poorly equipped to meet challenges of the 21st century because their employees lack the necessary skills in information technology, science, economics and management," and it remains to be seen if agencies will recruit more easily after the 2001 tragedy. On the other hand, the Internal Revenue Service sees no increase in cheating on taxes.[46] By many accounts, government officials and legislators have become less corrupt than they were a few decades ago.[47] Voluntary mail return of census forms increased to 67 percent in 2000, reversing a thirty-year decline since 1970.[48] Voting rates have declined from 62 percent to 50 percent over the past forty years, but the decline stopped in 2000, and the current rate is not as low as in the 1920s. Moreover, polls show that nonvoters are no more alienated or mistrustful of government than voters are.[49] Behavior does not seem to have changed as dramatically as have responses to poll questions. If so, the effect on the ability of our government to produce and use hard power has been limited.

Despite predictions of institutional crisis expressed in the aftermath of the tightly contested 2000 presidential election, the incoming Bush administration was able to get off to an effective start, even before his rise in the polls after September 2001. Nor does the decline in confidence in government seem to have greatly diminished American soft power, if only because most other developed countries seem to be experiencing a similar phenomenon. Canada, Britain, France, Sweden, and Japan—just to name a few—have seen a similar trend. The causes of the expressed loss of confidence in institutions may be rooted in deeper trends in attitudes toward greater individualism and less deference to authority that are characteristic of post-modern societies. As we saw above with regard to social change, when such attitudes are typical of most advanced societies, it is impossible to make invidious comparisons that undercut our attractiveness compared to the others. Thus far there have been few effects of the changes in confidence in government on our soft power.[50]

A significant decay in our social institutions could also erode our power by diminishing both our capacity for collective action and the overall attractiveness of our society. Robert Putnam's influential book *Bowling Alone* suggested that America's stock of social capital—the social networks and norms of reciprocity and trust that make a country more productive and effective—has been declining. The French nobleman Alexis de Tocqueville famously observed in 1830 that American individualism and tendencies to leave the greater society to look after itself are counterbalanced by a propensity to join voluntary associations "of a thousand different types—religious, moral, serious, futile, very general and very limited, immensely large and very minute."[51] While not all voluntary organizations are good for society—witness the Ku Klux Klan—states that rank high on social capital, such as Minnesota and South Dakota, outperform low-ranking states, such as Mississippi and Arkansas, on such issues as safety, health, child welfare, and prosperity.[52] In Putnam's terms, social capital makes "light touch government" more efficient. Police officers close more cases, child welfare departments work better when neighbors provide social support, and public schools teach better when parents volunteer.[53]

How serious are these changes in social capital for the effectiveness of American institutions? Putnam himself notes that community bonds have not weakened steadily over the last century. On the contrary, American history carefully examined is a story of ups and downs in civic engagement, not just downs—a story of collapse and renewal.[54] He suggests a number of policies that might contribute to a renewal early in the twenty-first century analogous to that created by the Progressive movement at the beginning of the last century. Moreover, Putnam's critics argue that his evidence confirms social transformation rather than decline. As Alan Wolfe argues, "Of course civic life has changed; how in a dynamic and entrepreneurial society could it be otherwise? To use the language of decline as Putnam so often does, is to show that people at one period of time were somehow better than at another period of time. . . . If my experience is at all typical, Americans have lost community but gained opportunity. Each is valuable, but I know of no social science research that can prove that one is more valuable than the other."[55]

Leaving aside the value judgment, the effects on American hard and soft power are likely to be limited. The changes in social capital do not seem to have eroded our national capacity for collective action on foreign policy, and since we compare well with other countries, our soft power is unlikely to be diminished. For one thing, the absolute levels of engagement remain remarkably high on many indicators. For example, there was a tremendous upwelling of community spirit and volunteering after the September 2001 tragedy, ranging from flag flying to donations to community support groups. Three-quarters of Americans feel connected to their communities and say the quality of life there is excellent or good. According to a 2001 poll, 111 million Americans volunteered their time to help solve problems in their communities in the past twelve months, and 60 million volunteered on a regular basis.[56] Moreover, as Putnam himself points out, Americans remain more likely to be involved in voluntary organizations than most countries, with the exception of a few small nations of northern Europe.[57] And Americans are far more involved in their churches than Western Europeans—only 10 percent of British and French and 3 percent of Scandinavians attend as often as once a month.[58] As the historian Robert Fogel points out, "The role of American evangelical churches in promoting popular democracy, radical social reform, and new political alignments stands in sharp contrast to that of European churches."[59] While many of the trends that Putnam identifies may be troubling in and of themselves, it does not seem that they are seriously eroding America's hard or soft power in the world.

IT'S THE ECONOMY, STUPID!

While the cultural and social problems discussed thus far do not threaten to weaken American power, a failure in the performance of the American economy would be a real showstopper. By economic failure, I do not mean the depressed condition of the stock market after the September 2001 terrorist attacks or the recessions of a year or so that are typical of all capitalist economies; rather, I refer to decreases in the level of productivity and the loss of the capacity for sustained high levels of growth measured over a decade or more. Not only does economic growth provide the sinews of hard power, it also burnishes the reputation and self-confidence of the country and thus contributes equally to soft power. When the U.S. economy slowed down in 2001, some skeptics were ready to say "I told you so." What matters, however, is not one- or two-year corrections in the business cycle but whether the American economy can return to the higher productivity that developed in the second half of the 1990s.

A decade and a half ago, many observers believed that the U.S. economy had run out of steam. Technological dominance had been lost in several manufacturing sectors, including automobiles and consumer electronics. The annual rate of increase of labor productivity, which averaged 2.7 percent in the two decades after World War II, had slipped to 1.4 percent in the 1980s. Although the American standard of living was still the highest among the seven largest market economies, it had grown only a quarter as fast as the others since 1972. According to a leading business magazine in 1987, "the nation is in a growth crisis. . . . Both personal and national agendas that were once unquestioned suddenly seem too expensive."[60] Japan and Germany were believed to be overtaking America, and this undercut both our hard and soft power. We seemed to have lost our competitive edge. As the new century began, the picture looked very different, with the World Economic Forum ranking the United States first in growth competitiveness.[61]

Can it last? Will the new levels of productivity and growth extend American influence well into the new century? Or will the United States merely follow Japan in a cycle of ups and downs? Long-run optimists argue that there is a "new economy" that has removed the prior speed limits on American growth, but an IMF study is more cautious about the term: "Despite the amount of attention that the 'new economy' has received, there is very little consensus on what is now different about the U.S. economy and whether such a difference has fundamentally changed the way the economy works." What is clear is that the United States leads in the production and use of information technology (IT). The IT sector accounts for a larger share of GDP than in the other major industrial countries.[62] That puts the United States at the forefront of the information revolution, with the attendant implications for power described in chapter 2.[63] As *The Economist* summarized the debate early in 2001: "That many 'new economy' claims look flawed does not necessarily mean that all are. There is evidence that structural productivity growth has quickened, but not as much as is widely believed. Those who think that productivity growth of 3% or more is sustainable are saying that IT will have a bigger economic impact than the era of electricity and cars in the 1920s. That was, and remains, a bold claim."[64]

Productivity

While there were no notable productivity growth differences between the United States and Europe in the first half of the 1990s, after 1995, a noticeable change in the rate of decline in the cost of computing power enhanced American productivity. Productivity is crucial because the more that workers can produce per hour, the more the economy can grow without shortages and inflation. And sustained noninflationary growth provides the resources we can invest in hard power as well as an attractive economic model that enhances our soft power. Productivity can increase because of new investment in tools or new forms of organization. Moore's law, which is a generalization about the rate of development in computing speed, continued to predict the doubling of semiconductor speed every eighteen months. Productivity also improved as companies began using the Internet intensively for commercial purposes and the government deregulated the American telecommunications industry.[65] And while information technology was a fairly small part of the economy (8.3 percent in 2000), it accounted for a third of all output growth from 1995 and 1999.[66]

Information technology was not the only source of the new productivity. Globalization, deregulation, and competition also spurred business process improvements.[67] The *Economic Report of the President* argued that information technology, business practices, and economic policies reinforced each other. The information revolution (discussed in chapter 2) and economic globalization (described in chapter 3) both spurred the American economy. "Indeed globalization and the recent advances in information technology at the core of the New Economy are inextricably linked. On the one hand, globalization has played a crucial role in promoting the technological innovation and investment and facilitating the organizational restructuring that built the New Economy. On the other hand, improvements in information technology have spurred deeper integration between the United States and the world economy."[68]

The key question for the future of American power is whether increases we see in rates of productivity are merely cyclical (and thus likely to be reversed) or structural (and thus capable of being sustained over long periods). For a number of years economists puzzled over why the rise in investment in new information technology tools was seen "everywhere except the productivity figures." This now seems to be changing, though there are differences over whether the structural gains are limited to the information industry alone or have spilled over into the rest of the economy. Some skeptics about the new economy attributed most of the gains to the manufacture rather than the use of computers, but other economists, such as Yale's William Nordhaus, found that the other sectors contributed roughly half of the recent upturn in productivity growth.[69] The White House Council of Economic Advisors argued that the 2.6 percent rate of growth in productivity in the second half of the 1990s was not merely cyclical and that the improvement in the ways capital and labor are used throughout the economy were important to the increase. *The Economist* estimated that the noncyclical structural productivity rate might be closer to 2 percent, but "productivity growth of 2% would still be pretty impressive by historical standards."[70] As Alan Greenspan warned Congress, even if one believes the gains are not ephemeral, "the rate of growth of productivity cannot continue to increase indefinitely. At some point, it must at least plateau."[71] But if it maintains the new plateau, and the risk premium associated with terrorism does not become too high, the "speed limit" on American economic growth that was presumed to be in effect a decade ago will have been raised, with positive implications for American hard and soft power.[72]

Saving and Investment

In addition to the question of whether the new rates of productivity are sustainable, other concerns about the future of American economic power include our low rate of personal savings and the current-account deficit (which means that Americans are becoming more indebted to foreigners). Personal savings are difficult to calculate and such estimates are subject to error, but the trend is clearly down, from 9.7 percent of personal incomes in the 1970s to near zero today. In part this is attributed to an increased culture of consumerism and easier access to credit. How much it matters is difficult to determine. Despite the drop in personal savings, a broader measure of savings, the national savings rate, which includes government and corporate savings, has held up.[73] The switch from government deficits to surpluses in the 1990s represented a significant gain in savings. If recent budget changes and tax cuts return us to a persistent pattern of deficit spending, the results would be costly for both our hard and soft power.

However, the key to economic growth and power is not savings but investment. Japan, for example, has kept up a high savings rate, but its economy has stagnated. When the figures are corrected for the fact that capital goods are cheaper in the United States, American real investment compared favorably with other OECD countries.[74] Moreover, competitive American capital markets and shareholder demands on managers have made the United States more efficient in the use of capital, thus getting more bang for the same buck of savings. A unit of capital invested in the American business sector creates half again as much output as it does in either Germany or Japan. American business earned an average real rate of return of 9 percent per year, compared to 7 percent in Germany and Japan. "If rates of return are higher in America, then it makes sense for America to have a net inflow of foreign capital: excess savings in Japan and elsewhere can be invested more profitably in America than at home.[75] In an open economy, if the current-account deficit leads to greater investment (rather than merely consumption), it can leave a country stronger. The danger is that in a severe recession foreigners might withdraw their investments rapidly and add to instability in the economy. American income would be even higher and dangers of instability lessened if the United States financed more of its investment through higher savings.[76]

Education

A well-educated labor force is another key to economic success in an information age. At first glance, the United States does well compared to other rich countries. Eighty-three percent of adults have graduated from high school, and 24 percent have graduated from college. The United States ranks seventh in high school graduation rates, slightly lower than Japan or Germany, but higher than most countries.[77] American university graduation rates are also higher than most countries, and the United States spends twice as much on higher education as a percentage of GDP than does France, Germany, Britain, or Japan. The American higher education system is very strong, and American universities have widened their lead in academic reputation over competitors in Britain, Continental Europe, and Japan over the past few decades.[78] The number of graduate degrees awarded annually has quadrupled since the 1960s.[79] Americans win more Nobel prizes than do citizens of any other country. These accomplishments enhance both our economic power and our soft power.

However, while American education is strong at the top, it is less impressive at lower levels. American education at its best—much of the university system and the top slice of the secondary system—meets or sets the global standard. But American education at its worst—too many of our primary and secondary schools, especially in less affluent districts—lags badly. This may mean that the quality of our labor force will not keep up with the rising standards of an information-based economy. Student test scores showed slow but steady gains over the 1990s, but the nation failed to achieve the ambitious "Goals 2000" aim (set in 1989) of achieving 90 percent high school graduation, being first in the world in math and science, and demonstrating competence in other subjects.[80] A national assessment of educational progress found that only between a fifth and a quarter of students were at or above the proficient level in math, and between a third and two-fifths scored at that level in reading.[81] Twenty-nine percent of all college freshmen require remedial classes in basic skills.[82] In adult literacy, 24 percent of Americans fell in the lowest category of comprehending documents (twice as bad as Germany, four times worse than Sweden).[83] Some American children get much better access to educational resources than do others; there are significant disparities in per pupil spending both between states and between districts within the same state.[84] The achievement gap between well-off children and others is above the average for the twenty-nine industrialized nations of the Organization for Economic Cooperation and Development. American teachers were paid only 1.2 times the average per capita income, whereas in Germany, Ireland, South Korea, and Switzerland, teachers earn twice or more the per capita income.[85]

Contrary to alarmist talk, there is no reliable evidence that students are performing worse than in the past, but "American students do not seem to be improving their knowledge and skills to keep pace with an advancing economy, nor do they compare particularly well in science and math with their counterparts in other countries."[86] In a recent test of 180,000 eighth graders in thirty-eight countries, Americans did worse in math and science than children in Singapore, Taiwan, Russia, Canada, Finland, and Australia, and worse in comparisons than they did as fourth graders in 1995.[87] While average SAT scores have improved slightly over the past two decades, the question is whether the changes are enough to cope with an information-based economy. Forty years ago, a high school dropout could use a hammer in a foundry; today he or she is likely to have to work a numerically controlled machine tool. And as productivity increases in manufacturing, jobs switch to services that often require the use of computers. Increasingly, college is becoming a requirement for a middle-class lifestyle, and workers who use computers are paid more than those who do not. We will have to continue to work on improving our educational system if we are to meet the standards needed in an information-based economy.

Income Inequality

The changing shape of the nation's income distribution also poses a problem for the American economy. From 1947 to 1968, census data show, inequality in family income decreased. From 1968 to 1993, inequality increased. Data collected since 1993 suggest that the increase has slowed or halted, but it is too soon to be sure. The nationwide poverty rate, which stood at 22 percent in 1960, fell to 11 percent in 1973 but worsened to 15 percent in 1993. The economic growth in the second half of the 1990s brought it back down to 11.8 percent.[88] Shifts in labor demand away from less-educated workers are perhaps a more important explanation of eroding wages than the shift out of manufacturing.[89]

The problem is not only a question of justice but one of whether inequality may lead to political reactions that could curb the productivity of the economy and slow the high rates of economic growth that are the foundation of our hard and soft power. As the Council of Economic Advisors points out, "Dislocation is an unavoidable effect of economic growth and technological change." The price of progress is what the economist Joseph Schumpeter called "creative destruction," but the burdens are not equally borne. The evidence suggests that worker displacement is largely the result of technology rather than import competition. In the 1990s, employment by American corporations at home and overseas rose in tandem rather than one at the cost of the other. Nonetheless, even though the country as a whole benefits, globalization and technological change are especially threatening to less-skilled and less-educated workers. Unless policies ensure that they are not left behind, they may provide a political basis for a reaction that could slow American growth.[90]

Despite these problems and uncertainties, it seems likely that with the right policies the American economy will continue to function well in producing hard power for the country. The wild card would be if repeated terrorist attacks so damaged confidence that a long period of recession occurs. Soft power is a more open question. Clearly many people admire the success of the American economy, but not all extol it as a model. Government plays a lighter role in the U.S. economy, spending (and taxing) one-third of GDP, while Europe is nearer one-half. Competitive market forces are stronger, social safety nets weaker. Unions are weaker and labor markets less regulated. Cultural attitudes, bankruptcy laws, and financial structures more strongly favor entrepreneurship. While foreigners extol many of these virtues, some object to the price of inequality and insecurity that accompanies this greater reliance on market forces.

The area where the American model clearly excelled was in job creation, with less than half the rate of unemployment in Germany (though about the same as Japan). As *The Economist* noted, "Overall, however, the notion that the American economy stands on top of the world is questionable. It is also vulnerable to criticism because of its wider income inequality. It is often asserted that America has traded higher inequality for faster growth; yet over the past decade, average incomes have risen by similar amounts in the three countries, despite America's bigger income differentials. . . . The poorest 20% in Japan are about 50% better off than America's poorest 20%."[91] The lowest 10 percent of people in America's income distribution had only the thirteenth highest average income when compared with relatively poor people in other advanced economies. The superior job performance of the American economy will not lead Europeans and others to see it as the best model unless we alleviate the effects of inequality.[92] How we deal at home with those who are left behind has an important effect on our soft power.

HOW AMERICANS VIEW THE WORLD

Even if social cleavages do not disrupt internal stability, institutional capacities remain adequate, and the economy grows over the long run, the United States might fall short in converting its power resources into effective influence if American public opinion were to turn inward after September 2001, as it did after World War I. If Atlas shrugs, what happens to hegemony?

In the initial response, this does not seem to be happening, though some worry that it may. The Chicago Council on Foreign Relations polled Americans about foreign policy every four years after 1974. It found continuing support for an active role for the United States in the world, with 61 percent of the public and 96 percent of leaders favoring such activism. Some three-quarters of the public and leaders foresaw an even greater role for the country in ten years. A majority of the public believed there would be more violence in the twenty-first century, and terrorism was considered the number one threat to U.S. vital interests, followed by chemical and biological weapons and nuclear proliferation. Concern about the development of China as a world power was rising among leaders. Superficially, American attitudes seemed appropriate.

Overall public commitment to engagement coexists with reluctance to support the use of American troops overseas, although leaders continue to be more willing to deploy troops abroad. We prefer multilateral approaches over going it alone. Fifty-seven percent of the public agree the United States should take part in UN peacekeeping forces, and 72 percent of the public (but only 48 percent of leaders) think the United States should not take action alone in international crises if it does not have the support of allies. On the question of globalization, 54 percent of the public and 87 percent of leaders believe it is mostly good for the United States. Sixty-three percent of the public and 89 percent of leaders believe that a country's economic strength is more important than its military strength as a measure of power and influence in the world.

So far, so good. Most Americans are not isolationist, and they do not focus solely on military hegemony. They want to engage the world through multilateral institutions. So what's wrong with this picture? Why are we having such a hard time defining our national interest? Why was our policy so often arrogantly unilateralist? For example, why did we undercut our own influence in the United Nations during the 1990s by refusing to pay our dues when polls showed that two-thirds of the public supported the UN?

In a word, the problem was indifference. After the Cold War and before the September 2001 terrorist attacks, Americans became preoccupied with domestic affairs, turning to the present and past rather than a concern about the global future. Foreign policy played little role in our presidential elections. As Henry Kissinger has observed, "Ironically, America's preeminence is often treated with indifference by its own people. . . . Hence prudence impels aspiring politicians to avoid discussions of foreign policy and to define leadership as a reflection of current popular sentiments rather than as a challenge to raise America's sights."[93]

When the majority are indifferent, they leave the battlefields of foreign policy to those with special interests. The result is a narrow definition of our national interest that often alienates other countries. Take the apparent paradox of our refusal to pay UN dues despite a majority being in favor of the United Nations. A large part of the reason was the intensity of preferences of a minority. Many of the political activists who turned out to vote in Republican primaries (often only a fifth of the electorate), strongly believed that the UN was a threat to national sovereignty, and for them, the dues issue was very important. Though they constituted a minority of the public, theirs was the voice that Congress heard in determining the American interest.[94] Moreover, that voice was amplified by the ideology of important committee chairs such as Senator Jesse Helms, and by special-interest tactics of linking payment of dues to extraneous issues such as abortion.

The polls were very clear on the issue of indifference. Americans' interest in the news, particularly news about foreign countries, declined after the end of the Cold War. Only 29 percent of the public are "very interested" in news about other countries, and 22 percent were "hardly interested." When asked about the biggest problems facing the country, foreign policy issues made up the smallest portion (7 percent) for the public. (For leaders, the number was 19.5 percent.) "In a post–Cold War world, without a clear-cut 'us vs. them' mentality, the relevance of world events appears less evident for many Americans."[95] Some people describe these attitudes as "soft isolationism."[96] Others call it "tempered internationalism."[97] The problem is not one of rejection of foreign concerns, which characterized American attitudes toward Europe in the 1930s. It is more a question of indifference and internal preoccupation.

The danger of public indifference is that the special interests— economic, ethnic, ideological—always present in a democracy develop an even stronger voice than normal in defining the national interest. During the Cold War, containment of Soviet power provided a north star to guide American foreign policy. Historically, the Cold War era was an anomalous period of consensus about the central concern of foreign policy (and even it involved bitter disputes

over Vietnam and Central America). In fact, confusion has more often been the rule. For example, ethnic differences colored appraisals
of whether the United States should enter World War I, and economic interests have always played an important role in the making
of American foreign policy.[98] A careful study of American definitions
of national interests in the 1890s, 1930s, and 1980s concludes that "there
is no single national interest. Analysts who assume that American has a
discernible national interest whose defense should determine its relations with other nations are unable to explain the persistent failure to
achieve domestic consensus on international objectives."[99] But never
before have we been so preponderant. Public indifference made our
situation before September 2001 all the more poignant when it came to
deciding how to use and preserve our power.

Congress pays attention to squeaky wheels, and the special interests
press it to legislate the tactics of foreign policy and codes of conduct
with sanctions for other countries. As Henry Kissinger points out,
"What is presented by foreign critics as America's quest for domination is very frequently a response to domestic pressure groups." The
cumulative effect "drives American foreign policy toward unilateral
and bullying conduct. For unlike diplomatic communications, which
are generally an invitation to dialogue, legislation translates into a
take-it-or-leave-it prescription, the operational equivalent of an ulti-
matum."[100] The September 2001 wake up call wiped away indifference
for now, but the isolationist and unilateral temptations remain. "To
the extent that the United States turns unilateralism into a habit or
cuts its contribution to the production of public goods, others will
feel the sting of American power more strongly. And the incentive to
discipline Mr. Big will grow."[101]

Attitudes toward globalization could prove to be another Achilles
heel for American power. Americans are not immune to protectionist
backlash, and support for economic globalization may be more fragile than at first appears. A wide range of public opinion surveys report that a plurality or majority oppose policies to further liberalize
trade, immigration, and foreign direct investment. These attitudes—
which align strongly with labor market skills, with lower-wage employees more likely to be negative—reflect not simply ignorance of

the benefits but a feeling that the costs of economic insecurity may be more important.[102] Such attitudes may be reinforced by the new anxiety about terrorism.

Polls show that the sharpest divergence in the attitudes of the public and leaders is in response to questions about the priority to be given to "protecting the jobs of American workers." Four-fifths of the public rank this "very important," compared to 45 percent for leaders.[103] Less skilled workers—a group that constitutes the majority of the U.S. labor force—"have experienced close to zero or even negative real-wage growth, despite renewed progress in recent years, and have also seen sharp declines in their wages relative to more-skilled workers . . . Popular support for further liberalization is likely to be conditioned on effective governmental assistance to help workers adjust to its adverse effects."[104] Leeway to exercise our power abroad depends in part on the policies we follow at home. If the United States were to turn in a more protectionist direction, we would not only reduce the economic growth that underpins our hard power but set an unfortunate example that would reduce our soft power.

Some argue that the costs of exercising power eventually overburden all empires and that terrorist attacks will make the American public weary of "imperial overstretch."[105] But the financial burdens have not increased, as defense and foreign affairs expenditures have declined as a share of GNP over the past several decades. Furthermore, our vulnerabilities cannot be removed by turning inward. It is true that American attitudes are more permissive than strongly supportive of leaders' efforts to convert the country's power resources into effective influence in the world. If economic slowdown occurs or inequality grows, or if we fail to cope with terrorism, significant groups may deny permission, particularly with regard to trade liberalization and immigration. Nonetheless, public opinion is a set of constraints, like dams and dikes, rather than a direct determinant of foreign policy.[106] The polls show that these constraints are quite broad. The problem of the home front is less the feared prospects of social and political decay or economic stagnation than developing and popularizing a vision of how the United States should define its national interest in a global information age. We turn to that question next.

5

REDEFINING THE
NATIONAL INTEREST

How should the United States define its interests in this global information age? How shall we decide how much and when to join with others? What should we do with our unprecedented power? Isolationists who think we can avoid vulnerability to terrorism by drawing inward fail to understand the realities of a global information age. At the same time, the new unilateralists who urge us to unashamedly deploy it on behalf of self-defined global ends are offering a recipe for undermining our soft power and encouraging others to create the coalitions that will eventually limit our hard power. We must do better than that.

When Condoleezza Rice, now the national security advisor, wrote during the 2000 campaign that we should "proceed from the firm ground of the national interest and not from the interest of an illusory international community," what disturbed our European allies was "the assumption that a conflict between the pursuit of national interest and commitment to the interests of a far-from-illusory international community necessarily exists."[1] The ties that bind the international community may be weak, but they matter. Failure to pay proper respect to the opinion of others and to incorporate a broad conception of justice into our national interest will eventually come to hurt us. As our allies frequently remind us, even well-intentioned

American champions of benign hegemony do not have all the answers. While our friends welcomed the multilateralism of the Bush administration's approach after September 2001, they remained concerned about a return to unilateralism.

Democratic leaders who fail to reflect their nation's interest are unlikely to be reelected, and it is in our interest to preserve our preeminent position. But global interests can be incorporated into a broad and farsighted concept of the national interest. After all, terrorism is a threat to all societies; international trade benefits us as well as others; global warming will raise sea levels along all our coasts as well as those of other countries; infectious diseases can arrive anywhere by ship or plane; and financial instability can hurt the whole world economy. In addition to such concrete interests, many Americans want global values incorporated into our national interest. There are strong indications that Americans' values operate in a highly global context—that our sphere of concern extends well beyond national boundaries. Seventy-three percent agreed with the poll statement "I regard myself as a citizen of the world as well as a citizen of the United States," and 44 percent agreed strongly.[2] We need a broad definition of our national interest that takes account of the interests of others, and it is the role of our leaders to bring this into popular discussions. An enlightened national interest need not be myopic—as September 2001 reminded us.

Traditionalists distinguish between a foreign policy based on values and a foreign policy based on interests. They describe as vital those interests that would directly affect our safety and thus merit the use of force—for example, to prevent attacks on the United States, to prevent the emergence of hostile hegemons in Asia or Europe, to prevent hostile powers on our borders or in control of the seas, and to ensure the survival of U.S. allies.[3] Promoting human rights, encouraging democracy, or developing specific economic sectors is relegated to a lower priority.

I find this approach too narrow, as I believe that humanitarian interests are also important to our lives and our foreign policy. Certainly national strategic interests are vital and deserve priority, because if we fail to protect them, our very survival would be at stake. For example, today countering and suppressing catastrophic terrorism will deserve the priority that was devoted to containing Soviet power during the Cold War.[4] Survival is the necessary condition of foreign policy, but it is not all there is to foreign policy. Moreover, the connection between some events (for example, Iraq's invasion of Kuwait, or a North Korean missile test) and a threat to our national survival may involve a long chain of causes. People can disagree about how probable any link in the chain is and thus about the degree of the threat to our survival. Consequently, reasonable people can disagree about how much "insurance" they want our foreign policy to provide against remote threats to a vital interest before we pursue other values such as human rights.

In my view, in a democracy, the national interest is simply what citizens, after proper deliberation, say it is. It is broader than vital strategic interests, though they are a crucial part. It can include values such as human rights and democracy, particularly if the American public feels that those values are so important to our identity or sense of who we are that people are willing to pay a price to promote them. Values are simply an intangible national interest. If the American people think that our long-term shared interests include certain values and their promotion abroad, then they become part of the national interest. Leaders and experts may point out the costs of indulging certain values, but if an informed public disagrees, experts cannot deny the legitimacy of their opinion.

Determining the national interest involves more than just poll results. It is opinion after public discussion and deliberation. That is why it is so important that our leaders do a better job of discussing a broad formulation of our national interest. Democratic debate is often messy and does not always come up with the "right" answers. Nonetheless, it is difficult to see a better way to decide on the national interest in a democracy. A better-informed political debate is the only way for our people to determine how broadly or narrowly to define our interests.

THE LIMITS OF AMERICAN POWER

Even when we agree that values matter, the hard job is figuring out how to bring them to bear in particular instances. Many Americans find Russia's war in Chechnya disturbing, but there are limits to what we can do because Russia remains a nuclear power and we seek its help on terrorism. As our parents reminded us, "Don't let your eyes get bigger than your stomach, and don't bite off more than you can chew." Given our size, the United States has more margin of choice than most countries do. But as we have seen in the earlier chapters, power is changing, and it is not always clear how much we can chew. The danger posed by the outright champions of hegemony is that their foreign policy is all accelerator and no brakes. Their focus on unipolarity and hegemony exaggerates the degree to which the United States is able to get the outcomes it wants in a changing world.

I argued in chapter 1 that power in a global information age is distributed like a three-dimensional chess game. The top military board is unipolar, with the United States far outstripping all other states, but the middle economic board is multipolar, with the United States, Europe, and Japan accounting for two-thirds of world product, and the bottom board of transnational relations that cross borders outside the control of governments has a widely dispersed structure of power. While it is important not to ignore the continuing importance of military force for some purposes, particularly in relation to the preindustrial and industrial parts of the world, the hegemonists' focus on military power can blind us to the limits of our power. As we have seen, American power is not equally great in the economic and transnational dimensions. Not only are there new actors to consider in these domains, but many of the transnational issues—whether financial flows, the spread of AIDS, or terrorism—cannot be resolved without the cooperation of others. Where collective action is a necessary part of obtaining the outcomes we want, our power is by definition limited and the United States is bound to share.

We must also remember the growing role of soft power in this global information age. It matters that half a million foreign students want to study in the United States each year, that Europeans and Asians want to watch American films and TV, that American liberties are attractive in many parts of the world, and that others respect us and want to follow our lead when we are not too arrogant. Our values are significant sources of soft power. Both hard and soft power are important, but in a global information age, as we saw in chapter 2, soft power is becoming even more so than in the past. Massive flows of cheap information have expanded the number of transnational channels of contacts across national borders. As we also noted earlier, global markets and nongovernmental groups—including terrorists—play a larger role, and many possess soft power resources. States are more easily penetrated and less like the classic military model of sovereign billiard balls bouncing off each other.

The United States, with its open democratic society, will benefit from the rapidly developing global information age if we develop a better understanding of the nature and limits of our power. Our institutions will continue to be attractive to many and the openness of our society will continue to enhance our credibility. Thus as a country, we will be well placed to benefit from soft power. But since much of this soft power is the unintended by-product of social forces, the government will often find it difficult to manipulate.

The good news is that the social trends of the global information age are helping to shape a world that will be more congenial to American values in the long run. But the soft power that comes from being a shining "city upon a hill" (as the Puritan leader John Winthrop first put it) does not provide the coercive capability that hard power does. Soft power is crucial, but alone it is not sufficient. Both hard and soft power will be necessary for successful foreign policy in a global information age. Our leaders must make sure that they exercise our hard power in a manner that does not undercut our soft power.

GRAND STRATEGY AND GLOBAL PUBLIC GOODS

How should Americans set our priorities in a global information age? What grand strategy would allow us to steer between the "imperial overstretch" that would arise out of the role of global policeman while avoiding the mistake of thinking the country can be isolated in this global information age? The place to start is by understanding the relationship of American power to global public goods. On one hand, for reasons given above, American power is less effective than it might first appear. We cannot do everything. On the other hand, the United States is likely to remain the most powerful country well into this century, and this gives us an interest in maintaining a degree of international order. More concretely, there is a simple reason why Americans have a national interest beyond our borders. Events out there can hurt us, and we want to influence distant governments and organizations on a variety of issues such as proliferation of weapons of mass destruction, terrorism, drugs, trade, resources, and ecological damage. After the Cold War, we ignored Afghanistan, but we discovered that even a poor, remote country can harbor forces that can harm us.

To a large extent, international order is a public good—something everyone can consume without diminishing its availability to others.[5] A small country can benefit from peace in its region, freedom of the seas, suppression of terrorism, open trade, control of infectious diseases, or stability in financial markets at the same time that the United States does without diminishing the benefits to the United States or others. Of course, pure public goods are rare. And sometimes things that look good in our eyes may look bad in the eyes of others. Too narrow an appeal to public goods can become a self-serving ideology for the powerful. But these caveats are a reminder to consult with others, not a reason to discard an important strategic principle that helps us set priorities and reconcile our national interests with a broader global perspective.

If the largest beneficiary of a public good (like the United States) does not take the lead in providing disproportionate resources toward its provision, the smaller beneficiaries are unlikely to be able to produce it because of the difficulties of organizing collective action when large numbers are involved.[6] While this responsibility of the largest often lets others become "free riders," the alternative is that the collective bus does not move at all. (And our compensation is that the largest tends to have more control of the steering wheel.)

This puts a different twist on former secretary of state Madeleine Albright's frequent phrase that the United States is "the indispensable nation." We do not get a free ride. To play a leading role in producing public goods, the United States will need to invest in both hard power resources and the soft power resources of setting a good example. The latter will require more self-restraint on the part of Congress as well as putting our own house in order in economics, environment, criminal justice, and so forth. The rest of the world likes to see the United States lead by example, but when "America is seen, as with emission standards, to put narrow domestic interests before global needs, respect can easily turn to disappointment and contempt."[7]

Increasing hard power will require an investment of resources in the nonmilitary aspects of foreign affairs, including better intelligence, that Americans have recently been unwilling to make. While Congress has been willing to spend 16 percent of the national budget on defense, the percentage devoted to international affairs has shrunk from 4 percent in the 1960s to just 1 percent today.[8] Our military strength is important, but it is not sixteen times more important than our diplomacy. Over a thousand people work on the staff of the smallest regional military command headquarters, far more than the total assigned to the Americas at the Departments of State, Commerce, Treasury, and Agriculture.[9] The military rightly plays a role in our diplomacy, but we are investing in our hard power in overly militarized terms.

As Secretary of State Colin Powell has pleaded to Congress, we need to put more resources into the State Department, including its information services and the Agency for International Development (AID), if we are going to get our messages across. A bipartisan report on the situation of the State Department recently warned that "if the 'downward spiral' is not reversed, the prospect of relying on military force to protect U.S. national interests will increase because Washington will be less capable of avoiding, managing or resolving crises through the use of statecraft."[10] Moreover, the abolition of the United States Information Agency (which promoted American government views abroad) as a separate entity and its absorption into the State Department reduced the effectiveness of one of our government's important instruments of soft power.[11] It is difficult to be a superpower on the cheap—or through military means alone.

In addition to better means, we need a strategy for their use. Our grand strategy must first ensure our survival, but then it must focus on providing *global* public goods. We gain doubly from such a strategy: from the public goods themselves, and from the way they legitimize our power in the eyes of others. That means we should give top priority to those aspects of the international system that, if not attended to properly, would have profound effects on the basic international order and therefore on the lives of large numbers of Americans as well as others. The United States can learn from the lesson of Great Britain in the nineteenth century, when it was also a preponderant power. Three public goods that Britain attended to were (1) maintaining the balance of power among the major states in Europe, (2) promoting an open international economic system, and (3) maintaining open international commons such as the freedom of the seas and the suppression of piracy.

All three translate relatively well to the current American situation. Maintaining regional balances of power and dampening local incentives to use force to change borders provides a public good for many (but not all) countries. The United States helps to "shape the environment" (in the words of the Pentagon's quadrennial defense review) in various regions, and that is why even in normal times we keep roughly a hundred thousand troops forward-based in Europe, the same number in Asia, and some twenty thousand near the Persian Gulf. The American role as a stabilizer and reassurance against aggression by aspiring hegemons in key regions is a blue chip issue. We should not abandon these regions, as some have recently suggested, though our presence in the Gulf could be handled more subtly.

Promoting an open international economic system is good for American economic growth and is good for other countries as well. As we saw in chapter 3, openness of global markets is a necessary (though not sufficient) condition for alleviating poverty in poor countries even as it benefits the United States. In addition, in the long term, economic growth is also more likely to foster stable, democratic middle-class societies in other countries, though the time scale may be quite lengthy. To keep the system open, the United States must resist protectionism at home and support international economic institutions such as the World Trade Organization, the International Monetary Fund, and the Organization for Economic Cooperation and Development that provide a framework of rules for the world economy.

The United States, like nineteenth-century Britain, has an interest in keeping international commons, such the oceans, open to all. Here our record is mixed. It is good on traditional freedom of the seas. For example, in 1995, when Chinese claims to the Spratly Islands in the South China Sea sparked concern in Southeast Asia, the United States avoided the conflicting claims of various states to the islets and rocks, but issued a statement reaffirming that the sea should remain open to all countries. China then agreed to deal with the issue under the Law of the Seas Treaty. Today, however, the international commons include new issues such as global climate change, preservation of endangered species, and the uses of outer space, as well as the virtual commons of cyberspace. But on some issues, such as the global climate, the United States has taken less of a lead than is necessary. The establishment of rules that preserve access for all remains as much a public good today as in the nineteenth century, even though some of the issues are more complex and difficult than freedom of the seas.

These three classic public goods enjoy a reasonable consensus in American public opinion, and some can be provided in part through unilateral actions. But there are also three new dimensions of global public goods in today's world. First, the United States should help develop and maintain international regimes of laws and institutions that organize international action in various domains—not just trade and environment, but weapons proliferation, peacekeeping, human rights, terrorism, and other concerns. Terrorism is to the twenty-first century what piracy was to an earlier era. Some governments gave pirates and privateers safe harbor to earn revenues or to harass their enemies. As Britain became the dominant naval power in the nineteenth century, it suppressed piracy, and most countries benefited from that situation. Today, some states harbor terrorists in order to attack their enemies or because they are too weak to control powerful groups. If our current campaign against terrorism is seen as unilateral or biased, it is likely to fail, but if we continue to maintain broad coalitions to suppress terrorism, we have a good prospect of success. While our antiterrorism campaign will not be seen as a global public good by the groups that attack us, our objective should be to isolate them and diminish the minority of states that give them harbor.

We should also make international development a higher priority, for it is an important global public good as well. Much of the poor majority of the world is in turmoil, mired in vicious circles of disease, poverty, and political instability. Large-scale financial and scientific help from rich countries is important not only for humanitarian reasons but also, as Harvard economist Jeffrey Sachs has argued, "because even remote countries become outposts of disorder for the rest of the world."[12] Here our record is less impressive. Our foreign aid has shrunk to 0.1 percent of our GNP, roughly one-third of European levels, and our protectionist trade measures often hurt poor countries most. Foreign assistance is generally unpopular with the American public, in part (as polls show) because they think we spend fifteen to twenty times more on it than we do. If our political leaders appealed more directly to our humanitarian instinct as well as our interest in stability, our record might improve. As President Bush said in July 2001, "This is a great moral challenge."[13] To be sure, aid is not sufficient for development, and opening our markets, strengthening accountable institutions, and discouraging corruption are even more important.[14] Development will take a long time, and we need to explore better ways to make sure that our help actually reaches the poor, but both prudence and a concern for our soft power suggest that we should make development a higher priority.

As a preponderant power, the United States can provide an important public good by acting as a mediator. By using our good offices to mediate conflicts in places such as Northern Ireland, the Middle East, or the Aegean Sea, the United States can help in shaping international order in ways that are beneficial to us as well as to other nations. It is sometimes tempting to let intractable conflicts fester, and there are some situations where other countries can more effectively play the mediator's role. Even when we do not want to take the lead, our participation can be essential—witness our work with Europe to try to prevent civil war in Macedonia. But often the United States is the only country that can bring together mortal enemies as in the Middle East peace process. And when we are successful, we enhance our reputation and increase our soft power at the same time that we reduce a source of instability.

Table 5.1   *A Strategy Based on Global Public Goods*

1. Maintain the balance of power in important regions
2. Promote an open international economy
3. Preserve international commons
4. Maintain international rules and institutions
5. Assist economic development
6. Act as convenor of coalitions and mediator of disputes.

HUMAN RIGHTS AND DEMOCRACY

A grand strategy for protecting our traditional vital interests and promoting global public goods addresses two-thirds of our national interest. Human rights and democracy are the third element, but they are not easily integrated with the others. Other countries and cultures often interpret these values differently and resent our intervention in their sovereign affairs as self-righteous unilateralism. As Malaysian prime minister Mahathir Mohamed complained of the Clinton administration: "No one conferred this right on this crusading President." Or in the words of a Republican critic (now a high official in the Pentagon): "America is genuinely puzzled by the idea that American assertiveness in the name of universal principles could sometimes be seen by others as a form of American unilateralism." Yet this charge is levied by many countries, including some of our friends. "Wilsonian Presidents drive them crazy—and have done ever since the days of Woodrow Wilson."[15]

Americans have wrestled with how to incorporate our values with our other interests since the early days of the republic, and the four main views cut across party lines. Isolationists hark back to John Quincy Adams's famous 1821 assertion that the United States "goes not abroad in search of monsters to destroy," while realists focus on his pragmatic advice that we should not involve ourselves "beyond the power of extrication in all the wars of interest and intrigue."[16] At least since the days of Woodrow Wilson, liberals have stressed democracy and human rights as foreign policy objectives, and Jimmy

Carter reestablished them as a priority. Even Ronald Reagan, certainly a conservative, resorted to the language of human rights, and today's neoconservatives "represent, in fact, a Reaganite variant of Wilsonianism."[17] President George W. Bush frequently reiterated the realist warning that the United States "cannot become the world's 911," but two dozen leading neoconservatives, including William Bennett and Norman Podhoretz, have urged him to make human rights, religious freedom, and democracy priorities for American foreign policy and "not to adopt a narrow view of U.S. national interests."[18]

Geopolitical realists deplore Wilsonian idealism as dangerous. As Robert Frost ironically noted, good fences can help to make good neighbors. While the erosion of sovereignty may help advance human rights in repressive regimes, it also portends considerable disorder. The Peace of Westphalia in the seventeenth century created a system of sovereign states to curtail vicious civil wars over religion. The fact that sovereignty is changing is generally a constraint for policy, not an objective of policy. But whether the realist strategists like it or not, humanitarian cases such as Somalia, Bosnia, Rwanda, Haiti, Kosovo, and East Timor will force themselves to the foreground because of their ability to command attention in a global information age. And their number will continue to burgeon. As we saw in chapter 3, globalization is disrupting traditional lifestyles, and the weak states left in the aftermath of the collapse of the Soviet empire and old European empires in Africa are particularly vulnerable. If there are clashes of civilizations, they occur more often within countries or regions over what Freud called the narcissism of small differences rather than a grand clash between "the West and the rest."[19] This in turn leads to increased violence and violation of human rights—all in the presence of television cameras and the Internet. The result puts a difficult set of issues on our foreign policy agenda and presents a challenge to our values. And, of course, our values are an important source of our soft power.

So where do human rights and democracy fit in the strategy? Human rights is an important *part* of foreign policy, but it is not foreign policy itself, because foreign policy is an effort to accomplish several objectives: security and economic benefits as well as humanitarian results. During the Cold War, this often meant that we reluctantly had to tolerate human rights abuses by regimes that were crucial to balancing Soviet power, such as in South Korea before its transition to democracy. Similar problems persist in the current period—witness the absence of an American policy to promote democracy in Saudi Arabia, or the need to balance human rights in Russia with our interest in forming an anti-terrorist coalition.

Former Clinton administration officials William Perry and Ashton Carter have suggested a scheme to evaluate risks to U.S. security and help reassert national priorities in cases that might involve the use of force. At the top of their hierarchy are A-list threats, of the scale that the Soviet Union presented to our survival. A threatening China or the spread of nuclear materials would also fit this category. The B list of imminent threats to our interests (but not to our survival) includes situations such as those on the Korean Peninsula and in the Persian Gulf. Their C list of important "contingencies that indirectly affect U.S. security but do not directly threaten U.S. interests" includes "the Kosovos, Bosnias, Somalias, Rwandas, and Haitis."[20]

What is striking, however, is that their C list of humanitarian interventions often dominates the foreign policy agenda. Carter and Perry speculated that this was because of the absence of A-list threats after the end of the Cold War. To some extent this is true, but another reason is the ability of C-list issues to dominate media attention in the global information age. Dramatic visual portrayals of immediate human conflict and suffering are far easier to convey to the public than A-list abstractions such as the possibility of a "Weimar Russia," the importance of our alliance with Japan, or the potential collapse of the international system of trade and investment. Few Americans can look at television pictures of starving people or miserable refugees on the evening news just before dinner and not feel that we should do something about it if we can. Some cases are quite easy, such as hurricane relief to Central America or the early stages of famine relief in Somalia. But as with Somalia, apparently simple cases can turn out to be extremely difficult, and others, such as Kosovo, are difficult from the start.

The problem with such cases is that the humanitarian interest that instigates the action often turns out to be quite shallow when it encounters significant costs in lives or money. The impulse to help starving Somalis (whose food supply was being interrupted by various warlords) vanished in the face of an image of a dead American being dragged through the streets of Mogadishu. This is sometimes attributed to popular reluctance to accept casualties. That is too simple. Americans went into the Gulf War expecting more than ten thousand casualties. More properly expressed, Americans are reluctant to accept casualties when their *only* interests are unreciprocated humanitarian interests. Ironically, the reaction against such cases may not only divert attention and limit willingness to support A-list interests but also interfere with action in more serious humanitarian crises. One of the direct effects of the Somalia disaster was an American failure (along with other countries) to support and reinforce the United Nations peacekeeping force in Rwanda, which could have limited a true genocide in 1994.[21]

There are no easy answers for such cases. We could not simply turn off the television or unplug our computers even if we wanted to. We cannot simply ignore the C list, nor should we. But there are certain rules of prudence for humanitarian interventions that may help us integrate our values and our security interests, to steer a path between the dangers of unfettered Wilsonianism and the narrow realism that George W. Bush articulated in his 2000 campaign.

First, there are many degrees of humanitarian concern and many degrees of intervention, such as condemnation, sanctions targeted on individuals, broad sanctions, and various uses of force. We should save the violent end of the spectrum for only the most egregious cases discussed below. Second, when we do use force, it is worth remembering some principles of just war: having a just cause in the eyes of others, discrimination in means so that we do not unduly punish the innocent, proportionality of our means to our ends, and a high probability (rather than wishful thinking) of good consequences. Such considerations would keep us from sending troops into civil wars in Congo or Chechnya, where the difficulty and costs of achieving our ends would exceed our means.

Third, we should generally (except in cases of genocide) avoid the use of force unless our humanitarian interests are reinforced by the existence of other national interests, because we are unlikely to have the necessary staying power. This was the case in the Gulf War, where we were concerned not only with the aggression against Kuwait but also with energy supplies and regional allies. This was not the case in Somalia, where, as we have seen, the absence of other interests made the intervention unsustainable when costs mounted. In the former Yugoslavia (Bosnia and Kosovo), our other interests flowed from our European allies and NATO.

Fourth, we should try to involve other regional actors, letting them lead where possible. In East Timor, Australia took the lead, while the United States offered support in logistics and intelligence. In Sierra Leone, Britain took the lead. After our failure in Rwanda, the United States belatedly offered to help African countries with training, intelligence, logistics, and transportation if they would provide the troops for a peacekeeping force. If regional states are unwilling to do their part, we should be wary of going it alone. In Europe, we should welcome the idea of combined joint task forces, including the planned European Rapid Reaction Force, that would be able to act in lesser contingencies where we did not need to be involved. We should encourage a greater European willingness and ability to take the lead on such issues as keeping the peace in the Balkans.

Fifth, the American people have a real humanitarian interest in not letting another holocaust occur, as we did in Rwanda in 1994. We need to do more to organize prevention and response to real cases of genocide. Unfortunately, the genocide convention is written so loosely and the word is so abused for political purposes that there is danger of the term becoming trivialized by being applied to any hate crimes. We should follow the recommendations of a 1985 UN study that recommended that "in order that the concept of genocide should not be devalued or diluted by the inflation of cases . . . considerations both of proportionate scale and of total numbers are relevant."[22] Regardless of the wording of the convention and the efforts of partisans in particular cases, we should focus our military responses on instances of intent to destroy large numbers of a people.

Finally, we should be very wary about intervention in civil wars over self-determination, such as demands for secession by groups in Indonesia, Central Asia, or in many African countries. Sometimes we

Table 5.2   *Rules of Prudence for Humanitarian Interventions*

1. Distinguish degrees of intervention and proportionality
2. Determine that there is just cause and probable success
3. Reinforce humanitarian interests with other interests
4. Give priority to other regional actors
5. Be clear about genocide
6. Be wary of civil wars over self-determination

will be drawn in for other reasons as in the cases mentioned above, but we should avoid taking sides among ethnic groups as much as possible. Albanians killing Serb civilians after the Kosovo war is no more justifiable than Serbs killing Albanian civilians before the war. In a world of nearly ten thousand ethnic and linguistic groups and only about two hundred states, the principle of self-determination presents the threat of enormous violence. It is dangerously ambiguous in moral terms. Atrocities are often committed by activists on both sides (reciprocal genocide), and the precedent we would create by endorsing a general right of self-determination could have disastrous consequences.

None of these rules will solve all the problems of determining our national interest in hard cases. They would have led to intervention in former Yugoslavia and stronger action in Rwanda, but greater caution in Somalia and many African civil wars. Somewhere between being the world's 911 and sitting on the sidelines, we will need some such prudential rules to help us meld our strategic, economic, and human rights interests into a sustainable foreign policy.

Finding a formula for deciding when humanitarian intervention is justified is necessary but not sufficient for the integration of human rights into foreign policy. How we behave at home also matters. Amnesty International is overly harsh in its declaration that "today the United States is as frequently an impediment to human rights as it is an advocate," but by ignoring or refusing to ratify human rights treaties (such as those concerning economic, social, and cultural rights and discrimination against women), the United States under-

cuts our soft power on these issues.[23] Sometimes the causes of our reluctance are minor while the costs to our reputation are considerable. For instance, it took six years for the United States to sign the
Protocol on Involvement of Children in Armed Conflict because the
Pentagon wanted to recruit seventeen-year-olds (with parental consent). It turned out that this affected fewer than 3,000 of the 1.4 million Americans in uniform.[24]

The promotion of democracy is also a national interest and a
source of soft power, though here the role of force is usually less central and the process is of a longer-term nature. The United States has
both an ideological and a pragmatic interest in the promotion of
democracy. While the argument that democracies never go to war
with each other is too simple, it is hard to find cases of *liberal* democracies doing so.[25] Illiberal populist democracies such as Peru,
Ecuador, Venezuela, or Iran, or countries going through the early
stages of democratization, may become dangerous, but liberal
democracies are less likely to produce refugees or engage in terrorism.[26] President Clinton's 1995 statement that "ultimately the best
strategy to ensure our security and to build a durable peace is to support the advance of democracy elsewhere" has a core of truth if approached with the caveats just described.[27] The key is to follow tactics
that are likely to succeed over the long term without imposing inordinate costs on other foreign policy objectives in the near term.

At the beginning of the twentieth century, the United States was
among a handful of democracies. Since then, albeit with setbacks, the
number has grown impressively. A third wave of democratization began in southern Europe in the 1970s, spread to Latin America and parts
of Asia in the 1980s, and hit Eastern Europe in the 1990s.[28] Prior to the
1980s, the United States did not pursue aid to democracy on a wide basis, but since the Reagan and Clinton administrations, such aid has become a deliberate instrument of policy. By the mid-1990s, a host of
U.S. agencies (State Department, Defense Department, AID, Justice
Department, National Endowment for Democracy) were spending
over $700 million on such work.[29] Our economic and soft power helps
promote democratic values, and at the same time, our belief in human
rights and democracy helps to increase our soft power.

THE BATTLE BETWEEN UNILATERALISTS
AND MULTILATERALISTS

How should we engage with other countries? There are three main approaches: isolation, unilateralism, and multilateralism. Isolationism persists in public opinion, but it is not a major strategic option for American foreign policy today. While some people responded to the September 2001 terrorist attacks by suggesting that we cut back on foreign involvements, the majority realized that such a policy would not curtail our vulnerability and could even exacerbate it. The main battle lines are drawn among internationalists, between those who ad-vocate unilateralism and those who prefer multilateral tactics. In William Safire's phrase, "Uni- is not iso-. In our reluctance to appear imperious, we could all too quickly abdicate leadership by catering to the envious crowd."[30] Of course, the differences are a matter of degree, and there are few pure unilateralists or multilateralists. When the early actions of the Bush administration led to cries of outrage about unilateralism, the president disclaimed the label and State Depart-ment officials described the administration's posture as selective mul-tilateralism. But the two ends of the spectrum anchor different views of the degree of choice that grows out of America's position in the world today. I will suggest below some rules for the middle ground.

Some unilateralists advocate an assertive damn-the-torpedoes ap-proach to promoting American values. They see the danger as a flag-ging of our internal will and confusion of our goals, which should be to turn a unipolar moment "into a unipolar era." In this view, a princi-pal aim of American foreign policy should be to bring about a change of regime in undemocratic countries such as Iraq, North Korea, and China.[31] Unilateralists believe that our intentions are good, American hegemony is benevolent, and that should end the discussion. Multilat-eralism would mean "submerging American will in a mush of collec-tive decision-making—you have sentenced yourself to reacting to events or passing the buck to multilingual committees with fancy acronyms."[32] They argue that "the main issue of contention between the United States and those who express opposition to its hegemony is not American 'arrogance.' It is the inescapable reality of American power in its many forms. Those who suggest that these international resentments could somehow be eliminated by a more restrained American foreign policy are engaging in pleasant delusions."[33]

But Americans are not immune from hubris, nor do we have all the answers. Even if it happened to be true, it would be dangerous to act according to such an idea. "For if we were truly acting in the interests of others as well as our own, we would presumably accord to others a substantive role and, by doing so, end up embracing some form of multilateralism. Others, after all, must be supposed to know their interests better than we can know them."[34] As one sympathetic European correctly observed, "From the law of the seas to the Kyoto Protocol, from the biodiversity convention, from the extraterritorial application of the trade embargo against Cuba or Iran, from the brusk calls for reform of the World Bank and the International Monetary Fund to the International Criminal Court: American unilateralism appears as an omnipresent syndrome pervading world politics."[35] When Congress legislated heavy penalties on foreign companies that did business with countries that the United States did not like, the Canadian foreign minister complained, "This is bullying, but in America, you call it 'global leadership.'"[36]

Other unilateralists (sometimes called sovereigntists) focus less on the promotion of American values than on their protection, and they sometimes gain support from the significant minority of isolationist opinion that still exists in this country. As one put it, the strongest and richest country in the world can afford to safeguard its sovereignty. "An America that stands aloof from various international undertakings will not find that it is thereby shut out from the rest of the world. On the contrary, we have every reason to expect that other nations, eager for access to American markets and eager for other cooperative arrangements with the United States, will often adapt themselves to American preferences."[37] In this view, Americans should resist the encroachment of international law, especially claims of universal jurisdiction. Instead, "the United States should strongly espouse national sovereignty, the bedrock upon which democracy and self-government are built, as the fundamental organizing principle of the international system."[38] Or as Senator Jesse Helms warned, the United Nations can be a useful instrument for America's world role, but if it "aspires to establish itself as the central moral authority of a new international order . . . then it begs for confrontation and, more important, eventual U. S. withdrawal."[39]

This battle between multilateralists and unilateralists, often played out in a struggle between the president and Congress, has led to a somewhat schizophrenic American foreign policy. The United States played a prominent role in promoting such multilateral projects as the Law of the Seas Treaty, the Comprehensive Test Ban Treaty, the Land Mines Treaty, the International Criminal Court, the Kyoto Protocol on climate change, and others, but it has failed to follow through with congressional ratification. In some instances, the result has been what *The Economist* calls "parallel unilateralism—a willingness to go along with international accords, but only so far as they suit America, which is prepared to conduct policy outside their constraints."[40] For instance, the United States asserts the jurisdictional limits of the unratified Law of the Seas Treaty. It has pledged not to resume testing nuclear weapons, but because of the unilateral nature of the decision, it does not gain the benefits of verification and the ability to bind others. In other instances, such as antipersonnel land mines, the United States has argued that it needs them to defend against tanks in Korea, but it has undertaken research on a new type of mine that might allow it to join by 2006.[41] In the case of the Kyoto Protocol, President Bush refused to negotiate and peremptorily pronounced it "dead." The result was a foreign reaction of frustration and anger that undermined our soft power.

During the 2000 political campaign, George W. Bush aptly described the situation: "Our nation stands alone right now in the world in terms of power. And that's why we've got to be humble and yet project strength in a way that promotes freedom. . . . If we are an arrogant nation, they'll view us that way, but if we're a humble nation, they'll respect us."[42] Yet our allies and other foreign nations considered the early actions of his administration arrogantly unilateral. Within a few months, America's European allies joined other countries in refusing for the first time to reelect the United States to the UN Human Rights Commission. The secretary of defense, Donald

Rumsfeld, said that "gratitude is gone,"[43] and the secretary of state, Colin Powell, explained that "the 'sole superpower' charge is always out there and that may have influenced some."[44] In the less temperate words of television commentator Morton Kondracke, "We're the most powerful country in the world by far, and a lot of pipsqueak wannabes like France resent the hell out of it. . . . When they have a chance to stick it to us, they try."[45] The House of Representatives responded by voting to withhold funds from the UN. But the situation was more complicated than such responses acknowledged.

At the beginning of the last century, as America rose to world power, Teddy Roosevelt advised that we should speak softly but carry a big stick. Now that we have the stick, we need to pay more attention to the first part of his admonition. And we need not just to speak more softly but to listen more carefully. As Chris Patten, the EU commissioner for external affairs and former British Conservative leader, explained a year earlier, the United States is a staunch friend with much to admire, "but there are also many areas in which I think they have got it wrong, the UN, for example, environmental policy, and a pursuit of extraterritorial powers combined with a neuralgic hostility to any external authority over their own affairs."[46] In the words of one observer, at the start of his administration President Bush "contrived to prove his own theory that arrogance provokes resentment for a country that, long before his arrival, was already the world's most conspicuous and convenient target."[47]

The United States should aim to work with other nations on global problems in a multilateral manner whenever possible. I agree with the recent bipartisan commission on our national security, chaired by former senators Gary Hart and Warren Rudman, which concluded that "emerging powers—either singly or in coalition—will increasingly constrain U.S. options regionally and limit its strategic influence. As a result we will remain limited in our ability to impose our will, and we will be vulnerable to an increasing range of threats." Borders will become more porous, rapid advances in information and biotechnologies will create new vulnerabilities, the United States will become "increasingly vulnerable to hostile attack on the American homeland, and the U.S. military superiority will not entirely protect us."[48] This means we must develop multilateral laws and institutions that constrain others and provide a framework for cooperation. In the words of the Hart-Rudman Commission, "America cannot secure and advance its own interests in isolation."[49] As the terrorist attacks of September 11 showed, even a superpower needs friends.

Granted, multilateralism can be used as a strategy by smaller states to tie the United States down like Gulliver among the Lilliputians. It is no wonder that France prefers a multipolar and multilateral world, and less developed countries see multilateralism as in their interests, because it gives them some leverage on the United States.[50] But this does not mean multilateralism is not generally in American interests as well. "By resting our actions on a legal basis (and accepting the correlative constraints), we can make the continued exercise of our disproportionate power easier for others to accept."[51]

Multilateralism involves costs, but in the larger picture, they are outweighed by the benefits. International rules bind the United States and limit our freedom of action in the short term, but they also serve our interest by binding others as well. Americans should use our power now to shape institutions that will serve our long-term national interest in promoting international order. "Since there is little reason for believing that the means of policy will be increased, we are left to rely on the greater cooperation of others. But the greater cooperation of others will mean that our freedom of action is narrowed."[52] It is not just that excessive unilateralism can hurt us; multilateralism is often the best way to achieve our long-run objectives.

Action to shape multilateralism now is a good investment for our future. Today, as we have seen, "worried states are making small adjustments, creating alternatives to alliance with the United States. These small steps may not look important today, but eventually the ground will shift and the U.S.-led postwar order will fragment and disappear."[53] These tendencies are countered by the very openness of the American system. The pluralistic and regularized way in which foreign policy is made reduces surprises. Opportunities for foreigners to raise their voice and influence the American political and governmental system not only are plentiful but constitute an important incentive for alliance.[54] Ever since Athens transformed the Delian

League into an empire, smaller allies have been torn between anxieties over abandonment or entrapment. The fact that American allies are able to voice their concerns helps to explain why American alliances have persisted so long after Cold War threats receded.

The other element of the American order that reduces worry about power asymmetries is our membership in a web of multilateral institutions ranging from the UN to NATO. Some call it an institutional bargain. The price for the United States was reduction in Washington's policy autonomy, in that institutional rules and joint decision making reduced U.S. unilateralist capacities. But what Washington got in return was worth the price. America's partners also had their autonomy constrained, but they were able to operate in a world where U.S. power was more restrained and reliable.[55] Seen in the light of a constitutional bargain, the multilateralism of American preeminence is a key to its longevity, because it reduces the incentives for constructing alliances against us. And to the extent that the EU is the major potential challenger in terms of capacity, the idea of a loose constitutional framework between the United States and the societies with which we share the most values makes sense.[56]

Of course, not all multilateral arrangements are good or in our interests, and the United States should occasionally use unilateral tactics in certain situations, which I will describe below. The presumption in favor of multilateralism that I recommend need not be a straitjacket. Richard Haass, the State Department's director of policy planning, says, "What you're going to get from this administration is 'à la carte multilateralism.' We'll look at each agreement and make a decision, rather than come out with a broad-based approach."[57] So how should Americans choose between unilateral and multilateral tactics? Here are seven tests to consider.

First, in cases that involve vital survival interests, we should not rule out unilateral action, though when possible we should seek international support for these actions. The starkest case in the last half century was the 1962 Cuban missile crisis. American leaders felt obliged to consider unilateral use of force, though it is important to note that President Kennedy also sought the legitimacy of opinion expressed in multilateral forums such as the United Nations and the

Organization of American States. Strikes against terrorist camps and safe havens are a current example, but again, unilateral actions are best when buttressed by multilateral support.

Second, we should be cautious about multilateral arrangements that interfere with our ability to produce stable peace in volatile areas. Because of our global military role, the United States sometimes has interests and vulnerabilities that are different from those of smaller states with more limited interests—witness the role of land mines in preventing North Korean tanks crossing the demilitarized zone into South Korea. Thus the multilateral treaty banning land mines was easier for other countries to sign. As noted previously, the United States announced that it would work to develop new mines that might allow it to sign by 2006. Similarly, given the global role of American military forces, if the procedures of the International Criminal Court cannot be clarified to ensure protection of American troops from unjustified charges of war crimes, they might deter the United States from contributing to the public good of peacekeeping. The ICC procedures currently proposed give primary jurisdiction over alleged war crimes by American servicemen to the United States, but there is still a danger of overzealous prosecutors egged on by hostile NGOs in instances where the United States finds no case. We should seek further assurances such as clarifying declarations by the UN Security Council. While the ICC has problems, helping to shape its procedures would be a better policy than abetting the current trend toward national claims of universal legal jurisdiction that are evolving in ad hoc fashion beyond our control.[58]

Third, unilateral tactics sometimes help lead others to compromises that advance multilateral interests. The multilateralism of free trade and the international gold standard in the nineteenth century were achieved not by multilateral means but by Britain's unilateral moves of opening its markets and maintaining the stability of its currency.[59] America's relative openness after 1945 and, more recently, trade legislation that threatened unilateral sanctions if others did not negotiate helped create conditions that prodded other countries to move forward with the WTO dispute settlement mechanism. Sometimes the United States is big enough to set high standards and get away with it—witness our more stringent regulations for financial markets. Such actions can lead to the creation of higher international standards. The key is whether the unilateral action was designed to promote a global public good.

The Kyoto Protocol, which caused President Bush such trouble at the beginning of his presidency, could have been another case in point had it been handled differently. Many who accept the reality of global warming and support the Framework Convention on Climate Change (the Rio agreement signed by President George H. Bush and ratified by the Senate in 1992) believed that the Kyoto agreement was badly flawed because it did not include developing countries and because its target for emission cuts, according to *The Economist,* "could not be done except at ruinous cost, and perhaps not even then." A longer-term plan based on milder reductions at the start followed by more demanding targets farther out would provide time for capital stocks to adjust and market-based instruments such as tradable permits to lower the costs of emissions reductions.[60] It would also reduce the trade-off with economic growth, which benefits a wide range of nations, including the poor.[61] If, instead of resisting the science and abruptly pronouncing the protocol dead on grounds of domestic interest, the Bush administration had said, "We will work on a domestic energy policy that cuts emissions and at the same time negotiate with you for a better treaty," his initial unilateralism would arguably have advanced multilateral interests.[62]

Fourth, the United States should reject multilateral initiatives that are recipes for inaction, promote others' self-interest, or are contrary to our values.[63] The New International Information Order proposed by the UN Educational, Scientific and Cultural Organization (UNESCO) in the 1970s would have helped authoritarian governments to restrict freedom of the press. Similarly, the New International Economic Order fostered by the General Assembly at the same time would have interfered with the public good of open markets. Sometimes multilateral procedures are obstructive—for example, Russia's and China's efforts to prevent Security Council authorization of intervention to stop the human rights violations in Kosovo in 1999. Ultimately the United States decided to go ahead without Security

Council approval, but even then the American intervention was not purely unilateral but taken with strong support of our allies in NATO.

Fifth, multilateralism is essential on intrinsically cooperative issues that cannot be managed by the United States without the help of other countries. Climate change is a perfect example. Global warming will be costly to us, but it cannot be prevented by the United States alone cutting emissions of carbon dioxide, methane, and particulates. The United States is the largest source of such warming agents, but three-quarters of the sources originate outside our borders. Without cooperation, the problem is beyond our control. The same is true of a long list of items: the spread of infectious diseases, the stability of global financial markets, the international trade system, the proliferation of weapons of mass destruction, narcotics trafficking, international crime syndicates, transnational terrorism. All these problems have major effects on Americans, and their control ranks as an important national interest—but one that cannot be achieved except by multilateral means.

Sixth, multilateralism should be sought as a means to get others to share the burden and buy into the idea of providing public goods. Sharing helps foster commitment to common values. Even militarily, the United States should rarely intervene alone. Not only does this comport with the preferences of the American public, but it has practical implications. The United States pays a minority share of the cost of UN and NATO peacekeeping operations, and the legitimacy of a multilateral umbrella reduces collateral political costs to our soft power.

Seventh, in choosing between multilateral and unilateral tactics, we must consider the effects of the decision on our soft power. If we continue to define our power too heavily in military terms, we may fail to understand the need to invest in other instruments. As we have seen, soft power is becoming increasingly important, but soft power is fragile and can be destroyed by excessive unilateralism and arrogance. In balancing whether to use multilateral or unilateral tactics, or to adhere to or refuse to go along with particular multilateral initiatives, we have to consider how we explain it to others and what the effects will be on our soft power.

Table 5.3   *Checklist for Multilateral Versus Unilateral Tactics*

1. Survival interests at stake
2. Effect on military and peace
3. Leadership increases public goods
4. Consistency with our values
5. Intrinsically cooperative issues
6. Helps on burden sharing
7. Effects on our soft power

In short, American foreign policy in a global information age should have a general preference for multilateralism, but not all multilateralism. At times we will have to go it alone. When we do so in pursuit of public goods, the nature of our ends may substitute for the means in legitimizing our power in the eyes of others. If, on the other hand, the new unilateralists try to elevate unilateralism from an occasional temporary tactic to a full-fledged strategy, they are likely to fail for three reasons: (1) the intrinsically multilateral nature of a number of important transnational issues in a global age, (2) the costly effects on our soft power, and (3) the changing nature of sovereignty.

SOVEREIGNTY, DEMOCRACY, AND GLOBAL INSTITUTIONS

As we saw in chapter 3, at this point in history democracy works best in sovereign nation-states, and that is likely to change only slowly. Giving too much power to global institutions could lead to a loss of democracy in decision making for the United States as well as other countries.[64] But *sovereignty* is a slippery term. Those who resist multilateralism define sovereignty narrowly as domestic authority and control. But as we have seen, unilateral control may be impossible on some global issues. In instances where we do not have the unilateral capability to produce the outcomes we want, our sovereign control may be enhanced by membership in good standing in the regimes that make up the substance of international life.[65]

We saw in chapters 2 and 3 that sovereignty remains important but that its content is changing under the influence of transnational forces of information and globalization. Sovereign states have always been porous to some degree, but today, less than ever, we cannot protect our homeland simply by protecting our borders.[66] As we found after September 2001, the only way to deal with many transnational intrusions is to mount a forward defense that involves cooperation in intelligence and law enforcement with other countries behind their borders and inside ours. Other countries' governments are quite often better placed to identify and arrest terrorists. Their cooperation is essential, and obtaining it will depend on both our hard and soft power.

Transnational relations and multiple identities also undermine our impermeability. Who we are is harder to define when Japanese firms are major exporters from the United States, American firms produce more overseas than they export, and the NGOs and political leaders who pressed for the land mines treaty included large numbers of Americans, including prominent senators. Mixed coalitions crisscross borders, and the price of stopping them would be prohibitive in terms of our basic democratic values and civil liberties.

Some sovereigntists believe that "America does not have to play by the rules that everybody else plays by because nobody can make it play by them—and besides it has its own set of more important ones."[67] But the costs are high in terms of rejection of U.S. leadership by states that otherwise would defer to our views, as well as our inability to achieve all our objectives alone. Moreover, American corporations are vulnerable to foreign and NGO reactions, and when they are hurt, they will press the government for relief at national or state levels. As columnist Tom Friedman observed, the smart activists are saying, "Okay, you want to play markets? Let's play." After Exxon supported the Bush administration's killing of the Kyoto Protocol, activists in Europe started a boycott of its products. Shell and BP, on the other hand, had withdrawn from the oil industry lobby that had been dismissing climate change.[68] And American corporations send armies of lobbyists to Brussels and Geneva, where the EU, the WTO, and the International Telecommunications Union shape new global rules on matters such as electronic commerce, intellectual property, and technical standards. "No government, no matter how powerful, can unilaterally impose or enforce its will on these issues. They embroil too many actors and interests in too many countries to be susceptible to brute, hegemonic force."[69] And when our rejection of cooperation appears narrowly self-interested and arrogant, we undercut our soft power. A consistently unilateral view of sovereignty will prove too costly to sustain.

At the same time, the problem of democratic accountability of multilateral institutions, discussed in chapter 3, remains a real one. As the lawyer Kal Raustiala notes, "It is the process of multilateral lawmaking, rather than the substance, that largely creates tensions with democracy and sovereignty. . . . The threats to sovereignty and democracy from multilateral cooperation are not large but they are real."[70] Rather than rejecting such institutions, as the sovereigntists advise, there are several things that the United States should do to respond to the concerns about a democratic deficit and to enhance the accountability and legitimacy of the multilateral institutions and networks that provide the necessary governance for globalism.

Most important, perhaps, is to try to design multilateral institutions that preserve as much space as possible for domestic democratic processes to operate. The real policy challenge is making the world safe for different brands of national economies to prosper side by side. The answer involves multilateral procedures, modest barriers, and rules of the game that allow countries to reimpose restrictions when not doing so would jeopardize a legitimate national objective.[71] Here the WTO is illustrative. While its dispute settlement procedures intrude on domestic sovereignty, as mentioned above, a country can respond to domestic democratic processes and reject a judgment if it is willing to pay carefully limited compensation to the trade partners injured by its actions. And if a country does defect from its trade agreements, the procedure limits the tit-for-tat downward spiral of retaliation that so devastated the world economy in the 1930s. In a sense, the procedure is like having a fuse in the electrical system of a house—better the fuse blows than the house burns down. The danger, however, is that our governments will legalize rather than negotiate too many of their trade disputes and eventually overburden an institution that, contrary to the protesters' arguments, leaves room for domestic democratic processes.

In addition, better accountability can start at home in democracies. If the American people believe that environmental standards are not adequately taken into account at WTO meetings in Geneva, we can press our government to include EPA officials in our delegations. Congress can hold hearings before or after meetings, and legislators can themselves become members of the national delegations to various organizations.

Moreover, Americans should understand that democratic accountability can be quite indirect. Accountability is ensured in multiple ways, not only through voting, even in well-functioning democracies. In the United States, for example, the Supreme Court and the Federal Reserve system are responsive to elections only indirectly through a long chain of delegation. Professional norms and standards also help to keep judges and bankers accountable. IMF and World Bank officials are accountable to executive directors who are accountable to governments. There is no reason in principle that indirect accountability should be inconsistent with democracy, or that international institutions should be held to a higher standard than domestic institutions.

Increased transparency—that is, curtailing secrecy of procedures—is essential if international institutions are to be held accountable. In addition to voting, people in democracies communicate and agitate over issues through a variety of means ranging from letters and polls to protests. Interest groups and a free press play an important role in creating transparency in our domestic democratic politics. We call the press the essential fourth branch of government, and this is a role that the press and NGOs can play at the international level as well. NGOs are self-selected, not democratically elected, but they can play a positive role in increasing transparency. They deserve a voice but not a vote. For them to fill this role, they need to be provided with information and included in dialogues with institutions. In some instances, such as judicial procedures or market interventions, it is unrealistic to provide the information in advance, but records and justifications of decisions can later be provided for comment and criticism, as the Fed and the Supreme Court do in our domestic politics. We should press international institutions and networks to put more information on the Internet.[72] (The same standards of transparency should be applied to NGOs themselves.)

The private sector can also contribute to accountability. Private associations and codes, such as those established by the international chemical industry in the aftermath of the explosion of Union Carbide's plant in the Indian city of Bhopal in 1984, can prevent a race to the bottom in standards. The practice of naming and shaming has helped consumers to hold accountable transnational firms in the toy and apparel industries—as Mattel and Nike can attest. And while people have unequal votes in markets, in the aftermath of the Asian financial crisis, accountability through markets may have led to more increases in transparency by corrupt governments than any formal agreements did. Open markets can help to diminish the undemocratic power of local monopolies and can reduce the power of entrenched and unresponsive government bureaucracies, particularly in countries where parliaments are weak. Moreover, efforts by investors to increase transparency and legal predictability can have beneficial spillover effects on political institutions.

If multilateral institutions are to be preserved, we will need to engage in experiments designed to improve accountability. Transparency is essential, and international organizations can provide more access, even if it requires delayed release of records in the manner practiced by the Supreme Court and Federal Reserve. NGOs could be welcomed as observers (as the World Bank has done) or allowed to file amicus curiae briefs in WTO dispute settlement cases (although the privilege might be extended only to those who are transparent about their own membership and finances). In some cases, such as the Internet Corporation for Assigned Names and Numbers (ICANN, which is incorporated as a nonprofit institution under the laws of California), experiments with direct voting for board members may prove fruitful, though the danger of capture by well-organized interest groups remains a problem. Hybrid network organizations that combine governmental, intergovernmental, and nongovernmental representatives, such as the World Commission on Dams or Kofi Annan's Global Compact, are other avenues to explore.

Table 5.4   *Enhancing Accountability of Global Institutions*

1. Design institutions to protect domestic processes (e.g., WTO)
2. Involve legislators in delegations and advisory groups
3. Make use of indirect accountability (e.g., reputations, markets)
4. Increase transparency through the press, NGOs, Web sites
5. Encourage private sector accountability
6. Experiment with new forms (e.g., ICANN, World Commission on Dams, Global Compact)

Congressmen could attend assemblies of parliamentarians associated with some organizations to hold hearings and receive information, even if not to vote (for reasons given earlier).

There is no single answer to the question of how to reconcile the necessary global multilateral institutions with democratic accountability. Highly technical organizations may be able to derive their legitimacy from their efficacy alone. But the more that an institution deals with broad values, the more the legitimacy of democratic accountability becomes relevant. Americans concerned about democracy will need to think harder about norms and procedures for the governance of globalization. Demands for withdrawal, direct elections, or control by unelected NGOs will not solve the problem. Changes in processes that increase transparency and take advantage of the multiple forms of accountability that exist in modern democracies will be necessary to preserve the multilateral options that we will need to deal with global problems.

PEERING INTO THE FUTURE

The September 2001 wake-up call means that Americans are unlikely to slip back into the complacency that marked the first decade after the Cold War. If we respond effectively, it is highly unlikely that terrorists could destroy American power, but the campaign against terrorism will require a long and sustained effort. At the same time, the

United States is unlikely to face a challenge to its preeminence unless it acts so arrogantly that it helps other states to overcome their built-in limitations. The one entity with the capacity to challenge the United States in the near future is the European Union if it were to become a tight federation with major military capabilities and if the relations across the Atlantic were allowed to sour. Such an outcome is possible but would require major changes in Europe and considerable ineptitude in American policy to bring it about. Nonetheless, even short of such a challenge, the diminished fungibility of military power in a global information age means that Europe is already well placed to balance the United States on the economic and transnational chessboards. Even short of a military balance of power, other countries may be driven to work together to take actions to complicate American objectives. Or, as the French critic Dominique Moisi puts it, "The global age has not changed the fact that nothing in the world can be done without the United States. And the multiplicity of new actors means that there is very little the United States can achieve alone."[73]

The United States can learn useful lessons about a strategy of providing public goods from the history of Pax Britannica. An Australian analyst may be right in her view that if the United States plays its cards well and acts not as a soloist but as the leader of a concert of nations, "the Pax Americana, in terms of its duration, might . . . become more like the Pax Romana than the Pax Britannica."[74] If so, our soft power will play a major role. As Henry Kissinger has argued, the test of history for the United States will be whether we can turn our current predominant power into international consensus and our own principles into widely accepted international norms. That was the greatness achieved by Rome and Britain in their times.[75]

Unlike Britain, Rome succumbed not to the rise of a new empire, but to internal decay and a death of a thousand cuts from various barbarian groups. We saw in chapter 4 that while internal decay is always possible, none of the commonly cited trends seems to point strongly in that direction at this time. At the start of the century, terrorist threats notwithstanding, American attitudes are both positive and realistic. The initial response to September 2001 was encouraging. The public did not turn to isolationism and the Congress and administration curbed their unilateralism. The public is also realistic about the limits of American power and expresses a willingness to share. "While 28% say America will remain the major world power in the next 100 years, 61% believe the United States will share this status with a few other countries. (Fewer than one in 10 thinks the U.S. will no longer be a major power.)"[76] Large majorities oppose a purely unilateralist approach. "Upwards of two-thirds of the public oppose, in principle, the U.S. acting alone overseas without the support of other countries."[77] The American public seems to have an intuitive sense for soft power even if the term is unfamiliar.

On the other hand, it is harder to exclude the barbarians. The dramatically decreased cost of communication, the rise of transnational domains (including the Internet) that cut across borders, and the democratization of technology that puts massive destructive power (once the sole preserve of governments) into the hands of groups and individuals all suggest dimensions that are historically new. In the last century, men such Hitler, Stalin, and Mao needed the power of the state to wreak great evil. "Such men and women in the 21st century will be less bound than those of the 20th by the limits of the state, and less obliged to gain industrial capabilities to wreak havoc. . . . Clearly the threshold for small groups or even individuals to inflict massive damage on those they take to be their enemies is falling dramatically."[78] Countering such terrorist groups must be a top priority. Homeland defense takes on a new importance and a new meaning and will require an intelligent combination of hard and soft power. If such groups were to produce a series of events involving even greater destruction and disruption of society than occurred in September 2001, American attitudes might change dramatically, though the direction of the change is difficult to predict. Isolationism might make a comeback, but greater engagement in world events is equally plausible.

Other things being equal, the United States is well placed to remain the leading power in world politics well into the twenty-first century or beyond. This prognosis depends upon assumptions that can be spelled out. For example, it assumes that the long-term productivity of the American economy will be sustained, that American society will not decay, that the United States will maintain its military strength but not become overmilitarized, that Americans will not become so unilateral and arrogant in their strength that they squander the nation's considerable fund of soft power, that there will not be some catastrophic series of events that profoundly transforms American attitudes in an isolationist direction, and that Americans will define their national interest in a broad and farsighted way that incorporates global interests. Each of these assumptions can be questioned, but they currently seem more plausible than their alternatives. If the assumptions hold, America will continue to be number one, but even so, in this global information age, number one ain't gonna be what it used to be. To succeed in such a world, America must not only maintain its hard power but understand its soft power and how to combine the two in the pursuit of national and global interests.

NOTES

PREFACE

1. Jim Rutenberg, "Networks Move to Revive Foreign News," *New York Times,* September 24, 2001, C10.

2. Gary Hart and Warren Rudman, cochairmen, United States Commission on National Security/21st Century, *New World Coming: American Security in the 21st Century, Phase I Report* (Washington, D.C.: U.S. Commission on National Security/21st Century, 1999), 4.

3. Joseph S. Nye Jr. and R. James Woolsey, "Perspective on Terrorism," *Los Angeles Times,* June 1, 1997, M5.

4. Anwar ul-Haque quoted in Colin Nickerson, "Some in Region See a Robin Hood Story," *Boston Globe,* September 24, 2001, 1.

5. King Abdallah quoted in Thomas Friedman, "The Big Terrible," *New York Times,* September 18, 2001, 31.

6. Jim Yardley, "Training Site Is Questioned About Links to Hijackers," *New York Times,* September 13, 2001, A4.

7. Thomas Pickering quoted in "The FP Interview," *Foreign Policy,* July-August 2001, 38.

8. Robert Kagan and William Kristol, "The Present Danger," *The National Interest,* spring 2000, 58, 64, 67.

9. Robert W. Tucker, "American Power—For What?" (symposium), *Commentary,* January 2000, 46.

10. Patrick Tyler and Jane Perlez, "World Leaders List Terms to Join U.S. in Coalition and Press Multilateralism," *New York Times,* September 19, 2001, 1.

11. Elaine Sciolino and Steven Lee Meyers, "U.S., Preparing to Act Largely Alone, Warns Taliban That Time Is Running Out," *New York Times,* October 7, 2001, A1.

12. Karen DeYoung, "Allies Are Cautious on Bush Doctrine," *Washington Post,* October 16, 2001, p. 1.

13. Associated Press, "Britain Ratifies Treaty Creating Criminal Court," *International Herald Tribune,* October 5, 2001.

CHAPTER 1: THE AMERICAN COLOSSUS

1. "America's World," *The Economist,* October 23, 1999, 15.

2. Lara Marlowe, "French Minister Urges Greater UN Role to Counter US Hyperpower," *The Irish Times,* November 4, 1999, 14. In 1998, Védrine coined the term "hyperpower" to describe the United States because "the word 'superpower' seems to me too closely linked to the cold war and military issues." Hubert Védrine with Dominique Moisi, *France in an Age of Globalization* (Washington, D.C.: Brookings Institution Press, 2001), 2.

3. Robert Kagan and William Kristol, "The Present Danger," *The National Interest,* spring 2000.

4. William Drozdiak, "Even Allies Resent U.S. Dominance," *Washington Post,* November 4, 1997, 1.

5. See Charles Krauthammer, "The Unipolar Moment," *Foreign Affairs,* winter 1990–91, 23–33; Christopher Lane, "The Unipolar Illusion: Why New Great Powers Will Arise," *International Security,* spring 1993, 5–51; Charles Kupchan, "After Pax Americana: Benign Power, Regional Integration and the Sources of Stable Multipolarity," *International Security,* fall 1998.

6. William Wohlforth, "The Stability of a Unipolar World," in Michael Brown et al., *America's Strategic Choices,* rev. ed. (Cambridge, MA: MIT Press, 2000), 305, 309; also from a liberal perspective, G. John Ikenberry, "Institutions, Strategic Restraint, and the Persistence of American Postwar Order," *International Security,* winter 1998–99, 43–78.

7. Charles Krauthammer, "The New Unilateralism," *Washington Post,* June 8, 2001, 29.

8. Kenneth Waltz, "Globalization and Governance," *Political Science and Politics,* December 1999, 700.

9. Sunanda K. Datta-Ray, "Will Dream Partnership Become Reality?" *The Straits Times* (Singapore), December 25, 1998, 46.

10. Hugo Chavez quoted in Larry Rohter, "A Man with Big Ideas, a Small Country . . . and Oil," *New York Times,* September 24, 2000, "Week in Review" section, 3.

11. "When the Snarling's Over," *The Economist,* March 13, 1999, 17.

12. Paul Kennedy, *The Rise and Fall of the Great Powers: Economic Change and Military Conflict from 1500–2000* (New York: Random House, 1987); Lester Thurow, *The Zero Sum Solution* (New York: Simon and Schuster, 1985).

13. Martilla and Kiley, Inc. (Boston, MA), *Americans Talk Security,* no. 6, May 1988, and no. 8, August 1988.

14. Quoted in Barbara Tuchman, *The March of Folly: From Troy to Vietnam* (New York: Knopf, 1984), 221.

15. Daniel Bell, *The Coming of Post-Industrial Society: A Venture in Social Forecasting* (New York: Basic Books, 1999 [1973]), new introduction, passim.

16. William Pfaff, *Barbarian Sentiments: America in the New Century,* rev. ed. (New York: Hill and Wang, 2000), 280.

17. On the complexities of projections, see Joseph S. Nye Jr., "Peering into the Future," *Foreign Affairs,* July-August 1994; see also Robert Jervis, "The Future of World Politics: Will It Resemble the Past?" *International Security,* winter 1991–92.

18. A. J. Taylor, *The Struggle for Mastery in Europe, 1848–1918* (Oxford: Oxford University Press, 1954), xxix.

19. Whether this would change with the proliferation of nuclear weapons to more states is hotly debated among theorists. Deterrence should work with most states, but the prospects of accident and loss of control would increase. For my views, see Joseph S. Nye Jr., *Nuclear Ethics* (New York: Free Press, 1986).

20. Robert Cooper, *The Postmodern State and the World Order* (London: Demos, 2000), 22.

21. John Mueller, *Retreat from Doomsday: The Obsolescence of Major War* (New York: Basic Books, 1989).

22. Thomas Friedman, *The Lexus and the Olive Tree: Understanding Globalization* (New York: Farrar, Straus and Giroux, 1999), chapter 6.

23. Richard N. Rosecrance, *The Rise of the Trading State* (New York: Basic Books, 1986), 16, 160.

24. Thucydides, *History of the Peloponnesian War,* trans. Rex Warner (London: Penguin, 1972), book I, chapter 1.

25. And in turn, as industrialization progressed and railroads were built, Germany feared the rise of Russia.

26. Henry Kissinger portrays four international systems existing side by side: the West (and Western Hemisphere), marked by democratic peace; Asia, where strategic conflict is possible; the Middle East, marked by religious conflict; and Africa, where civil wars threaten weak postcolonial states. "America at the Apex," *The National Interest,* summer 2001, 14.

27. Robert O. Keohane and Joseph S. Nye Jr., *Power and Interdependence,* 3rd ed. (New York: Longman, 2000), chapter 1.

28. James Carville quoted in Bob Woodward, *The Agenda: Inside the Clinton White House* (New York: Simon and Schuster, 1994), 302.

29. For a more detailed discussion, see Joseph S. Nye Jr., *Bound to Lead: The Changing Nature of American Power* (New York: Basic Books, 1990), chapter 2. This builds on what Peter Bachrach and Morton Baratz called the "second face of power" in "Decisions and Nondecisions: An Analytical Framework," *American Political Science Review,* September 1963, 632–42.

30. Védrine, *France in an Age of Globalization,* 3

31. The distinction between hard and soft power is one of degree, both in the nature of the behavior and in the tangibility of the resources. Both are aspects of the ability to achieve one's purposes by affecting the behavior of others. Command power—the ability to change what others do—can rest on coercion or inducement. Co-optive power—the ability to shape what others want—can rest on the attractiveness of one's culture and ideology or the ability to manipulate the agenda of political choices in a manner that makes actors fail to express some preferences because they seem to be too unrealistic. The forms of behavior between command and co-optive power range along a continuum: command power, coercion, inducement, agenda setting, attraction, co-optive power. Soft power resources tend to be associated with co-optive power behavior, whereas hard power resources are usually associated with command behavior. But the relationship is imperfect. For example, countries may be attracted to others with command power by myths of invincibility, and command power may sometimes be used to establish institutions that later become regarded as legitimate. But the general association is strong enough to allow the useful shorthand reference to hard and soft power.

32. Josef Joffe, "Who's Afraid of Mr. Big?" *The National Interest,* summer 2001, 43.

33. See Cooper, *Postmodern State;* Bell, *The Coming of Post-Industrial Society.*

34. Nixon quoted in James Chace and Nicholas X. Rizopoulos, "Towards a New Concert of Nations: An American Perspective," *World Policy Journal,* fall 1999, 9.

35. Jack S. Levy, *War in the Modern Great Power System, 1495–1975* (Lexington: University Press of Kentucky, 1983), 97.

36. Margaret Thatcher, "Why America Must Remain Number One," *National Review,* July 31,1995, 25.

37. Josef Joffe, "Envy," *The New Republic,* January 17, 2000, 6.

38. Kenneth Waltz, "Globalization and American Power," *The National Interest,* spring 2000, 55–56.

39. Stephen Walt, "Alliance Formation and the Balance of Power," *International Security,* spring 1985.

40. Robert Gilpin, *War and Change in World Politics* (New York: Cambridge University Press, 1981), 144–45; Charles Kindleberger, *The World in Depression, 1929–1939* (Berkeley: University of California Press, 1973), 305.

41. Joshua S. Goldstein, *Long Cycles: Prosperity and War in the Modern Age* (New Haven: Yale University Press, 1988), 281.

42. See Robert O. Keohane, *After Hegemony: Cooperation and Discord in the World Political Economy* (Princeton: Princeton University Press, 1984), 235.

43. Over the years, a number of scholars have tried to predict the rise and fall of nations by developing a general historical theory of hegemonic transition. Some have tried to generalize from the experience of Portugal, Spain, the Netherlands, France, and Britain. Others have focused more closely on Britain's decline in the twentieth century as a predictor for the fate for the United States. None of these approaches has been successful. Most of the theories have predicted that America would decline long before now. Vague definitions and arbitrary schematizations alert us to the inadequacies of such grand theories. Most try to squeeze history into procrustean theoretical beds by focusing on particular power resources while ignoring others that are equally important. Hegemony can be used as a descriptive term (though it is sometimes fraught with emotional overtones), but grand hegemonic theories are weak in predicting future events. See Immanuel Wallerstein, *The Politics of the World Economy: The States, the Movements, and the Civilizations: Essays* (New York: Cambridge University Press, 1984), 38, 41; George Modelski, "The Long Cycle of Global Politics and the Nation-State," *Comparative Studies in Society and History,* April 1978; George Modelski, *Long Cycles in World Politics* (Seattle: University of Washington Press, 1987). For a detailed discussion, see Nye, *Bound to Lead,* chapter 2.

44. Wohlforth, "The Stability of a Unipolar World."

45. Stephen Walt, "Keeping the World 'Off-Balance': Self-Restraint and US Foreign Policy," Kennedy School Research Working Paper Series 00–013, October 2000.

46. William Safire, "Putin's China Card," *New York Times,* June 18, 2001, A29.

47. Patrick Tyler, "Bush and Putin Look Each Other in the Eye," *New York Times*, June 17, 2001, A10.

48. Ikenberry, "Institutions, Strategic Restraint," 47; also Ikenberry, "Getting Hegemony Right," *The National Interest*, spring 2001, 17–24.

49. Josef Joffe, "How America Does It," *Foreign Affairs*, September-October 1997.

50. Michael Brown et al., *The Rise of China* (Cambridge, MA: MIT Press, 2000).

51. Coral Bell, *"TK," The National Interest*, fall 1999, 56.

52. "American Opinion," *Wall Street Journal*, September 16, 1999, A9.

53. Arthur Waldron, "How Not to Deal with China," *Commentary*, March 1997; Robert Kagan, "What China Knows That We Don't," *The Weekly Standard*, January 20, 1997.

54. "China Lashes Out at U.S. 'Gunboat Diplomacy,'" *Financial Times* (London), September 4, 1999, 4.

55. John Pomfret, "U.S. Now a 'Threat' in China's Eyes," *Washington Post*, November 15, 2000, 1.

56. Richard K. Betts and Thomas J. Christensen, "China: Getting the Questions Right," *The National Interest*, winter 2000–1, 17.

57. Thucydides, *History of the Peloponnesian War*, 62.

58. Asian Development Bank, *Emerging Asia* (Manila: ADB, 1997), 11.

59. Figures were calculated using data from *CIA World Fact Book 2000* (*http://www.cia.gov/cia/publications/factbook/*) (for purchasing power parities) and the World Bank (http://www.worldbank.org/data/wdi2001/pdfs/tab1_1.pdf) for official exchange rates. Size was measured by purchasing power parities that correct for the costs of goods in different currencies; equality in size would not occur until 2056 if measured by official exchange rates. If the United States grows at 3 percent per year, the convergence would occur between 2022 and 2075 (depending on the measure). My thanks to Kennedy School graduate students Ebrahim Afsah and Francisco Blanch for lending their computational skills.

60. Ibid.

61. Dwight Perkins, "Institutional Challenges for the Economic Transition in Asia," paper presented at Australian National University, September 2000, 48.

62. See Merle Goldman, Raja Menon, Richard Ellings, "Letters from Readers," *Commentary*, February 2001, 13, 19.

63. Charles Wolf Jr., Anil Bamezai, K. C. Yeh, and Benjamin Zycher, *Asian Economic Trends and Their Security Implications* (Santa Monica: RAND, 2000), 19–22.

64. David M. Lampton and Gregory C. May, *A Big Power Agenda for East Asia: America, China and Japan* (Washington, D.C.: The Nixon Center, 2000), 13. These calculations use constant dollars at market exchange rates and are higher than official Chinese figures.

65. David Shambaugh, "Containment or Engagement in China? Calculating Beijing's Responses," *International Security,* fall 1996, 21.

66. Paul Dibb, D. D. Hale, and P. Prince, "Asia's Insecurity," *Survivor,* autumn 1999, 5–20.

67. Robert Kagan, "What China Knows That We Don't," *The Weekly Standard,* January 20, 1997.

68. Thomas J. Christensen, "Posing Problems Without Catching Up: China's Rise and Challenges for U.S. Security Policy," *International Security,* spring 2001, 36.

69. "Hour of Power?" *Newsweek,* February 27, 1989, 15.

70. Jacques Attali, *Lignes d'Horizon* (Paris: Fayard, 1990); George Friedman and Meredith LeBard, *The Coming War with Japan* (New York: St. Martin's, 1992).

71. Herman Kahn and B. Bruce-Biggs, *Things to Come* (New York: Macmillan, 1972), ix.

72. They were questioned by some—see, for example, Bill Emmott, *The Sun Also Sets* (New York: Simon and Schuster, 1989).

73. Paul Bairoch, "International Industrialization Levels from 1750 to 1980," *Journal of European Economic History,* spring 1982, 14n.

74. Joseph S. Nye Jr., "Asia's First Globalizer," *The Washington Quarterly,* autumn 2000.

75. Prime Minister's Commission, *The Frontier Within* (Tokyo: Cabinet Secretariat, 2000).

76. Hisashi Owada, "The Shaping of World Public Order and the Role of Japan," *Japan Review of International Affairs,* spring 2000, 11.

77. Christopher Layne, "From Preponderance to Offshore Balancing," *International Security,* summer 1997, 86–124.

78. Lampton and May, *A Big Power Agenda for East Asia,* 51.

79. Li Jingjie, "Pillars of the Sino-Russian Partnership," *Orbis,* fall 2000, 530.

80. Mikhail Nosov, *Challenges to the Strategic Balance in East Asia on the Eve of the 21st Century: A View from Russia* (Alexandria, VA: Center for Naval Analysis, 1997), 32.

81. Gilbert Rozman, "A New Sino-Russian-American Triangle?" *Orbis,* autumn 2000, 541–55.

82. Mikhail Gorbachev, speech to Soviet writers, quoted in "Gorbachev on the Future: 'We Will Not Give In,'" *New York Times,* December 22, 1986, A20.

83. Quoted in Stephen Sestanovich, "Gorbachev's Foreign Policy: A Diplomacy of Decline," *Problems of Communism,* January-February 1988, 2–3.

84. World Bank data from http://www.worldbank.org/data/databy-topic/databytopic.html.

85. Peter Semler, "The Russian Economy: Progress and Challenge," *The Atlantic Council Bulletin,* January 2001, 3.

86. Michael Wines, "For All of Russia, Biological Clock Is Running Out," *New York Times,* December 28, 2000, A1.

87. National Intelligence Council, *Global Trends 2015: A Dialogue About the Future with Nongovernment Experts* (Langley, VA: Central Intelligence Agency, 2000), 17, 69.

88. Neal M. Rosendorf, "Social and Cultural Globalization: Concepts, History, and America's Role," in Joseph S. Nye Jr. and John D. Donahue, eds., *Governance in a Globalizing World* (Washington, D.C.: Brookings Institution Press, 2000), 122.

89. National Intelligence Council, *Global Trends 2015,* 66.

90. Again, my thanks to Kennedy School students Ebrahim Afsah and Francisco Balch for their number crunching.

91. Lampton and May, *A Big Power Agenda for East Asia,* using SIPRI data that correct for difficulties in calculating Chinese budgets in Western terms, 13, 31.

92. Wolf et al., *Asian Economic Trends,* 47.

93. Samuel Huntington, "The U.S.—Decline or Renewal?" *Foreign Affairs,* winter 1988–89, 93.

94. David Pryce-Jones, "Bananas Are the Beginning: The Looming War Between America and Europe," *National Review,* April 5, 1999.

95. Martin Feldstein, "EMU and International Conflict," *Foreign Affairs,* November-December 1997.

96. Cherise M. Valles, "Setting the Course on Data Privacy," *International Herald Tribune,* May 28, 2001, 13.

97. Pippa Norris, "Global Governance and Cosmopolitan Citizens," in Nye and Donahue, eds., *Governance in a Globalizing World,* 157.

98. John Vinocur, "Jospin Envisions an Alternative EU," *International Herald Tribune,* May 29, 2001, 1.

99. Andrew Moravscik, "Despotism in Brussels?" *Foreign Affairs,* May-June 2001, 121.

100. Roger Cohen, "A European Identity: Nation-State Losing Ground," *New York Times,* January 14, 2000, A3.

101. Roger Cohen, "Tiffs over Bananas and Child Custody," *New York Times,* May 28, 2000, News of the Week section, 1.

102. Joseph S. Nye Jr., "The US and Europe: Continental Drift?" *International Affairs,* January 2000.

103. Stephen M. Walt, "The Ties That Fray," *The National Interest,* winter 1998–99.

104. Gianna Riotta, "The Coming Identity War," *Foreign Policy,* September-October 2000, 87.

105. John J. Mearsheimer, "Back to the Future: Instability in Europe After the Cold War," *International Security,* summer 1990.

106. "Weathering the Storm," *The Economist,* September 9, 2000, 23.

107. National Intelligence Council, *Global Trends 2015,* 75.

108. Ibid.

109. Roger Cohen, "Tiffs over Bananas."

110. Robert D. Blackwill, *The Future of Transatlantic Relations* (New York: Council on Foreign Relations, 1999).

111. Pascal Boniface, "The Specter of Unilateralism," *The Washington Quarterly,* summer 2001,158.

112. Samuel Huntington, "The Lonely Superpower," *Foreign Affairs,* March-April 1999, 48.

113. International Institute for Strategic Studies (IIIS), *Strategic Survey 2000–2001* (Oxford: Oxford University Press, 2000), entries on noted states.

114. "The Global Giants," *Wall Street Journal,* September 25, 2000, R24; Robert Preston, "Rising and Midnight Suns Shine Brightly," "*Financial Times* Survey," *FT500 Annual Review 2000,* May 4, 2000, 3.

115. James Cox, "US Success Draws Envy, Protests," *USA Today,* August 3, 2000, 1B.

116. Rosendorf, "Social and Cultural Globalization."

117. "Snapshot of Report on Study-Abroad Programs," *Chronicle of Higher Education,* November 17, 2000 (http://chronicle.com/weekly/v47/i12/12a07402.htm).

118. Richard Adams, "U.S. the Dominant Economic Model," *Financial Times Annual Survey: Markets 2000,* January 11, 2000, 24.

119. Figures drawn from *CIA World Factbook 2000* (*http://www.cia. gov/cia/publications/factbook/*) and the World Bank (http://www.world-bank.org/data/wdi2001/pdfs/tab1_1.pdf); *United Nations Human Development Report 2000* (*http://www.undp.org/hdr2000/english/ HDR2000.html*); IISS *Strategic Survey 2000–2001*.

120. See Nye, *Bound to Lead,* chapter 1.

121. Herbert Block, *The Planetary Product in 1980: A Creative Pause?* (Washington, D.C.: U.S. Dept. of State, Bureau of Public Affairs, 1981), 18; Simon Kuznets, *Economic Growth and Structure* (New York: W. W. Norton, 1965); Council on Competitiveness, *Competitiveness Index* (Washington, D.C.: Council on Competitiveness, 1988), appendix II.

122. Adams, "U.S. the Dominant Economic Model," 24.

123. Harry Rowen, "The Prospects Before Us: A World Rich, Democratic, and (Perhaps) Peaceful," unpublished manuscript, June 1993, 29.

124. Kim Nossal, "Lonely Superpower or Unapologetic Hyperpower? Analyzing American Power in the Post-Cold War Era," paper for the South African Political Studies Association, July 1999, 12.

125. My friend Stanley Hoffmann first introduced me to the metaphor of multiple (though not three-dimensional) chess boards. See his *Primacy or World Order* (New York: McGraw-Hill, 1978), 119.

126. Samuel Huntington, "The U.S.—Decline or Renewal?"

127. Josef Joffe, "America the Inescapable," *New York Times* [Sunday] *Magazine,* June 8, 1997, 38.

128. Quoted in R. W. Apple Jr., "As the American Century Extends Its Run," *New York Times,* January 1, 2000, 3.

129. Sebastian Mallaby, "A Mockery in the Eyes of the World," *Washington Post,* January 31, 1999, B5.

CHAPTER 2: THE INFORMATION REVOLUTION

1. Robert Darnton, "An Early Information Society" (presidential address), *American Historical Review,* February 2000, 1.

2. Douglas McGray, "The Silicon Archipelago," *Daedalus,* spring 1999, 147–76.

3. Jeremy Greenwood, *The Third Industrial Revolution: Technology, Productivity, and Income Inequality* (Washington, D.C.: AEI Press, 1997), 20–23; "Electronic Commerce Helps to Fuel US Growth," *Financial Times* (Lon-

don), April 16, 1998, 5; Intel cofounder Gordon Moore formulated his now famous Moore's law of microprocessing power and cost in 1965—as Intel's Web site essay on Moore's law notes, "The average price of a transistor has fallen by six orders of magnitude due to microprocessor development. This is unprecedented in world history; no other manufactured item has decreased in cost so far, so fast" (*http://developer.intel.com/solutions/archive/issue2/focus.htm#OVER*); U.S. Department of Commerce, *The Emerging Digital Economy,* chapter 1, "The Digital Revolution" (*www.doc.gov/ecommerce/danc1.htm*); K. G. Coffman and Andrew Odlyzko, "The Size and Growth of the Internet," *First Monday: Peer-Reviewed Journal on the Internet* (www.firstmonday.dk/isues/issue3_10/coffman/index.html).

4. Richard Adams, "U.S. the Dominant Economic Model," *Financial Times Annual Survey: Markets 2000,* January 11, 2000, 26.

5. Pippa Norris, *The Digital Divide: Civic Engagement, Information Poverty, and the Internet Worldwide* (New York: Cambridge University Press, 2001), 8.

6. Hal Varian, "How Much Information Is There?" (http://www.sims.berkeley.edu/how-much-info/summary.html).

7. See, for example, Peter Drucker, "The Next Information Revolution," *Forbes,* August 24, 1998, 46–58; Alvin Toffler and Heidi Toffler, *The Politics of the Third Wave* (Kansas City, MO: Andrews and McMeel, 1995); Don Tapscott, *The Digital Economy: Promise and Peril in the Age of Networked Intelligence* (New York: McGraw-Hill, 1996); Richard Rosecrance, *The Rise of the Virtual State* (New York: Basic Books, 1999).

8. David S. Landes, *The Unbound Prometheus: Technological Change and Industrial Development in Western Europe from 1750 to the Present* (Cambridge: Cambridge University Press, 1969), chapters 2–3; David Thomson, *England in the Nineteenth Century, 1815–1914* (New York: Viking Penguin, 1978 [1950]), 63–68; Alfred Chandler Jr., *The Visible Hand: The Managerial Revolution in American Business* (Cambridge, MA: Belknap, 1977), 90–91.

9. Zane L. Miller, *The Urbanization of Modern America: A Brief History,* 2nd ed. (San Diego: Harcourt Brace Jovanovitch, 1987), passim.

10. Stuart W. Bruchey, *Growth of the Modern American Economy* (New York: Dodd Mead, 1975); Thomas McCraw, *Prophets of Regulation: Charles Francis Adams, Louis D. Brandeis, James M. Landis, Alfred E. Kahn* (Cambridge, MA: Belknap, 1984), chapters 1–5.

11. At the same time, one must be cautious with grand analogies. Revolution, defined as a disjunction of power, is often difficult to discern except in

retrospect. Moreover, historians differ on the dating and duration of earlier industrial revolutions. The term was not coined until 1886, a century after it began. While there may have been discontinuities in technological progress, with new leading sectors in each era, it has been difficult to specify the timing of long waves or cycles of economic growth. See Daniel Bell, *The Coming of Post-Industrial Society: A Venture in Social Forecasting* (New York: Basic Books, 1999 [1973]), 5. Also Nathan Rosenberg, *Exploring the Black Box: Technology, Economics, and History* (New York: Cambridge University Press, 1994), chapter 4.

12. Bell, *The Coming of Post-Industrial Society*, 94, 97.

13. William Fielding Ogburn, "The Influence of Inventions on American Social Institutions in the Future," *The American Journal of Sociology*, November 1937, 370.

14. Charles Kindleberger, *Centralization Versus Pluralism* (Copenhagen: Copenhagen Business School Press, 1996), 13. See also Gary Marks and Liesbet Hooghe, "Optimality and Authority: A Critique of Neo-Classical Theory," *Journal of Common Market Studies*, December 2000, 795–816.

15. Bell, *The Coming of Post-Industrial Society*, 94.

16. Lester Salamon, "The Rise of the Nonprofit Sector: A Global Associational Revolution," *Foreign Affairs*, July 1994, 109–22; Jessica T. Matthews, "Power Shift," *Foreign Affairs*, January 1997, 50–66; Ann Florini, ed., *The Third Force* (Washington, D.C.: Carnegie Endowment, 2000); *Nonprofit Almanac, 1996–97* (San Francisco: Jossey-Bass, 1996), 29.

17. Carl F. Friedrich and Zbigniew Brzezinski, *Totalitarian Dictatorship and Autocracy*, 2nd ed. (Cambridge, MA: Harvard University Press, 1965).

18. Marshall I. Goldman, *Gorbachev's Challenge: Economic Reform in the Age of High Technology* (New York: W. W. Norton, 1987), chapter 2.

19. Ibid., 15.

20. Abel Aganbegyan, "Economic Performance," in Abel Aganbegyan, ed., *Perestroika 1989* (New York: Scribner's, 1988), 101.

21. "Life Beyond the Kremlin," *New York Times*, May 30, 1988, 7–8.

22. "Soviets Launch Computer Literacy Drive," *Science*, January 10, 1986, 109–10; "Glasnost: Soviet Computer Lag, *Science*, August 26, 1988, 1034.

23. Sheila McNulty, "Equipping a Nation for the New Economy," *Financial Times* (London), September 15, 2000, 12.

24. Author's conversation with Lee Kuan Yew, Singapore, January 1999.

25. Tony Saich, "Globalization, Governance, and the Authoritarian State: China," in Joseph S. Nye Jr. and John Donahue, eds., *Governance in a Globalizing World* (Washington, D.C.: Brookings Institution Press), 222.

26. Wang Jisi, "The Internet in China: A New Fantasy?" *New Perspectives Quarterly*, winter 2001, 22; Richard McGregor, "Internet Chatrooms," *Financial Times* (London), November 13, 2000, viii.

27. Elizabeth Rosenthal, "China Struggles to Ride Herd on Ever More Errant Media," *New York Times*, March 17, 2001.

28. Susan Lawrence and David Murphy, "How to Start a Cold War," *Far Eastern Economic Review*, April 12, 2001, 15.

29. Saich, "Globalization, Governance, and the Authoritarian State," 223.

30. Lee Kuan Yew interview with John Thornhill and Sheil McNulty, *Financial Times* (London), April 11, 2001, 4.

31. John Thornhill, "Asia's Old Order Falls into the Net," *Financial Times* (London), March 17, 2001, 7.

32. Ibid.

33. Organization for Economic Cooperation and Development, "The Presence of Government in National Economies," table 1, "General Government Total Outlays" (www.oecd.org/puma/stats/window/index.htm#).

34. Susan Strange, *The Retreat of the State* (Cambridge, UK: Cambridge University Press, 1996), 14.

35. Douglass North, *Structure and Change in Economic History* (New York: W. W. Norton), 163–64. See also Paul A. David, "Understanding Digital Technology's Evolution and the Path of Measured Productivity Growth: Present and Future in the Mirror of the Past," in Erik Brynjolfsson and Brian Kahin, eds., *Understanding the Digital Economy* (Cambridge, MA: MIT Press, 2000), 50–92.

36. "Productivity: Lost in Cyberspace," *The Economist*, September 13, 1997, 72.

37. U.S. Department of Commerce, "Digital Economy 2000" (http://www.esa.doc.gov/de2000.pdf).

38. Drucker, "The Next Information Revolution."

39. Friedrich and Brzezinski, *Totalitarian Dictatorship and Autocracy*. On the other hand, as films, cassettes, and faxes spread, the later technologies of the second information revolution helped to undermine governmental efforts at information autarky—witness the Soviet Union and Eastern Europe. The overall effects were not always democratizing. In some cases, such as Iran, the technologies of the second information revolution merely changed the nature of the autocracy.

40. Lawrence Lessig, *Code and Other Laws of Cyberspace* (New York: Basic Books, 2000).

41. For example, Ian Clarke, the youthful Irish inventor of Freenet, says he is a free-speech absolutist who makes no exception for child pornogra-

phy or terrorism. "My point of view is not held by most people, but the technology has given me the ability to do what I think is right without having to convince anyone." "Entertainment Industry Vows to Fight Against Online Piracy," *Boston Globe,* May 31, 2000, 1.

42. Ithiel de Sola Pool, *Technologies of Freedom* (Cambridge, MA: Belknap, 1983).

43. Norris, *The Digital Divide,* 232.

44. For speculation on how the Internet will affect government, see Elaine Kamarck and Joseph S. Nye Jr., eds., *Democracy.com?* (Hollis, NH: Hollis Publishing, 1999), chapter 1.

45. See Toffler and Toffler, *The Politics of the Third Wave;* Drucker, "The Next Information Revolution."

46. Esther Dyson, *Release 2.1: A Design for Living in the Digital Age* (New York: Broadway Books, 1998).

47. Robert O. Keohane and Joseph S. Nye Jr., *Transnational Relations and World Politics* (Cambridge, MA: Harvard University Press, 1997).

48. Peter Spiro, "The New Sovereigntists," *Foreign Affairs,* November-December 2000.

49. John G. Ruggie, "Territoriality and Beyond: Problematizing Modernity in International Relations," *International Organization,* winter 1993, 143, 155.

50. Henry H. Perrritt Jr., "The Internet as a Threat to Sovereignty?" *Indiana Journal of Global Legal Studies,* spring 1998, 426.

51. Saskia Sassen, "On the Internet and Sovereignty," *Indiana Journal of Global Legal Studies,* spring 1998, 551.

52. Joseph Quinlan and Marc Chandler, "The U.S. Trade Deficit: A Dangerous Illusion," *Foreign Affairs,* May-June 2001, 92, 95.

53. Ruggie, "Territoriality and Beyond," 172.

54. Hendryk Spruyt, *The Sovereign State and Its Competitors* (Princeton: Princeton University Press, 1994).

55. Stephen Krasner, "Sovereignty," *Foreign Policy,* January-February 2001, 24; see also Linda Weiss, *The Myth of the Powerless State* (Ithaca, NY: Cornell University Press, 1998). See also "Geography and the Net," *The Economist,* August 11, 2001, 18–20.

56. Stephen E. Flynn, "Beyond Border Control," *Foreign Affairs,* November-December 2000, 57–68.

57. U.S. Commission on National Security in the Twenty-first Century, *Road Map for National Security: Imperative for Change* (http://www.nssg.gov/PhaseIIIFR.pdf), chapter 1.

58. James Adams, "Virtual Defense," *Foreign Affairs*, May-June 2001, 98–112.

59. Adam Roberts, "The So-called 'Right' of Humanitarian Intervention," *Yearbook of International Humanitarian Law*, summer 2001.

60. Harold Guetzkow, *Multiple Loyalties: Theoretical Approach to a Problem in International Organization* (Princeton: Princeton University Press, 1955).

61. Benedict Anderson, *Imagined Communities: Reflections on the Origin and Spread of Nationalism* (New York: Verso, 1991).

62. Norris, *The Digital Divide*, 191.

63. Florini, *The Third Force*, chapter 1; Margaret E. Keck and Kathryn Sikkink, *Activists Beyond Borders: Advocacy Networks in International Politics* (Ithaca, NY: Cornell University Press, 1998), chapter 2; James N. Rosenau, *Turbulence in World Politics* (Princeton: Princeton University Press, 1990), 409; "The Non-Governmental Order," *The Economist*, December 11, 1999.

64. Michael Edwards, *NGO Rights and Responsibilities* (London: The Foreign Policy Centre, 2000); Florini, *The Third Force*; Jessica T. Matthews, "Power Shift," *Foreign Affairs*, January 1997.

65. Peter M. Haas, "Introduction: Epistemic Communities and International Policy Coordination," *International Organization*, winter 1992.

66. At the beginning of the new century, the United States had 159 million computers in use; all of Latin America had only 18 million. Of 350 million Internet users, nearly half were in North America; less than 0.5 percent were in Latin America. North America had 493 Internet users per thousand population, Western Europe 221, the Middle East and Africa 8. "Innovation and Technology," *Wall Street Journal*, September 25, 2000, R6.

67. Norris, *The Digital Divide*, 8.

68. Editorial, "The Digital Divide," *Far Eastern Economic Review*, April 12, 2001, 6.

69. Robert Litan, "The Internet Economy," *Foreign Policy*, March-April 2001, 16.

70. See Suzanne Daly, "French Prosecutor Investigates US Global Listening System," *New York Times*, July 5, 2000, A7.

71. Douglas McGray, "The Silicon Archipelago," 167.

72. Clayton Christensen, "The Great Disruption," *Foreign Affairs*, March-April 2001.

73. "Top-Secret Kodak Moment in Space Shakes Global Security," *Christian Science Monitor*, March 21, 2000, 2.

74. Newt Gingrich, "Threats of Mass Destruction," *Information Security,* April 2001 (http://www.infosecuritymag.com/articles/april01/columns_se-curity_persp.shtml).

75. Joseph S. Nye Jr. and William A. Owens, "America's Information Edge," *Foreign Affairs,* March-April 1996.

76. I owe these distinctions to Robert O. Keohane. See Robert O. Keo-hane and Joseph S. Nye Jr., "Power and Interdependence in the Information Age," *Foreign Affairs,* fall 1998.

77. Herbert A. Simon, "Information 101: It's Not What You Know, It's How You Know It," *The Journal for Quality and Participation,* July-August 1998, 30–33.

78. Of course, as I argued above, soft power varies with the targeted audi-ence. Thus American individualism may be popular in Latin America at the same time that it appears offensively libertine in some Middle Eastern countries. Moreover, governments can gain and lose soft power depending on their performance at home.

79. Richard Pells, *Not Like Us* (New York: Basic Books, 1997), 31–32.

80. Ibid., 33, xiii.

81. Jerome C. Glenn, "Japan: Cultural Power of the Future," *Nikkei Weekly,* December 7, 1992, 7.

82. "Multinational Movies: Questions on Politics," *New York Times,* No-vember 27, 1990, D7.

83. "Japanese News Media Join Export Drive," *International Herald Tri-bune,* May 10, 1991; David Sanger, "NHK of Japan Ends Plan for Global News Service," *New York Times,* December 9, 1991.

84. Calvin Sims, "Japan Beckons and East Asia's Youth Fall in Love," *New York Times,* December 5, 1999, A3; "Advance of the Amazonesu," *The Econo-mist,* July 22, 2000, 61.

85. Mark Huband, "Egypt Tries to Tempt Back Broadcasters," *Financial Times* (London), March 7, 2000, 14.

86. John Kifner, "Tale of Two Uprisings," *New York Times,* November 18, 2000, A6.

87. Chris Hedges, "Iran Is Unable to Stem the West's Cultural Invasion," *New York Times,* March 28, 1992, A11.

88. United States Information Agency Office of Research, "European Opinion Alert," March 16, 1994, and May 27, 1994.

89. Josef Joffe, "America the Inescapable," *New York Times* [Sunday] *Mag-azine,* June 8, 1997, 38.

90. Dominique Moisi, "America the Triumphant," *Financial Times* (London), February 9, 1998, 12; Moisi, "The Right Argument at the Wrong Time," *Financial Times* (London), November 22, 1999, 13.

91. Quoted in Todd Gitlin, "World Leaders: Mickey, et al.," *New York Times*, May 3, 1992, Arts and Leisure section, 1.

92. Neal M. Rosendorf, "Social and Cultural Globalization: Concepts, History, and America's Role," in Nye and Donahue, eds., *Governance in a Globalizing World.*

93. Todd Gitlin, "Taking the World by (Cultural) Force," *The Straits Times* (Singapore), January 11, 1999, 2.

94. Elisabeth Rosenthal, "Chinese Test New Weapon From West: Lawsuits," *New York Times*, June 16, 2001.

95. Walter LaFeber, *Michael Jordan and the New Global Capitalism* (New York: Norton, 1999), 157.

96. Data drawn from *CIA World Factbook 2000* (*http://www.cia.gov/cia/publications/factbook/*) and *Hoover's Handbook of World Business 2001* (Austin: Reference Press, 2001).

97. Gordon Smith and Moises Naim, *Altered States: Globalization, Sovereignty and Governance* (Ottawa: International Development Research Centre, 2000), 10.

CHAPTER 3: GLOBALIZATION

1. "Mosquito Virus Exposes a Hole in the Safety Net," *New York Times*, October 4, 1999, A1.

2. See, for example, "Warning—*Bioinvasion*" (full-page advertisement), *New York Times*, September 20, 1999, A11.

3. David Held et al., *Global Transformations: Politics, Economics and Culture* (Stanford: Stanford University Press, 1999), 21–22. On early globalization, see "Economic Focus: 1492 and All That," *The Economist*, August 25, 2001, 61.

4. Karl Marx and Friedrich Engels, *The Communist Manifesto* (Oxford: Oxford University Press, 1992).

5. Adam Smith, *The Wealth of Nations* (New York: Random House, 1985), book 4, chapter 6, part 3.

6. Hubert Védrine with Dominique Moisi, *France in an Age of Globalization* (Washington, D.C.: Brookings Institution Press, 2001), 3.

7. Darrin McMahon, "The France That Says No," *Correspondence,* winter 1999–2000, 27.

8. Roger Cohen, "Fearful over the Future, Europe Seizes on Food," *New York Times,* August 29, 1999, section 4, l.

9. "Iranian, in Paris Speech, Aims a Barb at U.S.," *New York Times,* October 29, 1999, A8.

10. Barbara Wallraff, "What Global Language?" *The Atlantic Monthly,* November 2000.

11. Michael Elliott, "A Target Too Good to Resist," *Newsweek,* January 31, 2000, 27–28.

12. Anthony Giddens, *Runaway World: How Globalization Is Reshaping Our Lives* (New York : Routledge, 2000), 22.

13. Kishore Mahbubani, "The Rest of the West?" text of RSA/BBC World Lectures, London, June 1, 2000 (http://www.bbc.co.uk/worldservice/people/features/world_lectures/mahbub_lect.shtml), 26.

14. Indeed, one can trace an unbroken chain of European hostility and anxiety toward the United States from well back into the nineteenth century through the present. See Neal M. Rosendorf, "The Life and Times of Samuel Bronston, Builder of Hollywood in Madrid: A Study in the International Scope and Influence of American Popular Culture" (Ph.D. dissertation, Harvard University, 2000), "Appendix: The Power of American Pop Culture—Evolution of an Elitist Critique," 402–15 and passim.

15. Neal M. Rosendorf, "Social and Cultural Globalization: Concepts, History, and America's Role," in Joseph S. Nye Jr. and John D. Donahue, eds., *Governance in a Globalizing World* (Washington, D.C.: Brookings Institution Press, 2000), 133, n. 51.

16. Frederick Schauer, "The Politics and Incentives of Legal Transplantation," in Nye and Donahue, eds., *Governance in a Globalizing World.*

17. Walter LaFeber, *Michael Jordan and the New Global Capitalism* (New York: Norton, 1999), 110.

18. For a network of relationships to be considered global, it must include multicontinental distances, not simply regional networks. Globalization refers to the shrinkage of distance, but on a large scale. It can be contrasted with localization, nationalization, or regionalization. Globalism is the condition of worldwide interdependence. Globalization is the increase and deglobalization the decline of such interdependence.

19. United Nations Development Programme (UNDP), *Human Development Report* (New York: Oxford University Press, 1999).

20. Dani Rodrik, "Sense and Nonsense in the Globalization Debate," *Foreign Policy*, summer 1997, 19–37.

21. Keith Griffin, "Globalization and the Shape of Things to Come," *Macalester International: Globalization and Economic Space*, spring 1999, 3; "One World?" *The Economist*, October 18, 1997, 79–80.

22. John F. Helliwell, *How Much Do National Borders Matter?* (Washington, D.C.: Brookings Institution Press, 1998).

23. Samuel Huntington, *The Clash of Civilizations and the Remaking of World Order* (New York: Simon and Schuster, 1996).

24. William J. Broad, "Smallpox: The Once and Future Scourge?" *New York Times*, June 15, 1999, F1.

25. Jared Diamond, *Guns, Germs and Steel: The Fates of Human Societies* (New York: W. W. Norton, 1998), 202, 210; William H. McNeill, *Plagues and Peoples* (London: Scientific Book Club, 1979), 168; see as well Alfred W. Crosby, *Ecological Imperialism: The Biological Expansion of Europe, 900-1900* (Cambridge: Cambridge University Press, 1986).

26. United Kingdom Ministry of Defense, *The Future Strategic Context for Defence* (London, 2001), 6.

27. The foot and mouth disease that damaged European livestock in 2001 was an example in which "an Asian virus finding no natural defenses was able to propagate at an alarming rate." Barry James, "Mischievous Species Capitalize on Globalization," *International Herald Tribune*, May 21, 2001, 1.

28. Alfred Crosby, *The Columbian Exchange: Biological and Cultural Consequences of 1492* (Westport, CT: Greenwood Press, 1972).

29. Craig Smith, "150 Nations Start Groundwork for Global Warming Policies," *New York Times*, January 18, 2001, A7.

30. James J. McCarthy, "The Scope of the IPCC Third Assessment Report," *The Climate Report*, winter 2001, 3. I am indebted to Ted Parson for help on this point.

31. Katharine Q. Seelye, "In a Shift, White House Cites Global Warming as a Problem," *New York Times*, June 8, 2001, A18.

32. Held et al., *Global Transformations*, 295–96.

33. Karl Polanyi, *The Great Transformation* (New York: Rinehart, 1944), chapters 19, 20.

34. John G. Ruggie, "International Regimes, Transactions, and Change: Embedded Liberalism in the Postwar Economic Order," *International Organization*, spring 1982, quoted in Dani Rodrik, *Has Globalization Gone Too Far?* (Washington, D.C.: Institute for International Economics, 1997), 65.

35. Merilee S. Grindle, "Ready or Not: The Developing World and Globalization," in Nye and Donahue, eds., *Governance in a Globalizing World.*

36. Thomas Friedman, *The Lexus and the Olive Tree: Understanding Globalization* (New York: Farrar, Straus and Giroux, 1999), 7–8.

37. "A Semi-Integrated World," *The Economist,* September 11, 1999, 42.

38. Joseph Stiglitz, "Weightless Concerns," *Financial Times* (London), February 3, 1999, 14.

39. Robert Jervis, *System Effects: Complexity in Political and Social Life* (Princeton: Princeton University Press, 1997).

40. "One World?" *The Economist,* October 18 1997, 80.

41. Greenspan quoted in Friedman, *The Lexus and the Olive Tree,* 368.

42. Held et al., *Global Transformations,* 235.

43. "China Ponders New Rules of 'Unrestricted War,' " *Washington Post,* August 8, 1999, l.

44. The biggest change in velocity came with the steamship and especially the telegraph. The Atlantic cable of 1866 reduced the time of transmission of information between London and New York from well over a week to a few minutes—hence by a factor of about a thousand. The telephone, by contrast, increased the velocity of such messages by minutes (since telephone messages do not require decoding), and the Internet, as compared to the telephone, not much at all.

45. Friedman, *The Lexus and the Olive Tree,* 41–58.

46. John Maynard Keynes, *The Economic Consequences of the Peace* (London: Penguin, 1988), 11.

47. Frances Cairncross, *The Death of Distance: How the Communications Revolution Will Change Our Lives* (Boston: Harvard Business School Press, 1997).

48. Daniel Brass and Marlene Burckhardt, "Centrality and Power in Organizations," in Nitin Nohria and Robert Eccles, eds., *Networks and Organizations* (Boston: Harvard Business School Press, 1992); John Padgett and Christopher Ansell, "Robust Actors and the Rise of the Medici, 1400–1434," *American Journal of Sociology,* May 1993. I am indebted to David Lazer and Jane Fountain for help on this point.

49. Ronald Burt, *Structural Holes: The Social Structure of Competition* (Cambridge, MA: Harvard University Press, 1992), chapter 1.

50. Alec Klein, "Seeking to Conquer the Globe, AOL Is Advertising Local Appeal," *International Herald Tribune,* May 31, 2001, 1.

51. "Graphiti," *Red Herring,* January 30, 2001, 39.

52. Tony Saich, "Globalization, Governance, and the Authoritarian State: China," in Nye and Donahue, eds., *Governance in a Globalizing World,* 224.

53. "America's World," *The Economist,* October 23, 1999, 15.

54. Bill Joy et al., "Why the Future Doesn't Need Us," *Wired,* April 2000.

55. See "Multiple Modernities," special issue of *Daedalus,* winter 2000. See also John Tomlinson, *Globalization and Culture* (Chicago: University of Chicago Press, 1999).

56. Alex Inkeles, *One World Emerging? Convergence and Divergence in Industrial Societies* (Boulder: Westview, 1998), xiv–xv.

57. Sharon Moshavi, "Japan's Teens Take Trip to US Hip-Hop," *Boston Globe,* October 29, 2000, A18.

58. Mario Vargas Llosa, "The Culture of Liberty," *Foreign Policy,* January-February 2001 (http://www.foreignpolicy.com/issue_janfeb_2001/vargasllosa.html).

59. Frederick Schauer, "The Politics and Incentives of Legal Transplantation," in Nye and Donahue, eds., *Governance in a Globalizing World,* 258–60.

60. Jonathan Freedland, "A Subtle Form of Dissent," *Newsweek,* January 31, 2000, 22.

61. Giddens, *Runaway World,* 31.

62. Dan Barry, "Gaelic Comes Back on Ireland's Byways and Airwaves," *New York Times,* July 25, 2000, A6.

63. Raymond Vernon, *Sovereignty at Bay: The Multinational Spread of U.S. Enterprises* (New York: Basic Books, 1971).

64. Giddens, *Runaway World,* 59, 67.

65. UNDP, *Human Development Report,* 2–3.

66. The measurement of global inequality depends on assumptions and definitions used. If countries are treated equally (not weighted by population) and income is measured in purchasing power parity, then world income distribution has become more unequal over the past few decades. If people are treated equally (so China and India count more), then income distribution shows little change. Some recent World Bank studies based on household surveys (rather than average GDP) show rising inequality from 1988 to 1993, but these do not include public expenditures. Robert Wade, "Winners and Losers," and "Of Rich and Poor," *The Economist,* April 28, 2001, 72–74, 80.

67. Of the forty-three poorest countries, a third were quite open, but of the twenty-four poorest African countries that made opening reforms in the last decade, ten also suffered from wars or coups. "Not by Their Bootstraps Alone," *The Economist,* May 12, 2001, 74.

68. See Dani Rodrik, *The New Global Economy and Developing Countries: Making Openness Work* (Washington, D.C.: Overseas Development Council, 1999); also Richard N. Cooper, "Growth and Inequality: The Role of Trade and Investment," Weatherhead Center for International Affairs (Harvard University), Working Paper 01–07, 2001.

69. World Bank, *Knowledge for Development: World Development Report 1998–99* (New York: Oxford University Press, 1999), table 5, 198–99.

70. UNDP, *Human Development Report,* 3.

71. Ibid., 156.

72. Saich, "Globalization, Governance, and the Authoritarian State," 217–20.

73. Kevin O'Rourke and Jeffrey Williamson, *Globalization and History: The Evolution of a Nineteenth-Century Atlantic Economy* (Cambridge, MA: MIT Press, 1999), 9–10.

74. Polanyi, *The Great Transformation,* chapter 18.

75. John Tagliabue, "With Eye on Unequal World Wealth, Young Europeans Converge on Genoa," *New York Times,* July 22, 2001, A8.

76. "The FP Interview: Lori's War," *Foreign Policy,* Spring 2000.

77. Michael J. Sandel, *Democracy's Discontents* (Cambridge, MA: Harvard University Press, 1996), 338n.

78. See especially UNDP, *Human Development Report,* chapter 5.

79. David Lazer, "Regulatory Interdependence and International Governance," *Journal of European Public Policy,* June 2001, 474–92.

80. For opposing arguments, see, for example, Susan Strange, *The Retreat of the State: The Diffusion of Power in the World Economy* (New York : Cambridge University Press, 1996), and Linda Weiss, *The Myth of the Powerless State* (Ithaca: Cornell University Press, 1998).

81. Cary Coglianese, "Globalization and the Design of International Institutions," and Deborah Hurley and Viktor Mayer-Schoenberger, "Information Policy and Governance," both in Nye and Donahue, eds., *Governance in a Globalizing World.*

82. Robert O. Keohane and Joseph S. Nye Jr., "Transgovernmental Relations and International Organizations," *World Politics,* October 1972; Anne-Marie Slaughter, "The Real New World Order," *Foreign Affairs,* September-October 1997.

83. Saskia Sassen, "Embedding the Global in the National: Implications for the Role of the State," *Macalester International,* spring 1999 ("Globalization and Economic Space"), 39; see also Saskia Sassen, *Losing Control? Sovereignty in an Age of Globalization* (New York: Columbia University Press, 1996).

84. Edward Alden, "Brands Feel the Impact as Activists Target Customers," *Financial Times* (London), July 18, 2001, 7.

85. "Good Names," *Financial Times* (London), April 23, 2001, 24.

86. David Ignatius, "Try a Network Approach to Global Problem-Solving," *International Herald Tribune,* January 29, 2001, 8.

87. Richard Falk and Andrew Strauss, "Toward Global Parliament," *Foreign Affairs,* January-February 2001, 216.

88. Global Public Policy Project home page (http://*www.globalpublicpolicy.net*).

89. Dennis Thompson, "Democratic Theory and Global Society," *Journal of Political Philosophy,* June 1999.

90. Giddens, *Runaway World,* 97.

91. John Bolton quoted in Anne-Marie Slaughter, "Building Global Democracy," *Chicago Journal of International Law,* fall 2000, 225.

92. Robert Dahl, a leading democratic theorist, also argues that international organizations may be necessary for bargaining among countries, but they are not likely to be democratic. Robert Dahl, "Can International Organizations Be Democratic? A Skeptic's View," in Ian Shapiro and Casiano Hacker-Cordon, eds., *Democracy's Edges* (Cambridge: Cambridge University Press, 1999), 32.

93. "The FP Interview: Lori's War," 37, 47. See also Richard Longworth, "Government Without Democracy," *The American Prospect,* summer 2001, 19–22.

94. Pippa Norris, "Global Governance and Cosmopolitan Citizens," in Nye and Donahue, eds., *Governance in a Globalizing World.*

95. Falk and Strauss, "Toward Global Parliament," 212–13.

96. Slaughter, "Building Global Democracy," 225.

CHAPTER 4: THE HOME FRONT

1. Of course there were many more causes of this complex phenomenon. See Ramsay MacMullen, *Corruption and the Decline of Rome* (New Haven: Yale University Press, 1988).

2. The phrase is from the classic treatment by Cecil V. Crabb Jr. and Pat M. Holt, *Invitation to Struggle: Congress, the President and Foreign Policy* (Washington, D.C.: Congressional Quarterly Press, 1980).

3. Dexter Perkins, "What Is Distinctly American About the Foreign Policy of the United States?" in Glyndon Van Dusen and Richard Wade, eds., *For-

eign Policy and the American Spirit (Ithaca: Cornell University Press, 1957), 3–15.

4. James Schlesinger, *America at Century's End* (New York: Columbia University Press, 1989), 87.

5. "One Nation, Fairly Divisible, Under God," *The Economist*, January 20, 2001, 21–24.

6. Gertrude Himmelfarb, *One Nation, Two Cultures* (New York, Knopf, 1999), 20.

7. Robert H. Bork, *Slouching Toward Gomorrah: Modern Liberalism and American Decline* (New York: Reagan Books, 1996); Richard Neuhaus, "The End of Democracy? The Judicial Usurpation of Politics," *First Things*, November 1996, 18.

8. Alan Wolfe, *One Nation, After All: What Americans Really Think About God, Country, Family, Racism, Welfare, Immigration, Homosexuality, Work, the Right, the Left and Each Other* (New York: Viking, 1998), 15, 176, 165.

9. Derek Bok, *The State of the Nation* (Cambridge, MA: Harvard University Press, 1996), 359.

10. Gregg Easterbrook, "America the O.K.," *The New Republic*, January 4, 1999, 19–25.

11. Theodore Caplow, Louis Hicks, and Ben Wattenberg, *The First Measured Century: An Illustrated Guide to Trends in America, 1900–2000* (Washington, D.C.: AEI Press, 2001), 106.

12. David Whitman, *The Optimism Gap: The I'm OK—They're Not Syndrome and the Myth of American Decline* (New York: Walker, 1998).

13. Christopher Jencks, foreword to Whitman, *The Optimism Gap*, ix.

14. Charles Dickens, *Martin Chuzzlewit* (1844), quoted in Whitman, *The Optimism Gap*, 85.

15. Robert Samuelson, *The Good Life and Its Discontents* (New York: Times Books, 1995).

16. Himmelfarb, *One Nation, Two Cultures*, 141.

17. Bok, *The State of the Nation*, 7, 388, 395. See also "What a Lot of SterEUtypes," *The Economist*, October 23, 1999, 60.

18. Tamar Lewin, "Family Decay Global, Study Says," *New York Times*, May 30, 1995, 5.

19. Bok, *The State of the Nation*, 376.

20. Himmelfarb, *One Nation, Two Cultures*, 139.

21. Franklin quoted in George Borjas, *Heaven's Door: Immigration Policy and the American Economy* (Princeton: Princeton University Press, 1999), 3.

22. See, for example, Peter Brimelow, *Alien Nation: Common Sense About America's Immigration Disaster* (New York: Random House, 1995), and Chilton Williamson Jr., *The Immigration Mystique: America's False Conscience* (New York: Basic Books, 1996).

23. Wolfe, *One Nation, After All,* 138; Kenneth Scheve and Matthew Slaughter, *Globalization and the Perceptions of American Workers* (Washington, D.C.: Institute for International Economics, 2001), 35.

24. Arthur Schlesinger, *The Disuniting of America: Reflections on a Multicultural Society,* rev. ed. (New York: W. W. Norton, 1998).

25. Caplow, Hicks, and Wattenberg, *The First Measured Century,* 14–19.

26. U.S. Census Bureau, "The Foreign Born Population in the United States," *Current Population Reports,* March 2000, 1.

27. Borjas, *Heaven's Door,* 8n.

28. Eric Schmitt, "New Census Shows Hispanics Are Even with Blacks in US," *New York Times,* March 8, 2001, 1.

29. Steven Holmes, "Census Sees a Profound Ethnic Shift in U.S.," *New York Times,* March 14, 1996, 16.

30. Brimelow, *Alien Nation,* 258, 208, 217.

31. James Smith and Barry Edmonston, eds., *The New Americans: Economic, Demographic, and Fiscal Effects of Immigration* (Washington, D.C.: National Academy Press, 1997), 13.

32. "The New Americans," *The Economist,* March 11, 2000, survey 13–14.

33. Wolfe, *One Nation, After All,* 163.

34. Nicholas Eberstadt, "The Population Implosion," *Foreign Policy,* March-April 2001, 43, 49.

35. Barbara Crossette, "Against a Trend, U.S. Population Will Bloom, UN Says," *New York Times,* February 28, 2001, A6.

36. Nicholas Eberstadt, "World Population Prospects: The Shape of Things to Come," American Enterprise Institute, *On the Issue,* April 2001, 2.

37. "Silicon Valley's Skilled Immigrants: Generating Jobs and Wealth for California," Research Brief Issue 21, Public Policy Institute of California, June 1999, 2.

38. *Washington Post*/Kaiser Family Foundation/Harvard University Survey Project, 1996; Harris Poll, 1996; Hart-Teeter Poll for the Council of Excellence in Government, reported in the *Washington Post,* March 24, 1997. See also Seymour Martin Lipset and William Schneider, *The Confidence Gap* (Baltimore: Johns Hopkins University Press, 1987).

39. Harris Poll, 1966–1996. There are some exceptions. For example, confidence in science remains strong, and in Europe, confidence in business has risen.

40. See Samuelson, *The Good Life and Its Discontents.*

41. General Social Survey, spring 1994, National Opinion Research Center, Chicago. Congress received 58 percent and the executive branch received 63 percent. The survey, prepared by Survey Research Consultants International, is reprinted in Elizabeth Hann Hastings and Philip K. Hastings, eds., *Index to International Public Opinion*, 1994–1995 (Westport, CT: Greenwood Press, 1996). See as well Gallup poll of eighteen countries, "Satisfaction Index," survey no. 22–50001–018 in *The Gallup Poll, Public Opinion 1995* (Wilmington, DE: Scholarly Research, 1996).

42. Daniel Katz et al., *Bureaucratic Encounters: A Pilot Study in the Evaluation of Government Services* (Ann Arbor: Survey Research Center, University of Michigan, 1975) 178.

43. Lipset and Schneider, *The Confidence Gap*, 402.

44. Thomas E. Patterson, *Out of Order* (New York: Vintage, 1994). See also Gary Orren, "Fall from Grace: The Public's Loss of Faith in Government," in Joseph S. Nye Jr., Philip D. Zelikow, and David C. King, eds., *Why People Don't Trust Government* (Cambridge, MA: Harvard University Press, 1997).

45. S. Robert Lichter, Linda S. Lichter, and Daniel Amundson, *Images of Government in TV Entertainment* (Washington, D.C.: Council for Excellence in Government, 2001), 7, 17, 62 and passim.

46. Whitman, *The Optimism Gap*, 92.

47. Suzanne Garment, *Scandal: The Culture of Mistrust in American Politics* (New York: Doubleday, 1991).

48. Steven Holmes, "Defying Forecasts, Census Response Ends Declining Trend," *New York Times*, September 20, 2000, 23.

49. Richard Berke, "Nonvoters Are No More Alienated than Voters, a Survey Shows," *New York Times*, May 30, 1996, A21; also "Conventions and Their Enemies," *The Economist*, July 22, 2000, 34.

50. See Nye, Zelikow, and King, eds., *Why People Don't Trust Government*, chapters 9, 10, and conclusion. See also Pippa Norris, ed., *Critical Citizens: Global Support for Democratic Government* (New York: Oxford University Press, 1999).

51. Alexis de Tocqueville, *Democracy in America*, ed. J. Mayer, trans. George Lawrence (Garden City, NY: Doubleday, 1969), 513.

52. Robert D. Putnam, *Bowling Alone: The Collapse and Revival of American Community* (New York: Simon and Schuster, 2000), section 4.

53. Ibid., 346.

54. Ibid., 25.

55. Alan Wolfe, "American Society Unglued?" *Harvard Magazine,* July-August 2000, 28–29.

56. Pew Partnership for Civic Change, "New Survey Dispels Myths on Citizen Engagement" (*http://www*.pew-partnership.org/newsroom/rwa (pr).html).

57. Putnam, *Bowling Alone,* 48.

58. T. R. Reid, "Empty Naves Echo an Age's Loss of Faith," *International Herald Tribune,* May 7, 2001, 1.

59. Robert W. Fogel, *The Fourth Great Awakening and the Future of Egalitarianism* (Chicago: University of Chicago Press, 2000), 7.

60. "Can America Compete?" *Business Week,* April 20, 1987, 45.

61. Michael Porter and Jeffrey Sachs, *The Global Competitiveness Report 2000* (New York: Oxford University Press, 2000), 11.

62. International Monetary Fund, "United States of America: Selected Issues," IMF Staff Country Report no. 00/112, August 2000, 4.

63. The columnist Jeffrey Madrick warns that we have been here before: "If the economy of the 1990s was indeed 'new,' America enjoyed a new economy in every generation of its history, beginning with the cotton economy after the War of 1812, and extending through canals, water mills, steamships, mass retailers, steel and oil, railroads, electric appliances, autos and television over the course of the next two centuries." Jeffrey Madrick, "Tax Cuts Are in the Air, and Both Political Parties Have Their Heads in the Sand," *New York Times,* March 15, 2001, C2.

64. "Productivity, Profits and Promises," *The Economist,* February 10, 2001, 24.

65. Quoted in IMF Economic Forum, "The Information Economy: New Paradigm or Old Fashion," December 12, 2000 (*http://www*.imf.org/external/np/tr/2000).

66. *Economic Report of the President* (Washington, D.C.: U.S. Government Printing Office, 2001), 25.

67. IMF Economic Forum, "The Information Economy."

68. *Economic Report of the President,* 23, 145.

69. See "Productivity on Stilts," "Performing Miracles," and "Another Look at Productivity," *The Economist,* respectively June 10, 2000, 86; June 17,

2000, 78; and February 10, 2001, 78. See also William Nordhaus, "Productivity Growth and the New Economy," National Bureau of Economic Research Working Paper 8096, January 2001.

70. "A Spanner in the Productivity Miracle," *The Economist*, August 11, 2001, 55.

71. Richard Stevenson, "Fed Chief Calls Recent Rate of Growth Unsustainable," *New York Times*, October 29, 1999, C6.

72. Dale Jorgenson and Kevin Stiroh, "Raising the Speed Limit: US Economic Growth in the Information Age," manuscript, May 2000.

73. Sylvia Nasar, "Economists Simply Shrug as Savings Rate Declines," *New York Times*, December 21, 1998, A14.

74. Milka Kirova and Robert Lipsey, "Measuring Real Investment: Trends in the United States and International Comparisons," National Bureau of Economic Research, Working Paper 6404, 7.

75. "America's Fantastic Factories," *The Economist*, June 8, 1996, 17; "The Vice of Thrift," *The Economist*, March 21, 1998, 88.

76. Franco Modigliani and Robert Solow, "America Is Borrowing Trouble," *New York Times*, April 9, 2001, A17.

77. Ethan Bronner, "Long a Leader, US Now Lags in High School Graduation Rates," *New York Times*, November 24, 1998, A1.

78. Martin Wolf, "Mediocrity Flourishes When an Inspector Calls," *Financial Times* (London), April 16, 2001, 17.

79. Caplow, Hicks, and Wattenberg, *The First Measured Century*, 53, 65; Bok, *The State of the Nation*, 61; "A Sorry State," *The Economist*, July 1, 2000, 80.

80. Peter Applebome, "Student Test Scores Show Slow but Steady Gains at Nation's Schools," *New York Times*, September 3, 1997, B8; Richard Rothstein, "Goals 2000 Scoreboard: Failure Pitches a Shutout," *New York Times*, December 22, 1999, B15.

81. U.S. Department of Education, National Center for Educational Statistics, *The Condition of Education 2000* (Washington, D.C.: U.S. Government Printing Office, 2000).

82. Diane Ravitch, "Student Performance Today," Brookings Policy Brief no. 23, September 1997, 2.

83. Bok, *The State of the Nation*, 63.

84. National Center for Education Statistics, *The Condition of Education 2000*, 103.

85. Bronner, "Long a Leader, US Now Lags," 18.

86. Bok, *The State of the Nation*, 65.

87. Diana Schemo, "Students in U.S. Do Not Keep Up in Global Tests," *New York Times,* December 6, 2000, A1.

88. *Economic Report of the President,* 20–22.

89. United States Census Bureau, "The Changing Shape of the Nation's Income Distribution," *Current Population Reports,* June 2000, 1, 10.

90. *Economic Report of the President,* 174–75.

91. "Desperately Seeking a Perfect Model," *The Economist,* April 10, 1999, 67–68.

92. Even as sympathetic an observer as Martin Wolf of the *Financial Times* notes that "some of the most successful economies, in terms of high technology and low unemployment (though with a mixed record of productivity growth) have been the Nordic welfare states. Yet these are in some respects, the polar opposites of the US, notably on taxation and public spending. For all its success, it is unlikely that the US offers the only workable way to organize an advanced economy." Martin Wolf, "The Lure of the American Way," *Financial Times* (London), November 1, 2000, 25.

93. Henry Kissinger, *Does America Need a Foreign Policy? Toward a Diplomacy for the 21st Century* (New York: Simon and Schuster, 2001), 18.

94. Steven Kull, "What the Public Knows That Washington Doesn't," *Foreign Policy,* winter 1995–96, 114.

95. John E. Reilly, ed., *American Public Opinion and U.S. Foreign Policy 1999,* Chicago Council on Foreign Relations (http://www.ccfr.org/publications/opinion/AmPuOp99.pdf), 4–8.

96. James M. Lindsay, "The New Apathy," *Foreign Affairs,* September-October 2000.

97. Wolfe, *One Nation, After All,* 170.

98. Charles A. Beard, *The Idea of the National Interest* (New York: Macmillan, 1934).

99. Peter Trubowitz, *Defining the National Interest: Conflict and Change in American Foreign Policy* (Chicago: University of Chicago Press, 1998), 12.

100. Henry Kissinger, "America at the Apex," *The National Interest,* summer 2001, 15.

101. Josef Joffe, "Who's Afraid of Mr. Big?" *The National Interest,* summer 2001, 52.

102. Scheve and Slaughter, *Globalization and the Perceptions of American Workers,* 9.

103. United States Information Agency Opinion Analysis, M-162–99, August 20, 1999, 1.

104. Fred Bergsten, "Preface," in Scheve and Slaughter, *Globalization and the Perceptions of American Workers,* x.

105. Franz Nuscheler, "Multilateralism vs. Unilateralism," Development and Peace Foundation, Policy Paper 16, Bonn, 2001, 8.

106. Richard Sobel, *The Impact of Public Opinion on U.S. Foreign Policy Since Vietnam* (New York: Oxford University Press, 2001), 10.

CHAPTER 5: REDEFINING THE NATIONAL INTEREST

1. Peter Ludlow, "Wanted: A Global Partner," *The Washington Quarterly,* summer 2001, 167.

2. Program on International Policy Attitudes, "Americans on Globalization: A Study of US Public Attitudes," University of Maryland, 1999, 8.

3. *America's National Interests: A Report from the Commission on America's National Interests* (cochairs Robert Ellworth, Andrew Goodpaster, and Rita Hauser, 1996), 13.

4. See Ashton Carter, John Deutch, and Philip Zelikow, *Catastrophic Terrorism: Elements of a National Policy* (Cambridge, MA: Belfer Center for Science and International Affairs, Harvard University, 1998). See also Joseph S. Nye Jr. and R. James Woolsey, "Perspective on Terrorism," *Los Angeles Times,* June 1, 1997, M-5.

5. For a full discussion of the complexity and problems of definition, see Inge Kaul, Isabelle Grunberg, and Marc A. Stern, eds., *Global Public Goods: International Cooperation in the 21st Century* (New York: Oxford University Press, 1999). Strictly defined, public goods are nonrivalrous and nonexclusionary.

6. Mancur Olson, *The Logic of Collective Action: Public Goods and the Theory of Groups* (Cambridge, MA: Harvard University Press, 1965).

7. Philip Bowring, "Bush's America Is Developing an Image Problem," *International Herald Tribune,* May 31, 2001, 8.

8. Richard N. Gardner, "The One Percent Solution," *Foreign Affairs,* July-August 2000, 3.

9. Dana Priest, "A Four Star Foreign Policy?" *Washington Post,* September 28, 2000, 1.

10. Robin Wright, "State Dept. Mismanaged, Report Says," *Los Angeles Times,* January 30, 2001, 10.

11. The United States Advisory Commission on Public Diplomacy, *Consolidation of USIA into the State Department: An Assessment After One Year* (Washington, D.C.: October 2000).

12. Jeffrey Sachs, "What's Good for the Poor Is Good for America," *The Economist,* July 14, 2001, 32–33.

13. "Bush Proposes Aid Shift to Grants for Poor Nations," *New York Times,* July 18, 2001, A1.

14. William Easterly, "The Failure of Development," *Financial Times* (London), July 4, 2001, 32; Dani Rodrik, *The New Global Economy and Developing Countries: Making Openness Work* (Washington, D.C.: Overseas Development Council, 1999).

15. Peter Rodman, *Uneasy Giant: The Challenges to American Predominance* (Washington: The Nixon Center, 2000), 3, 15, 44.

16. Richard Bernstein, "To Butt In or Not in Human Rights: The Gap Narrows," *New York Times,* August 4, 2001, 15.

17. Rodman, *Uneasy Giant,* 40.

18. Steven Mufson, "Bush Nudged by the Right over Rights," *International Herald Tribune,* January 27–28, 2001, 3. See also "American Power— For What? A Symposium," *Commentary,* January 2000, 21n.

19. G. Pascal Zachary, "Market Forces Add Ammunition to Civil Wars," *Wall Street Journal,* June 12, 2000, 21. From 1989 to 1998, 108 armed conflicts broke out in seventy-three places around the world; 92 of them took place within a country rather than between countries.

20. Ashton B. Carter and William J. Perry, *Preventive Defense: A New Security Strategy for America* (Washington, D.C.: Brookings Institution Press, 1999), 11–15.

21. Samantha Power, "Bystanders to Genocide," *Atlantic Monthly,* September 2001, 84–108.

22. Samantha Power, *"A Problem from Hell": America's Failure to Prevent Genocide* (New York: Basic Books, 2002), chapter 5.

23. Norman Kempster, "US Is Sharply Criticized on Human Rights Issues," *International Herald Tribune,* May 31, 2001, 3.

24. Barbara Crossette, "Clinton Signs Agreements to Help Protect Children," *New York Times,* July 6, 2000, A7.

25. John M. Owen, "How Liberalism Produces Democratic Peace," *International Security,* fall 1994; John R. Oneal and Bruce Russett, "Assessing the Liberal Peace with Alternative Specifications: Trade Still Reduces Conflict," *Journal of Peace Research* (Oslo), July 1999; Fareed Zakaria, "The Rise of Illiberal Democracy," *Foreign Affairs,* November-December 1997. For a critical monographic look at the "liberal peace" thesis, see Joanne Gowa, *Ballots and Bullets: The Elusive Democratic Peace* (Princeton: Princeton University Press, 1999); for a favorable monographic assessment, see Spencer R. Weart,

Never at War: Why Democracies Will Not Fight One Another (New Haven: Yale University Press, 1998).

26. See Edward D. Mansfield and Jack Snyder, "Democratization and War," *Foreign Affairs*, May 1995.

27. Thomas Carothers, *Aiding Democracy Abroad: The Learning Curve* (Washington, D.C.: Carnegie Endowment, 1999), 5.

28. Samuel P. Huntington, *The Third Wave: Democratization in the Late Twentieth Century* (Norman: University of Oklahoma Press, 1991).

29. Ibid., 7.

30. William Safire, "The Purloined Treaty," *New York Times*, April 9, 2001, A21.

31. Robert Kagan and William Kristol, "The Present Danger," *The National Interest*, spring 2000, 58, 64, 67.

32. Charles Krauthammer, "The New Unilateralism," *Washington Post*, June 8, 2001, A29.

33. Kagan and Kristol, "The Present Danger," 67.

34. Robert W. Tucker in "American Power—For What? A Symposium," *Commentary*, January 2000, 46.

35. Harald Muller quoted in Franz Nuscheler, "Multilateralism vs. Unilateralism," Development and Peace Foundation, Bonn, 2001, 5.

36. Lloyd Axworthy quoted in Stewart Patrick, "Lead, Follow, or Get Out of the Way: America's Retreat from Multilateralism," *Current History*, December 2000, 433.

37. Quoted in Peter Spiro, "The New Sovereigntist," *Foreign Affairs*, November-December 2000, 12–13.

38. David B. Rivkin Jr. and Lee A. Casey, "The Rocky Shoals of International Law," *The National Interest*, winter 2000–1, 42.

39. Jesse Helms, "American Sovereignty and the UN," *The National Interest*, winter 2000–1, 34.

40. "Working Out the World," *The Economist*, March 31, 2001, 24.

41. James Glanz, "Study Optimistic on Safer Land Mines, but Says Push is Needed," *New York Times*, March 22, 2001, A18.

42. "2nd Presidential Debate Between Gov. Bush and Vice President Gore," *New York Times*, October 12, 2000, A20.

43. Brian Knowlton, "Bush Aide Calls UN Vote an Outrage," *International Herald Tribune*, May 7, 2001 (http://www.iht.com/articles/19081.html).

44. David Sanger, "House Threatens to Hold U.N. Dues in Loss of a Seat," *New York Times*, May 9, 2001, A1.

45. Quoted in *The Hotline: National Journal's Daily Briefing on Politics*, May 8, 2001, 4.

46. Barry James, "The EU Counterweight to American Influence," *International Herald Tribune*, June 16, 2000, 4.

47. Roger Cohen, "Arrogant or Humble? Bush Encounters Europeans' Hostility," *International Herald Tribune*, May 8, 2001, 1. Among the multilateral treaties and agreements that the administration opposed in its first six months were the International Criminal Court, the Comprehensive Test Ban Treaty, the ABM Treaty, the Kyoto Protocol, a small arms control pact, a biological weapons protocol, and an OECD measure to control tax havens. "By knocking off several of the hard-earned, high-profile treaties on arms control and the environment, Mr. Bush has been subjected to outrage from some of America's closest friends—who wonder what will replace a world ordered by treaties—as well as its adversaries who see arrogance in Mr. Bush's actions." Thom Shanker, "White House Says US Is Not a Loner, Just Choosy," *New York Times*, July 31, 2001, 1.

48. United States Commission on National Security in the Twenty-first Century, *New World Coming: American Security in the 21st Century* (Washington, D.C., 1999), 4.

49. United States Commission on National Security in the Twenty-first Century, *Roadmap for National Security: Imperative for Change, Phase III Report* (Washington, D.C., 2001), 2, 5.

50. Dominique Moisi, "The Right Argument, but the Wrong Tone," *Financial Times* (London), November 22, 1999, 13.

51. Joshua Muravchik in "American Power—For What? A Symposium," *Commentary*, January 2000, 41.

52. Robert W. Tucker in "American Power—For What? A Symposium," *Commentary*, January 2000, 46.

53. G. John Ikenberry, "Getting Hegemony Right," *The National Interest*, spring 2001, 19.

54. Robert O'Neill, "Working with the US: An Allied Perspective," lecture, All Souls Foreign Policy Studies Program, May 10, 2001.

55. Ikenberry, "Getting Hegemony Right," 21–22.

56. Mark A. Pollack and Gregory C. Shaffer, eds., *Transatlantic Governance in the Global Economy* (Lanham, MD: Rowman and Littlefield, 2001).

57. Shanker, "White House Says the US Is Not a Loner, Just Choosy."

58. The problems stem not only from foreign courts, but from a new trend in lawsuits brought in U.S. courts to challenge human rights abuses

around the world. American lawyers who boast about unilaterally export-ing our conception of law and who argue that the post–Cold War paradigm is the United States as global attorney fail to pay adequate attention to the costs of the doctrine of universal jurisdiction for the United States. William Glaberson, "U.S. Courts Become Arbiters of Global Rights and Wrongs," *The New York Times,* June 21, 2001, 1. See also Henry A. Kissinger, "The Pit-falls of Universal Jurisdiction," *Foreign Affairs,* July-August 2001, 86–96.

59. John Ruggie, *Constructing the World Polity* (London: Routledge, 1998), 118. Britain's unilateral willingness to bear the costs (and benefits) encour-aged free riding. American actions have been conditioned on reciprocity.

60. "Rage over Global Warming," *The Economist,* April 7, 2001, 18. For a careful study of Kyoto's flaws, see David Victor, *The Collapse of the Kyoto Protocol and the Struggle to Slow Global Warming* (Princeton: Princeton University Press, 2001).

61. Robert N. Stavins, "Give Bush Time on Climate Issues," *Boston Globe,* April 4, 2001, A21.

62. Andrew Revkin, "After Rejecting Climate Treaty, Bush Calls in Tutors to Give Courses and Help Set One," *New York Times,* April 28, 2001, A9.

63. I am indebted to Robert Keohane for help on this point.

64. John R. Bolton, "Should We Take Global Governance Seriously?" *Chicago Journal of International Law,* fall 2000.

65. For contrasting views, see Jeremy Rabkin, *Why Sovereignty Matters* (Washington, D.C.: AEI Press, 1998), and Abram Chayes and Antonia Han-dler Chayes, *The New Sovereignty: Compliance with International Regulatory Agreements* (Cambridge, MA: Harvard University Press, 1995), 27.

66. Stephen Krasner, *Sovereignty: Organized Hypocrisy* (Princeton: Princeton University Press, 1999).

67. Spiro, "The New Sovereigntists," 14.

68. Thomas Friedman, "Kyoto Will Come Back to Haunt Bush," *Interna-tional Herald Tribune,* June 2, 2001, 8.

69. Moises Naim, "New Economy, Old Politics," *Foreign Policy,* January-February 2001, 108.

70. Kal Raustiala, "Trends in Global Governance: Do They Threaten American Sovereignty?" *Chicago Journal of International Law,* fall 2000, 418.

71. Dani Rodrik, "The Global Fix," *New Republic,* November 2, 1998, 17.

72. For interesting suggestions on "virtual visibility," see Anne-Marie Slaughter, "Agencies on the Loose? Holding Government Networks Ac-countable," in George Bermann et al., eds., *Transatlantic Regulatory Cooper-ation* (New York: Oxford University Press, 2001), 528.

73. Dominique Moisi, "The Real Crisis over the Atlantic," *Foreign Affairs,* July-August 2001, 153.

74. Coral Bell, "American Ascendancy—and the Pretense of Concert," *The National Interest,* fall 1999, 60.

75. Henry Kissinger, "Our Nearsighted World Vision," *Washington Post,* January 10, 2000, A19.

76. Albert R. Hunt, "Americans Look to 21st Century with Optimism and Confidence," *Wall Street Journal,* September 16, 1999, A9.

77. Department of State, Opinion Analysis, "Sizable Majority of U.S. Public Supports Active, Cooperative Involvement Abroad," Washington, D.C., October 29, 1999.

78. United States Commission on National Security in the Twenty-first Century, *New World Coming,* 4.

INDEX